Student Study Guide

for use with

Child Development
Its Nature and Course

Fifth Edition

Ganie B. DeHart
State University of New York, Geneseo

L. Alan Sroufe
University of Minnesota

Robert G. Cooper
San Jose State University

Prepared by
Ganie B. DeHart
State University of New York, Geneseo

D1511294

Boston   Burr Ridge, IL   Dubuque, IA   Madison, WI   New York   San Francisco   St. Louis
Bangkok   Bogotá   Caracas   Kuala Lumpur   Lisbon   London   Madrid   Mexico City
Milan   Montreal   New Delhi   Santiago   Seoul   Singapore   Sydney   Taipei   Toronto

Student Study Guide for use with
CHILD DEVELOPMENT: ITS NATURE AND COURSE
DeHart/Sroufe/Cooper

Published by McGraw-Hill, an imprint of The McGraw-Hill Companies, Inc., 1221 Avenue of the Americas, New York, NY 10020. Copyright © 2004 (2000, 1996) by The McGraw-Hill Companies, Inc. All rights reserved.

ISBN-13: 978-0-07-249144-9
ISBN-10: 0-07-249144-2

4 5 6 7 8 9 0 CUS CUS 0 9 8 7

www.mhhe.com

TABLE OF CONTENTS

PAGE

HOW TO USE THIS STUDY GUIDE

This Study Guide is designed to help you organize and review your reading of DeHart, Sroufe, and Cooper's *Child Development: Its Nature and Course*, fifth edition. Each chapter includes:

> ! A **Chapter Review** and

> ! A **Self-Test**.

Here's a quick overview of each of these features:

CHAPTER REVIEWS
Each chapter in the Study Guide begins with a **Chapter Review**, which is intended as a guide for constructing a detailed chapter outline. The review follows the organization of the textbook chapter and includes the terms from the marginal glossary and a series of questions for each major section of the chapter. The **Chapter Review** is designed to help you structure your reading of the textbook, increase the amount of information you retain from reading, and construct notes that can be used in studying for exams.

> ! *Before reading each section of the chapter*, look at the key terms and questions included in that section of the **Chapter Review**, for a preview of what will be covered and an idea of what information to watch for.

> ! *As you finish each section or subsection of the chapter*, check your understanding of the key terms and answer the review questions.

> ! *As you study for exams*, use the review questions and your answers to them as a study guide. Many students also find it helpful to make flashcards to help them learn the key terms and review key points.

SELF-TESTS
The Chapter Review in each chapter is followed by a **Self-Test**, which includes multiple-choice, matching, short-answer, and essay questions. Answers to self-test items and sample essays are found at the end of the test. The **Self-Test** is intended as a means for you to check your understanding *after* reading and reviewing the chapter in the textbook and to identify areas that you need to study further.

> ! The multiple-choice questions include items with answers drawn directly from the book and items that require you to apply material from the book to identify

examples or reason about practical issues.

!   The matching questions are drawn from the items in the textbook's marginal glossary.

!   The short-answer questions include fill-in-the-blank items, questions that can be answered with one or two words, and questions that require you to provide lists or short explanations.

!   The essay questions are designed to let you practice formulating clear essays using material from the textbook. Some of the essay questions require fairly short responses, consisting of information recalled directly from your reading. Others require you to go beyond what you have read in the textbook, either applying the material to a practical issue or drawing logical implications from textbook information. The sample essays are not the only possible correct answers, but they provide you with a model for selecting and organizing information into a coherent essay.

One of the unique features of your textbook is the series of vignettes tracing the development of three children. The purpose of the vignettes is to help you relate the material in the textbook to the behavior of real children. To further this purpose, the Study Guide includes both multiple-choice and essay questions that draw on material from the vignettes.

CHAPTER 1
THE NATURE OF DEVELOPMENT
CHAPTER REVIEW

As you read the chapter, construct your own chapter outline by answering the following review questions and defining the *Key Terms*.

I. INTRODUCTION
    Key Terms: **development, qualitative change, quantitative change**
    A. Explain what it means to say that **development** is orderly, cumulative, and directional.

    B. What are the three major assumptions of the textbook's developmental perspective?

II. BASIC DEVELOPMENTAL CONCEPTS
    Key Terms: **behavioral reorganization, normative development, individual development**
    A. Explain the role of **qualitative change** and **behavioral reorganization** in development. Give an example of each.

    B. Explain the concepts of **normative development** and **individual development,** including the two types of individual differences in development. Give examples.

III. A FRAMEWORK FOR UNDERSTANDING DEVELOPMENT

Key Terms: **adaptation, natural selection, evolution, maturation**

A. List the three factors on which development depends and explain how they interact to produce development.

B. Explain how Darwin's theory of evolution is relevant to the study of child development.

C. Summarize Locke's and Rousseau's views on the roles of heredity and environment in development. What twentieth century theories of child development correspond most nearly to each of their views?

D. How does contemporary research demonstrate interaction between heredity, environment, and past development?

E. BOX: Summarize the evidence for genetic and environmental influences on intelligence.

IV. THEORETICAL PERSPECTIVES ON DEVELOPMENT

Key Terms: **theory, sensorimotor period, preoperational period, concrete operational period, formal operational period, information-processing theory, sociocultural theory, private speech, inner speech, zone of proximal development, psychoanalytic theory, id, ego, superego, fixation, social learning theory, modeling, adaptational theory**

A.   What are the two major functions of a scientific **theory**?

B.   List three criteria for judging the validity of a **theory**.

C.   Summarize Piaget's theory of cognitive development. How is it distinctive and how has it influenced developmental psychology?

D.   What are the major characteristics of **information-processing theory**? How is it different from Piaget's theory? Name a currently influential developmental researcher who uses an information-processing approach.

E.   What is the main emphasis in **sociocultural theory**? Summarize Vygotsky's major ideas and compare them to Piaget's.

F. Summarize Freud's ideas about human development. How has Freud influenced current ideas about children's development? How do Erikson's ideas differ from Freud's?

G. How does **social learning theory** explain human behavior? How does social learning theory compare to information-processing and Piagetian theories? Name an influential social learning theorist in the field of developmental psychology.

H. How was Bowlby's **adaptational theory** influenced by evolutionary, psychoanalytic, and cognitive theories? How did Bowlby explain the development of infant-caregiver attachment and the influence of early attachments on later development?

I. Explain why there is no single, universally accepted theory of human development.

V. MAJOR ISSUES IN DEVELOPMENT

A. Explain the issue of *gradual development versus stages*. What theories fall on each side of this issue? How is level of analysis involved in this issue?

B. Explain the issue of *early versus current experiences*. What theories fall on each side of this issue? How does Bowlby's theory occupy a middle ground?

C. Explain the two questions involved in the issue of *specificity versus generality*. For each question, what theories fall on each side of this issue?

VI. RESEARCH METHODS FOR STUDYING DEVELOPMENT

Key Terms: **hypothesis, experiment, ecological validity, nonexperimental methods, correlational methods, natural experiment, naturalistic observation, ethology, survey research, longitudinal study, cross-sectional study, cohort effect, subject attrition, accelerated longitudinal design**

A. List the advantages and disadvantages of **experiments**. Why do researchers sometimes use **nonexperimental methods** instead?

B. List the advantages and disadvantages of **natural experiments**. For what types of research questions are they most useful?

C. List the advantages and disadvantages of **naturalistic observation**. For what types of research questions is it most useful?

D. List the advantages and disadvantages of **survey research**. For what types of research questions is it most useful?

E. Summarize the advantages and disadvantages of **longitudinal** and **cross-sectional** research designs. Explain how an **accelerated longitudinal design** combines some of the advantages of both methods.

G. BOX: List the key characteristics of a strong prospective longitudinal study.

VII. THE THEMES OF THIS BOOK

List and explain the four major themes of the textbook.

SELF-TEST

After **you have studied the chapter, use the following questions to test your understanding.**

MULTIPLE-CHOICE QUESTIONS:

1. **Development** always moves toward greater complexity in behavioral organization. This means that development is:
   a. orderly.
   b. cumulative.
   c. directional.
   d. quantitative.

2. Adolescents are able to think of the world in terms of abstract concepts, while younger children tend to think of it in concrete terms. This is an example of:
   a. quantitative change.
   b. qualitative change.
   c. individual development.
   d. maturation.

3. Which of the following would be an example of **behavioral reorganization**?
   a. Sharp growth in the number of words a child knows during the second year of life.
   b. A child using visual, cognitive, and verbal skills in a new way to start reading aloud.
   c. A dramatic increase in a child's reading speed between first and second grade.
   d. A child changing from reading picture books to reading books without pictures.

4. The height and weight standards Maggie's pediatrician uses to evaluate her growth reflect _____ development; the height and weight records Christine keeps in Maggie's baby book reflect _____ development.
   a. individual; normative.
   b. individual; individual.
   c. normative; individual.
   d. normative; normative.

5. Darwin's concept of **natural selection** was intended to explain:
   a. why animals generally mate only with others of their species.
   b. how species become adapted to their environments.
   c. individual differences among humans.
   d. the connection between storks and high birth rates.

6. A major reason Darwin's theory of evolution is relevant to the study of child development is:
    a. it was the first systematic theory of child development.
    b. it explains why children are often different from their parents.
    c. it focuses on biological characteristics and downplays the role of the environment.
    d. it suggests how environment and heredity can interact to produce development.

7. Locke's ideas on the nature of children are reflected today in which of the following theories?
    a. Freudian theory
    b. Maturational theory
    c. Evolutionary theory
    d. Social learning theory

8. Concerning the nature-nurture controversy, most developmentalists today would agree that:
    a. heredity and environment interact to influence behavior.
    b. heredity is clearly more influential than environment.
    c. environment is clearly more influential than heredity.
    d. the influences of environment and heredity cannot be determined.

9. Research on genetic and environmental influences on intelligence has demonstrated that:
    a. identical twins usually have identical IQs, even if they are reared in different families.
    b. environmental enrichment has little or no impact on children's IQ scores.
    c. children's IQs are predicted better by biological parents' IQs than by adoptive parents' IQs.
    d. all of the above.

10. In the study of human development, a **theory** is:
    a. a collection of observations about children's behavior.
    b. a series of research results based on laboratory studies.
    c. a framework for interpreting findings and guiding research.
    d. a set of guesses about how things work.

11. The validity of a scientific theory can be judged on the basis of:
    a. how sensible and consistent it is.
    b. how well it organizes a set of research findings.
    c. how specific and testable it is.
    d. all of the above.

12. Which of the following statements would Piaget agree with?
    a. Cognitive development is a process of actively constructing understanding of the world.
    b. Cognitive development consists of gradually increasing skills and knowledge.
    c. Cognitive development can be significantly speeded up with appropriate training.
    d. Cognitive development varies dramatically from child to child.

13. **Information-processing theory** differs from Piaget's theory in that:
    a. it focuses more on normative development.
    b. it focuses less on individual development.
    c. it is more concerned with qualitative change.
    d. it is more concerned with quantitative change.

14. Vygotsky's **zone of proximal development** is the gap between:
    a. what children think and what they are able to talk about.
    b. children's experience and their understanding of the world around them.
    c. children's performance alone and with guidance from someone more skilled.
    d. children's past and current performance on the same task.

15. Erikson's theory of human development differs from Freud's in that Erikson:
    a. downplays the role of feelings and social relationships.
    b. focuses on broader developmental issues.
    c. proposes psychosexual stages.
    d. abandons the concept of developmental stages.

16. A little girl watches a peer sharing his crayons and being praised for that act. Later she does the same with her crayons. This is an example of:
    a. modeling.
    b. shaping.
    c. positive reinforcement.
    d. negative reinforcement.

17. A 10-month-old baby cries and tries to follow when his mother leaves the room. How would Bowlby's **adaptational theory** explain his behavior?
    a. Babies have a biologically built-in tendency to form attachments to caregivers.
    b. Babies try to stay close to the person they associate most with food.
    c. This particular baby has learned that crying will make his mother return.
    d. This particular baby has had a negative experience when separated from his mother.

18. Which of the following theories is LEAST concerned with **individual development**?
    a. Psychoanalytic theory.
    b. Piaget's cognitive developmental theory.
    c. Social learning theory.
    d. Bowlby's adaptational theory.

19. Which of the following theories holds that development is a process of gradual change?
    a. Psychoanalytic theory.
    b. Piaget's cognitive developmental theory.
    c. Social learning theory.
    d. Bowlby's adaptational theory.

20. Which of the following pays the LEAST attention to the age at which experiences occur?
    a. Freud's theory of psychosexual stages
    b. Erikson's theory of psychosocial stages
    c. Bowlby's adaptational theory
    d. Social learning theory

21. Which of the following theories was intended to be both domain- and culture-general?
    a. Piaget's theory of cognitive development
    b. Information-processing theory
    c. Sociocultural theory
    d. Social learning theory

22. A major advantage of laboratory **experiments** is:
    a. they have high ecological validity.
    b. they offer researchers maximum control.
    c. they are inexpensive and quick to do.
    d. they allow observation of naturally occurring behavior.

23. Placing a tape recorder under a baby's bed to record the sounds she makes when she is alone is an example of:
    a. an experiment.
    b. a natural experiment.
    c. survey research.
    d. naturalistic observation.

24. Comparing anxiety levels in a group of children from a high-crime neighborhood and a group of children from a similar neighborhood with lower crime rates is an example of:
    a. a cross-sectional study.
    b. a longitudinal study.
    c. a natural experiment.
    d. naturalistic observation.

25. **Cross-sectional studies** are useful when the researcher's goal is to:
    a. show how children of various ages differ.
    b. examine processes of development.
    c. examine individual change over time.
    d. all of the above.

MATCHING QUESTIONS:

Match the following key terms with their definitions:

1. ___ Behavioral reorganization

2. ___ Adaptation

3. ___ Maturation

4. ___ Sociocultural theory

5. ___ Social learning theory

6. ___ Psychoanalytic theory

7. ___ Adaptational theory

8. ___ Id

9. ___ Ego

10. ___ Superego

11. ___ Modeling

12. ___ Hypothesis

13. ___ Correlational methods

14. ___ Subject attrition

15. ___ Cohort effect

A. Learning by imitating others' behavior, especially behavior that has been observed to have positive consequences.

B. In a longitudinal study, the loss of participants over time.

C. A theory that emphasizes the role of social interaction and specific cultural practices in the development of cognitive skills.

D. Freud's term for the self; the part of the mind whose major role is to find safe, appropriate ways to express instinctual drives.

E. In a cross-sectional study, a difference between age groups due to a peculiarity in one of the groups being studied rather than to a general developmental difference.

F. Freud's term for the part of the mind that consists of primitive drives and instincts.

G. A change in a species that increases chances of survival in a particular environment.

H. Freud's term for the conscience; the part of the mind that has internalized rules and values governing behavior.

I. Research methods that allow researchers to examine relationships among factors but not to draw conclusions about cause and effect.

J. Any theory of development derived from the ideas of Freud.

K. Bowlby's developmental theory, integrating ideas from evolutionary, psychoanalytic, and cognitive theories to explain the development and impact of early attachment relationships.

L. Age-related physical changes guided by a genetic plan.

M. A theory that emphasizes the learning of behaviors through associations with different kinds of consequences, especially in a social context.

N. A testable proposition, often developed to check the validity of a theory.

O. A change in the way a developing child organizes and uses his or her capabilities; one way qualitative change occurs.

SHORT-ANSWER QUESTIONS:

1. The developmental perspective used in the textbook assumes that:
    (a)
    (b)
    (c)

2. What is the difference between **qualitative change** and **quantitative change**?

3. The three factors that interact to produce developmental changes are:
   (a)
   (b)
   (c)

4. The belief that children need strong shaping from their environment to develop properly matches the ideas of _____; the idea that children will naturally develop in positive ways as long as the environment does not interfere matches the ideas of _____.

5. List the two major functions of a scientific **theory**.
   (a)
   (b)

6. List and define the four stages in Piaget's theory of cognitive development.
   (a)

   (b)

   (c)

   (d)

7. Describe the process by which Vygotsky believed children developed self-regulation and cognitive skills.

8. How did Freud and Erikson each characterize the stage of infancy (birth-1 year)?

9. According to Bowlby, the tendency to form attachments is universal, but the *security* of an infant's attachments is determined by _____ _____.

10. Explain why there isn't one generally accepted theory of human development.

11. How does an **experiment** differ from a **natural experiment**?

12. Explain the concept of **ecological validity**.

13. List the major advantage and disadvantage of **naturalistic observation**.

14. A study in which a group of subjects is followed over time is a _____;
    a study in which subjects of different ages are compared at the same time is a
    _____.

15. List the four major themes of the textbook.
    (a)
    (b)
    (c)
    (d)

ESSAY QUESTIONS:

1. Explain the concepts of **normative** and **individual development**. Discuss ways in which focusing on each type of development might be useful to researchers, teachers, and parents.

2. Summarize Locke's and Rousseau's views on the roles of heredity and environment in development and discuss the implications of each view for child-rearing and education.

3. Discuss how **psychoanalytic theory** and **social learning theory** have influenced child-rearing ideas and practice in our culture.

4. Briefly explain the two questions in the issue of *specificity versus generality* and indicate which theories of development fall on each side of each question.

5. Piaget initially based his theory of cognitive development on detailed observations of his own children in their usual day-to-day surroundings. Discuss how this research approach might have influenced Piaget's theory--in particular, what strengths and weaknesses the theory might have as a result.

6. Explain the difference between **longitudinal** and **cross-sectional studies**. For each one, summarize the advantages and disadvantages and give an example of a research question for which it would be a particularly appropriate method.

7. List four basic principles of development that you think could be useful for parents or teachers to know. Explain why each would be useful and how it could be applied to child-rearing and education.

ANSWER KEY

MULTIPLE-CHOICE QUESTIONS:

1. c   See definition of *directionality*.

2. b   The change from concrete to abstract thinking involves a fundamental transformation, not just an increase in an existing ability.

3. b   Reading aloud involves organizing and using existing skills in a *new* way; increasing vocabulary and reading speed involve growth of existing skills and changing to books without pictures requires increased reading skill but not reorganization.

4. c   The pediatrician's height and weight standards reflect general changes typical of all children; Christine's records reflect any variation in Maggie's growth from the norms and also capture the continuity in her individual growth pattern.

5. b   Natural selection is the process by which adaptation occurs.

6. d   Darwin explained the development of species on the basis of interaction between genes and the environment; a similar process of interaction applies to human development.

7. d   Both Locke and social learning theory focus on environmental influences.

8. a   Some researchers focus more heavily on genetic or environmental influences, but all recognize that behavior is influenced by the interaction of environment and heredity.

9. c   Answers *a*, *b*, and *c* appear consistent with each other, but only *c* is true.

10. c   Answer *c* reflects the two major functions of scientific theory; theories go beyond observations and research results and are not just *guesses* about how things work.

11. d   See criteria for judging validity of a theory.

12. a   This is one of Piaget's major contributions. He believed development involved qualitative shifts, that training could not speed it up, and that it was similar for all children.

13. d   Unlike Piaget, information-processing theorists see development as quantitative change; like Piaget, they focus mainly on normative development.

14. c   See definition of zone of proximal development.

15. b   Like Freud, Erikson emphasized feelings, relationships, and developmental stages, but he focused on broader developmental issues rather than psychosexual ones.

16. a   See definition of modeling.

17. a   Crying and following are examples of what Bowlby saw as biologically built-in behaviors that promoted attachment; he did not believe these behaviors had to be learned.

18. b   Piaget was primarily interested in normative development; the other three theories all deal with individual development in some way.

19. c   Social learning theory is based on gradual change; the other three theories all involve developmental stages.

20. d   In social learning theory, the age at which an experience occurs is of little importance; the other three theories all attach special importance to experiences early in life.

21. a   Piaget *intended* his theory to describe cognitive structures and processes that cut across domains and were culturally universal. Information-processing and social learning theories were intended to be culturally universal but to explain development in specific domains. Sociocultural theory is intended to be both domain- and culture-specific.

22. b   Experiments offer researchers control, but they do not always generalize beyond the laboratory, involve naturally occurring behavior, or save time and money.

23. d   This is a good example of observing natural behavior in an everyday setting.

24. c   Anxiety is being compared in two naturally occurring groups of children.

25. a   Cross-sectional studies can demonstrate differences between children of different ages, but they cannot capture processes of development or individual change over time.

MATCHING QUESTIONS:

1. O	4. C	7. K	10. H	13. I
2. G	5. M	8. F	11. A	14. B
3. L	6. J	9. D	12. N	15. E

SHORT-ANSWER QUESTIONS:

1. (a) Development involves qualitative changes as well as quantitative changes; (b) children's later abilities, behavior, and knowledge emerge from earlier ones systematically; (c) each individual's development is coherent over time.

2. Qualitative change involves a fundamental transformation in an ability or characteristic; quantitative change simply involves an increase in the amount of an existing ability or characteristic.

3. (a) Developmental potentials provided by the genes; (b) developmental history; (c) current environment.

4. Locke; Rousseau

5. (a) To provide a framework for interpreting facts and research findings; (b) to guide scientific research.

6. (a) Sensorimotor period--the first two years of life, when awareness of the world is based on sensory awareness and motor acts; (b) preoperational period--ages 2-7, when children have mental representation but do not yet reason systematically; (c) concrete operational period--ages 7-11, when children start to use logical operations to reason about concrete objects; (d) formal operational period--beginning about age 12, when children become able to reason systematically about hypothetical and abstract problems.

7. According to Vygotsky, children develop both self-regulation and cognitive skills by learning them in social settings and gradually internalizing them. In particular, self-regulation develops by internalizing directives they originally hear from adults. At first they reproduce these directives themselves in audible private speech; gradually, they become able to regulate their behavior by means of inner speech, inaudible directives to themselves.

8. Freud described infancy as the oral stage, a period when sensual pleasure is obtained orally and feeding and weaning are important issues. Erikson described the basic issue of infancy as trust vs. mistrust; depending on the quality of care they receive, infants either learn to trust others to meet their needs and therefore develop feelings of self-worth, or they learn that they cannot trust others to take care of them.

18

9. the quality of care an infant receives

10. There is no one generally accepted theory of human development because different theories focus on different aspects of behavior and psychologists' knowledge of human development is a work in progress--as the store of knowledge about children's development increases, theories are revised and refined.

11. In an experiment, the researcher controls conditions, systematically manipulates variables, and randomly assigns research participants to groups for study. In a natural experiment, the researcher does not have as much control over variables and studies naturally occurring groups of people instead of randomly assigning people to groups.

12. Ecological validity is the degree to which experimental findings generalize to the world outside the laboratory. Laboratory results do not always generalize well to the outside world because people may behave differently in the laboratory than in other settings, because laboratory settings do not always accurately reproduce everyday situations, and because laboratory tasks do not always measure what they were intended to measure.

13. The major advantage of naturalistic observation is high ecological validity; its major disadvantage is low researcher control.

14. longitudinal study; cross-sectional study

15. (a) Development involves both change and continuity; (b) within a framework of normative development, each child shows a unique pattern of individual development; (c) context plays a critical role in development; (d) cognitive and social development work together.

ESSAY QUESTIONS:

1. Normative development refers to typical developmental changes that virtually all children experience. Individual development refers to individual variations around the norm and to individual children's developmental histories. (Some ways that focusing on each type might be useful follow; you may be able to think of others.) Focusing on normative development allows researchers to discover what children are typically like at various ages and how they change as they grow older, and gives parents and teachers standards for judging whether children are developing normally. Focusing on the first type of individual development allows researchers to find out how much variability there is in children's development and helps parents and teachers evaluate individual children's development and pinpoint possible problems. Focusing on the second type of individual development allows researchers to discover factors likely to produce benefits or problems later in

children's development and helps parents and teachers understand children's current behavior and provide appropriate support for further development.

2. Locke viewed the newborn as a *tabula rasa*, a blank slate waiting to be written on by experience. He believed children were inherently neither good nor bad, but were shaped almost entirely by their environments. Rousseau saw children as inherently good and believed they would turn out well if development was allowed to unfold naturally. Locke's view suggests that parents and teachers should provide children with plenty of structure, guidance, and correction, and that environmental enrichment will enhance development. Rousseau's view implies that parents and teachers should try not to interfere with the natural course of development, providing a supportive environment but not attempting to shape children in particular ways. (You could also discuss specific practices that would fit each approach.)

3. Both psychoanalytic theory and social learning theory have had considerable impact on child-rearing ideas and practices in our culture. Examples of influences from psychoanalytic theory include the widely accepted idea that early experiences are crucial, that early relationships with parents (especially mothers) have profound impacts on later development, that unresolved conflicts from childhood can cause problems in adulthood, that early day care is harmful because it interferes with the mother-infant relationship, that toilet-training is psychologically significant, and that sleeping with parents is psychologically unhealthy. Examples of social learning theory influences include such discipline methods as the time-out chair, the idea that positive reinforcement is more effective than punishment in changing children's behavior, that positive and negative role models have a strong effect on children's development, and that children can learn bad behavior by imitating what they see modeled on television. (You can probably think of additional ways these two theories have influenced child-rearing.)

4. The two questions in the issue of specificity versus generality are: (a) the question of domain specificity--whether developmental processes are specific to particular knowledge or skill domains or whether they apply more generally to a broad range of abilities, and (b) the question of cultural specificity--whether developmental processes are specific to particular social or cultural contexts or whether they are socially and culturally universal. Information-processing theory is a domain-specific theory of cognitive development; sociocultural, social learning, and Bowlby's adaptational theories are domain-specific theories that focus on social development. Of the theories discussed in Chapter 1, only sociocultural theory was intended to be culture-specific; the rest were intended to be culture-general. (However, cross-cultural research suggests that some aspects of all of these theories are actually culture-specific.)

5. To answer this question, you need to apply what you know about naturalistic observation to Piaget's early research. Two general ways Piaget's theory might have been influenced by his early reliance on observations of his own children are the fact that they were his children and the fact that he used observational research techniques. For example, his children may have been atypical in some way, meaning that his theory might not apply equally well to other children. Their behavior may have been affected by the fact that he was observing them, or his observations may have been affected by the fact that they were his own children. His use of observational techniques means that he based his theory on children's behavior in real-world situations, giving it ecological validity. But it also means that he did not control the situations in which he collected his data. As a result, his conclusions about causation in his children's behavior cannot be firm and remain open to testing through experimental means.

6. Longitudinal studies involve following the same group of people over time, whereas cross-sectional studies involve studying groups of people of different ages at the same time. The major advantages of longitudinal studies are that they allow researchers to look directly at developmental processes and to study individual development. Major disadvantages are that they are time-consuming, expensive, and may suffer from subject attrition (loss of subjects over time). Advantages of cross-sectional studies include the fact that they are relatively quick and inexpensive; disadvantages are that they cannot be used to study developmental processes or individual development and that they are subject to cohort effects (results due to peculiarities in the groups being studied rather than to genuine age differences). Appropriate research questions for longitudinal studies would be any that involve developmental processes or individual development, such as the processes by which children learn to read or the long-term effects of parent-infant attachment on later social relationships. Appropriate research questions for cross-sectional studies would be any that focus on age differences in children's thinking or behavior, such as comparisons of preschoolers' and elementary schoolers' memory abilities or the friendship patterns of 2nd graders and 5th graders.

7. Any of the principles of development discussed in this chapter could be used in answering this questions--for example, normative and individual development, qualitative and quantitative development, the coherence of individual development, the interaction of environment and heredity. For whatever principles you choose, the key is to be as concrete as possible in discussing *why* knowing about that principle would be useful for parents or teachers and *how* they could potentially apply it.

CHAPTER 2
THE CONTEXTS OF DEVELOPMENT

CHAPTER REVIEW

As you read the chapter, construct your own chapter outline by answering the following review questions and defining the *Key Terms*.

I. INTRODUCTION
    A. What is known about the effects of early environmental deprivation and institutionalization on children's development?

    B. BOX: What seems to be the major cause of developmental problems in children in institutions? What can be done to help infants in institutions develop normally?

II. AN OVERVIEW OF DEVELOPMENTAL CONTEXTS
    Describe Bronfenbrenner's model of developmental contexts and explain what is included at each level in the model.

III. THE CHILD'S BIOLOGICAL MAKEUP
    Key Term: canalization
    A. What are the major components of the child's biological makeup?

B.   What traits do human infants possess as part of their evolutionary heritage?

C.   How are individual genetic characteristics involved in the evolution of species? How do they influence individual development?

D.   What factors other than genetic inheritance influence a child's biological makeup? Explain the concept of **canalization** and some ways in which it can vary.

IV. THE CHILD'S IMMEDIATE ENVIRONMENT
     Key Terms: **bidirectional effects, transactional model, family day care**
     A.   List four ways the family context influences children's development.

B.   Why have researchers traditionally focused on mothers' influence on their children? Why is this approach inadequate?

C. Explain what it means to think of the family as a system. What are the major characteristics of family systems?

D. Explain the direct and indirect effects fathers and siblings can have on children's development.

E. What kinds of day-care arrangements are used most often in the United States? What have researchers discovered about the effects of day care on children's development?

F. What do children learn from experiences with peers?

G. How do neighborhoods influence children's development?

H. What are some ways schools influence children's development? How are normative and individual developmental reflected in schools and in their influence on children?

I. BOX: How does exposure to violence affect children?

V. THE SOCIAL AND ECONOMIC CONTEXT
Key Term: **socioeconomic status (SES)**
A. What is included in the social and economic context?

B. How have American families changed since the 1950's?

C. Summarize what is known about the impacts of the following on children's development:
1. Maternal employment

   2.   Single parenting

   3.   Homosexual parents

D.   What social class differences have been observed in parenting practices?

E.   How common is poverty for American children? Summarize the effects of poverty, homelessness, and unemployment on children's development.

VI. THE CULTURAL CONTEXT
   Key Terms: **culture, socialization, subcultures**
   A.   What is the same about child rearing across all cultures? What varies?

   B.   What are some ways children learn what is valued in their culture?

C. Explain what it means to say that different behaviors and child-rearing practices are *adaptive* in different cultures.

D. Give some examples of how cultural change has affected children's development.

E. Explain how differences between **subcultures** can influence children's development.

VII. DEVELOPMENT AS CONTEXT

Explain two ways that development itself becomes a context for further development.

VIII. CONTEXTS IN INTERACTION

Explain how contexts interact to influence children's development. What role does the family play in determining contextual influences on children?

SELF-TEST

After **you have studied the chapter, use the following questions to test your understanding.**

MULTIPLE-CHOICE QUESTIONS:

1. Research on children reared in institutions from an early age suggests that:
   a. early institutionalization has little or no impact on development.
   b. early institutionalization has little developmental impact, as long as children's physical needs are met.
   c. early institutionalization leads to long-term problems in all areas of development, often even after adoption.
   d. problems stemming from early institutionalization usually disappear once children leave the institution.

2. The center of Bronfenbrenner's model of developmental contexts represents:
   a. the immediate environment.
   b. the cultural context.
   c. the child's biological makeup.
   d. the social and economic context.

3. Which of the following would Bronfenbrenner consider part of the cultural context?
   a. A decision by the local school board that there is no room in the budget to buy a new reading series.
   b. The idea that teaching children to read is the most important task of elementary school.
   c. The particular series of reading books used in a school system.
   d. The reading test scores of the children in a school system.

4. Human infants' evolutionary heritage includes which of the following?
   a. A propensity for curiosity and problem solving.
   b. A built-in ability to acquire language.
   c. A predisposition to interact and form bonds with other humans.
   d. All of the above.

5. Strongly canalized genetic traits are those that are:
   a. most impervious to environmental influences.
   b. most susceptible to environmental influences.
   c. most variable in their susceptibility to the environment.
   d. most likely to appear soon after birth.

6. Sameroff's **transactional model** describes:
   a. cumulative bidirectional effects between parents and children.
   b. indirect effects parents have on children.
   c. direct effects parents have on children.
   d. short-term bidirectional effects between parents and children.

7. Which of the following statements about family systems is FALSE?
   a. Families are made up of many subsystems joined together in a coherent network.
   b. Families tend to be closed systems that are resistant to change and outside influences.
   c. Families often show cyclical influences that are repeated across generations.
   d. Each family member's behavior is affected by the behavior of the rest of the family.

8. Aggression by husbands against wives is associated with low-quality maternal care for the children in the family. This is an example of:
   a. bidirectional effects.
   b. reciprocal determinism.
   c. fathers' indirect effects.
   d. mothers' indirect effects.

9. As of 1999, which of the following child care arrangements was used most widely in the United States for children under 5 with employed mothers?
   a. In-home babysitter.
   b. Cared for by father.
   c. Cared for by other relatives.
   d. Child-care center or preschool.

10. Peer groups tend to influence development by providing a setting for:
    a. learning about unequal-status relationships.
    b. learning to manage interpersonal aggression.
    c. undermining cultural values and behavior standards.
    d. all of the above.

11. Neighborhoods seem to affect children's development primarily by means of:
    a. collective socialization.
    b. behavioral contagion.
    c. school influences.
    d. reciprocal determinism.

12. Impacts on children who are exposed to chronic high levels of violence include:
    a.   post-traumatic stress disorder.
    b.   declines in school achievement.
    c.   aggressive behavior.
    d.   all of the above.

13. Which of the following has NOT increased in the United States since 1970?
    a.   The proportion of married mothers employed outside the home.
    b.   The rate of births to unmarried women.
    c.   The number of births to teenagers.
    d.   The percentage of single-parent families.

14. Which of the following statements about the effects of maternal employment is FALSE?
    a.   Maternal employment has particularly strong effects on adolescents' adjustment and academic achievement.
    b.   The impact of maternal employment on children's development depends on how satisfied the mother is with her employment status.
    c.   Daughters of employed mothers have higher academic achievement and better emotional adjustment than daughters of nonemployed mothers.
    d.   Children of employed single mothers have stronger cognitive skills and fewer behavior problems than children of mothers receiving welfare.

15. Developmental problems are less likely for children born to adolescent mothers if:
    a.   adolescent motherhood is the norm in their culture.
    b.   the mothers receive strong social and emotional support from others.
    c.   the mothers finish high school.
    d.   all of the above.

16. Which of the following factors matters the LEAST in children's response to divorce?
    a.   age and gender of the children
    b.   type of custody arrangement
    c.   amount of conflict between parents after the divorce
    d.   amount of contact with both parents after the divorce

17. Which of the following statements about social class and parenting is FALSE?
    a.   Working-class parents use physical discipline more than middle-class parents do.
    b.   Middle-class parents reason with their children more than working-class parents do.
    c.   Low socioeconomic status generally produces poor quality parenting.
    d.   Different socioeconomic settings may demand different styles of parenting.

18. What proportion of children in the United States live in poverty?
    a. One in twenty.
    b. One in ten.
    c. One in six.
    d. One in three.

19. In Madsen's studies, American children showed high levels of competition, and Mexican children showed high levels of cooperation. An explanation of this based on the concept of cultural adaptiveness would be:
    a. Competition is needed to do well in American society, while cooperation is needed to do well in Mexican society.
    b. American parents do not realize how useful cooperation is in American society.
    c. Mexican parents are not as interested as American parents in teaching their children skills that will help them succeed as adults.
    d. American culture is less adaptive because it does not emphasize cooperation

20. When children who are members of a subculture enter school, they:
    a. invariably encounter problems because the school is structured to fit the values and norms of the dominant culture.
    b. usually encounter problems because their background is not as stimulating the background of children from the dominant culture.
    c. encounter problems if there is a cultural mismatch between their background and the way their school is set up.
    d. usually do not encounter problems because they are familiar with the dominant culture from watching television anyway.

21. Erikson's idea that a young adult's ability to achieve intimacy with another person is partly dependent on having achieved a personal identity is an example of the impact of:
    a. developmental history.
    b. physical maturation.
    c. socialization.
    d. reciprocal determinism.

22. Environmental influences from the various contexts in Bronfenbrenner's model tend to be funneled to children through:
    a. their families.
    b. their schools.
    c. their friends.
    d. the mass media.

23. One culturally influenced way in which family life will be different for the Williams

baby than for the Gordon baby or the Polonius baby is that he or she will:
a. be born to a single mother.
b. live in an extended family.
c. have a stay-at-home mother.
d. be expected to carry on the family name.

24. Which of the following issues seems most likely to create future problems for the Gordon baby?
a. Poverty
b. Maternal age
c. The neighborhood the family lives in
d. Conflict between the baby's parents

25. To minimize her baby's chances of developmental problems, Karen Polonius should:
a. move to her own apartment so that she and her baby can be independent from her family.
b. get a job right away so that she can be financially self-supporting.
c. find a way to stay in high school until she graduates.
d. all of the above.

MATCHING QUESTIONS:
Match the following key terms with their definitions:

1. ___ Transactional model

2. ___ Socialization

3. ___ Family day care

4. ___ Canalization

5. ___ Socioeconomic status (SES)

6. ___ Subcultures

7. ___ Bidirectional effects

8. ___ Culture

A. The extent to which genes constrain environmental influences on particular traits.

B. A system of beliefs, attitudes, values, and guidelines for behavior shared by a group of people.

C. Groups whose beliefs, attitudes, values, and guidelines for behavior differ in some ways from those of the dominant culture.

D. The process by which children acquire the rules, standards, and values of a culture.

E. A day-care setting in which a group of children is cared for in the home of a nonrelative.

F. Sameroff's model describing the cumulative effects of ongoing two-way influences between children and parents.

G. The grouping of people within a society on the basis of income, occupation, and education.

H. Two-way developmental influences between family members.

SHORT-ANSWER QUESTIONS:

1. List three major ways to improve care for infants in institutions.

   (a)

   (b)

   (c)

2. List the four levels in Bronfenbrenner's model.

   (a)
   (b)
   (c)
   (d)

3. What are the three major components of the child's biological makeup?

   (a)

   (b)

   (c)

4. A genetically based trait that is influenced only slightly by the environment is said to be strongly _____.

5. As children grow older and develop new abilities, parents tend to change the way they respond to them and the rules and expectations they have for them; in turn, the children's behavior changes in response. This is an example of _____ _____.

6. List four ways family members influence children's development.
   (a)

   (b)

   (c)

   (d)

7. Explain what it means to think of the family as a system.

8. List two ways siblings have direct effects on children's development.
   (a)

   (b)

9. What major issue about the effects of day care on children's development is still subject to the most debate?

10. List two ways normative developmental considerations are reflected in school structures and activities.
    (a)

    (b)

11. Explain how the social and economic context has both direct and indirect effects on children's development.

12. As of the year 2000, about _____ percent of American married women with children under 18 were employed outside the home.

13. List three negative outcomes often seen in children of unmarried adolescent mothers.

    (a)

    (b)

    (c)

14. List two major child-rearing tasks that are shared by adults in all cultures.

    (a)

    (b)

15. Explain why the same child-rearing practice, such as children sharing a bed with their parents, can have different meanings and different outcomes in different cultures.

ESSAY QUESTIONS:

1. Starting from what the textbook has to say about the effects of abnormal environments and about the range of child-rearing practices across cultures, suggest minimum requirements for an environment to be supportive of human development.

2. Using the levels in Bronfenbrenner's model, summarize what is distinctive about the developmental contexts each of the expected babies described in the vignettes will be born into.

3. Discuss the traits that children inherit as part of the evolutionary heritage shared by all humans.

4. List and explain the major characteristics of family systems.

5. Discuss what parents and teachers can do to counteract the effects of violence on children.

6. Summarize the effects of poverty on children's development and explain how those effects are brought about.

7. Explain two ways in which development itself provides a context for further development. Give an example of each.

ANSWER KEY

MULTIPLE-CHOICE QUESTIONS:

1. c   Research with children reared in institutions in Eastern Europe and elsewhere has found long-term problems in their physical, cognitive, social, and emotional development, which often continue even after children are adopted. The key factor seems to be lack of physical and social stimulation; meeting basic physical needs is not enough to prevent negative developmental consequences.

2. c   See the diagram of Bronfenbrenner's model.

3. b   The cultural context consists of abstract *ideas* that govern behavior and influence all the other contexts in Bronfenbrenner's model--beliefs, attitudes, values, etc. School board decisions, the particular reading series used in a school system, and reading test scores could all be *influenced* by cultural factors, but they would be found in other levels of the model, not at the cultural level.

4. d   All three characteristics listed are part of the evolutionary heritage shared by all infants. Answers *a* and *c* are shared with other primates; *b* is distinctive to the human species.

5. a   See the definition of **canalization.**

6. a   See the definition of **transactional model.**

7. b   Family systems are open, dynamic systems subject to change as well as continuity--by adding and losing members and through developmental changes in family members.

8. c   This is an indirect effect because the actions of the husband toward his wife have an impact on the children by affecting her behavior, even though the father has not behaved aggressively toward the children himself.

9. c   See Figure 2.2.

10. b   Peer groups provide a setting for learning about *equal*-status relationships, and they tend to *reinforce* cultural values and behavior standards.

11. a   Collective socialization by neighborhood adults appears to be a more important influence than behavioral contagion from peer influence. School influences and reciprocal determinism are not mentioned in the section on neighborhoods.

12. d   See the box on violence and children.

13. c   Although the *rate* of births to teenagers is higher now than in 1970, the *number* of births to teenagers actually peaked in the 1970s.

14. a   Maternal employment seems to have few effects on adolescents' adjustment or academic achievement; both positive and negative impacts are more noticeable in early and middle childhood.

15. d   Answers *a*, *b*, and *c* all help to decrease the likelihood of developmental problems.

16. b   The specific type of custody arrangement does not make much difference, as long as the arrangement that is chosen leads to reduced conflict between the divorcing parents.

17. c   Good and poor parenting are found in all social classes.

18. c   See statistics in the first paragraph under the heading **Poverty and Child Development.**

19. a   Competitiveness is *adaptive* in America because it helps children meet the demands of our culture. In Mexico cooperativeness is *adaptive* because it helps children meet the demands of Mexican culture, which are different from those in the U.S.

20. c   Children who are members of a subculture do not inevitably have problems in school; for example, many children of Asian immigrants do extremely well in American schools because the culture they are exposed to at home encourages educational achievement. Problems arise only when there is a mismatch between children's cultural background and the way their school is set up.

21. a   Erikson's entire theory is based on the idea that developmental history makes a difference in later adjustment.

22. a   Families provide the basis for children's biological makeup, establish their immediate environments, and determine the social/economic and cultural contexts in which they grow up to a greater extent than any other institution.

23. b   The Williams family is a good example of an extended family, with three generations living together and Momma Jo available to provide childcare for the new baby.

24. d   Answer *d* most accurately describes the situation in the Gordon family and its potential outcome.

25. c   If adolescent mothers graduate from high school, their babies have a reduced chance of developmental problems; getting a job might interfere with that goal, and moving to her own apartment might reduce Karen's chances of getting social support from her mother.

MATCHING QUESTIONS:

1. F	3. E	5. G	7. H
2. D	4. A	6. C	8. B

SHORT-ANSWER QUESTIONS:

1.   (a) Provide recurrent social interaction and emotional involvement with the same caregivers; (b) ensure continuity of care; (c) provide interesting sensory experiences on a daily basis.

2.   (a) Child's biological makeup; (b) immediate environment; (c) social and economic context; (d) cultural context.

3.   (a) The evolutionary heritage shared by all humans; (b) the child's individual genetic inheritance; (c) the biological results of interactions between genes and the environment.

4.   canalized

5.   bidirectional effects

6.   (a) They interact with the child on a daily basis, stimulating language and cognitive development; (b) they provide the child's first opportunity to form social relationships;
(c) they provide models for behavior; (d) the way the family is structured and the tasks the child is given foster the development of particular characteristics.

7.   Thinking of the family as a system implies that each family member's behavior is influenced by the behavior of the other family members and that all of them are affected by the organization of the family as a whole.

8.   (a) Younger siblings learn by imitating older siblings' behavior; (b) older siblings learn from the experience of having a younger sibling by taking on new roles and learning to interpret the younger child's behavior.

9.   The effects of day care on infants under a year old.

10. (a) In North America, nursery schools are flexibly structured; more formal instruction does not begin until middle childhood, when children are cognitively ready for it. (b) Children usually do not have different teachers for different subjects until middle school because a relationship with one central teacher is assumed to be emotionally important for elementary school children.

11. The social and environmental context affects children directly by influencing the resources available in their immediate environment; it affects them indirectly by influencing their parents' behavior through such factors as job stress and income level.

12. 70

13. Correct answers include developmental problems (including cognitive lags and behavior problems), school failure, delinquency, early sexual activity, and adolescent pregnancy.

14. (a) Providing infants with basic nurturance; (b) preparing children to function as adults in their particular social world.

15. The same child-rearing practice can have different means and different outcomes in different cultures because different cultures value and demand different personality characteristics and behavior; in other words, what is adaptive in one culture may not be adaptive in another.

ESSAY QUESTIONS:
1.   The research on environmental deprivation and on cross-cultural variation in child-rearing techniques suggests a number of requirements for a supportive environment. Obviously, the physical needs of the child must be met--food, clothing, cleanliness, a place to sleep, etc. However, the research on institutionalized infants suggests that meeting physical needs is not enough. Children also have a need for physical and social stimulation. Since humans have a predisposition to form bonds with other humans, it also seems that the *consistent* presence of one or more caregivers is necessary for healthy social and emotional development. The identity of these caregivers and the exact nature of their caregiving seem less important, since cultures have developed a variety of family organizations and child care practices.

2.   Here are some distinctive characteristics of each baby's developmental contexts (you may be able to think of others): At the biological level, the Williams baby will

be born to a mother over 35, which increases the risk of certain birth defects and pregnancy complications; the Polonius baby may also face certain risks as the result of being born to a teenage mother. At the level of the immediate environment, the three babies will be born into dramatically different family situations. The Williams baby will be part of an extended family, with a working mother and childcare from a grandmother. The Gordon baby will be the younger of two children, with an older sister and a mother who does not work outside the home. The Polonius baby will be the only child of a teenage mother, who lives with her own divorced mother. At the social and economic level, the Williams baby will face particular challenges as a result of being black (which could also be thought of as part of the biological context) and living in an inner city neighborhood. All of the babies are being born into families with some economic struggles, though the Polonius baby perhaps faces the greatest risk of being reared in poverty, as the child of an unmarried teenager. At the cultural level, the Williams baby will be raised in an African-American culture that differs in some ways from white American culture; this baby will also have to deal with culturally based attitudes of various white Americans toward blacks. The Gordon baby is being born into a family where culturally based attitudes about sex roles seem to be especially strong. The Polonius baby may have to deal with cultural stereotypes about unmarried teenage mothers and their children.

3. Your answer should include the fact that the evolutionary heritage shared by all humans includes some traits common to all mammals, some traits shared with other primates, and some unique to the human species. Specific traits mentioned in the chapter include the following: Like other mammals, human infants are born with a sucking reflex that allows them to get nourishment from their mothers immediately after birth, a tendency to act on the environment rather than being passive, and a capacity for learning. Like other primates, human infants have a tendency to seek social stimulation, form strong attachments with caregivers, and explore the environment and solve problems. Uniquely human characteristics include a timetable for developmental milestones; specific learning abilities, including the ability to acquire language; and behaviors that elicit caregiving responses from adults, such as crying, cooing, smiling, clinging, and following.

4. Three major characteristics of family systems are discussed in the textbook. The first major characteristic is that family systems are made up of many subsystems that form a coherent, interlocking network. Subsystems include relationships between siblings, between husband and wife, and between parent and child. Characteristics of each relationship have an impact on all of the other relationships in the system. Thus, each member of the family is affected not only by all of the other family members, but also by the way the whole family is organized. A second major characteristic is that a family is a dynamic, open system, subject to change as well as

continuity. Families change by adding and losing members and in response to changing external circumstances and developmental changes in family members. A third major characteristic of family systems is that they are subject to cyclical influences that can be repeated across generations. Family harmony or discord tends to be perpetuated from one generation to the next because the level of parents' marital harmony has an impact on children's personality development, which in turn influences their own marriage relationships. Parenting practices also tend to be passed down from one generation to the next. However, negative cycles can be broken if an adult from a harsh family background somehow manages to form a stable, supportive relationship with a marriage partner.

5. To answer this question, you need to use the information provided in the box on children and violence about factors that help to make the effects of violence on children less severe. These include a strong relationship with supportive and protective parents, family cohesiveness, support from outside the home, and the child's own intelligence, self-efficacy, and social and problem-solving skills. Suggestions for counteracting the effects of violence could be aimed at enhancing any of these factors. One important point is that efforts need not be directed specifically at violence-related issues; *general* abilities such as intelligence and social skills play a major role. For example, anything parents can do to increase family cohesiveness, to teach their children skills for dealing with conflict and other difficult social situations, and to enhance their children's basic intelligence and self-efficacy is helpful. In addition, parents can be encouraged to respond supportively and protectively when their children witness violence or are victimized by it. Parents may need help developing their own resources for dealing with a violent environment before they can help their children. Teachers can provide support from outside the family and can also help children both general intelligence, skills, and self-efficacy and more specific strategies for dealing with potential violence. It may also be helpful to think about the various effects that violence can have on children, as discussed in the box, and to direct your suggestions to counteracting specific effects.

6. The effects of poverty on children mentioned in the book include reduced IQ, vocabulary, and achievement test scores; increased likelihood of repeating grades, being placed in special education, and dropping out of school; and increased rates of problem behavior and delinquency. It is not simply being poor that produces these results. Instead, various factors that often go along with poverty tend to lead to problems. Prenatal problems may interfere with brain development, setting the stage for cognitive deficits. Exposure to lead in the environment and low cognitive stimulation may further impede cognitive development. Family stress and inadequate parenting may lead to social and emotional problems, often resulting in various kinds of problem behaviors.

7. One way that development provides a context for further development is in an individual's developmental history. That history gives the individual a set of expectations and ways of dealing with new demands, which in turn influences the course of future development. For example, the parent-infant relationship provides a basis for the toddler's later ability to comply with limits set by parents. Another way that development provides a context for further development is in maturation. Physical and cognitive maturational changes have a dramatic effect on how children interact with their environments. For example, toddlers become able to understand and use language as a result of physical and cognitive maturation.

CHAPTER 3
HEREDITY AND PRENATAL DEVELOPMENT
CHAPTER REVIEW

As you read the chapter, construct your own chapter outline by answering the following review questions and defining the *Key Terms*.

I. INTRODUCTION

   Key Terms: **prenatal period, differentiation**

   What are the four major themes of the chapter?

II. GENETIC PROCESSES

   Key Terms: **chromosome, gene, genome, somatic cells, mitosis, homologues, meiosis, germ cells, gamete, crossing over, random assortment, sex chromosomes, critical period, gonads, hormone, androgens, allele, homozygous, heterozygous, genotype, phenotype, sex-linked traits, polygenic**

   A. Explain the process of **mitosis** and what purpose it serves for an organism.

   B. Explain the process of **meiosis** and how the processes of **random assortment** and **crossing over** operate to produce genetic variability in a couple's children.

   C. Discuss how the environment affects the operation of **genes**. In particular, explain how genes and environment are involved in the development of physical gender.

D. Explain how **genes** interact with each other to influence development. In particular, explain the genetic basis of blood type in humans and how **sex-linked traits** operate.

III. CONCEPTION

Key Terms: **ovum, ovulation, zygote, dizygotic twins, monozygotic twins**

A. Describe the process of conception and the events leading up to it.

B. Explain the two ways that twinning can occur.

IV. PRENATAL DEVELOPMENT

Key Terms: **blastocyst, embryoblast, trophoblast, embryo, organogenesis, placenta, umbilical cord, amniotic sac, endoderm, mesoderm, ectoderm, embryonic induction, cephalocaudal development, proximodistal development, fetus, neural tube, neurons, neurogenesis, cerebral cortex, synapses**

A. List the three stages of prenatal development and state what is distinctive about each.

B. Summarize the events of the germinal period.

C. Summarize the events of the embryonic period. What principles are revealed by the timetable for embryonic development? Why is the embryonic period a particularly vulnerable period of development?

D. Summarize the events of the fetal period. How is the fetal period different from the embryonic period?

E. BOX: Summarize what takes place during prenatal brain development.

V. THE MOTHER'S EXPERIENCE OF PREGNANCY
    Key Term: **trimesters**
    Describe the typical experience of expectant mothers during each trimester of pregnancy.

VI. PROBLEMS IN PRENATAL DEVELOPMENT
Key Terms: **congenital (birth) defect, single-gene (Mendelian) disorder, chromosomal abnormality, sex chromosome abnormalities, teratogen, risk factors, fetal alcohol syndrome (FAS), estrogen, ultrasound, amniocentesis, chorionic villus sampling**

A. What are the major sources of **congenital defects** and what proportion of defects can be ascribed to each of these sources?

B. Explain the difference between **single-gene disorders** and **chromosomal abnormalities** and give examples of each.

C. Explain how **teratogens** cause their negative effects and how scientists have been able to identify effects of specific teratogens.

D. Explain the ways in which prenatal exposure to alcohol, tobacco, and illicit drugs can affect development. Summarize the effects of each.

E. BOX: Explain and give examples of how multiple **risk factors** can affect prenatal development.

F. Summarize the effects of various kinds of medications on prenatal development. What does the case of thalidomide illustrate about the action of **teratogens**?

G. Explain three different ways that maternal disease can affect an unborn child. Summarize the effects of various diseases on prenatal development.

H. Summarize the effects of maternal stress, maternal nutrition, and maternal age on prenatal development. Why is it sometimes difficult to interpret results of studies on these and other prenatal factors?

I.   Describe the prenatal diagnostic techniques now available and explain what kind of problems each can detect. Explain how genetic testing and counseling before conception can be useful.

VII. BIRTH

Key Terms: **Apgar scale, anoxia, premature, low birth weight, very low birth weight, cesarean section**

A.   Describe what happens during each of the three stages of labor.

B.   Explain what the **Apgar scale** measures and what it is used for.

C.   Explain how **anoxia** can occur and what risks it poses for a baby.

D.   What are the criteria for **prematurity**, for **low birth weight**, and for **very low birth weight**? Which low-birth-weight babies are at greatest risk? What factors are associated with low birth weight? What are the developmental outcomes for low-birth-weight babies?

E. Discuss cultural variations in childbirth practices and current trends in childbirth in the United States.

VIII. PRENATAL DEVELOPMENT IN CONTEXT
Explain how context influences prenatal development.

SELF-TEST

After **you have studied the chapter, use the following questions to test your understanding.**

MULTIPLE-CHOICE QUESTIONS:

1. The process by which embryonic cells take on specialized forms and functions is called:
    a. prenatal development.
    b. differentiation.
    c. reorganization.
    d. qualitative change.

2. Threadlike structures located in the nucleus of each cell that contain the organism's genetic instructions are called:
    a. genes.
    b. homologues.
    c. chromosomes.
    d. gametes.

3. Which of the following does NOT occur during the process of meiosis?
    a. Egg and sperm cells are formed.
    b. A total of two daughter cells are formed from one parent cell.
    c. New combinations of genes are created.
    d. The number of chromosomes in each cell is reduced.

4. Prenatal development of a female reproductive system results from:
    a. the presence of androgens.
    b. the presence of estrogens.
    c. the absence of androgens.
    d. a combination of androgens and estrogens.

5. If a couple both have Type O blood, which of the following blood types could be possible for their children?
    a. Type O.
    b. Type A.
    c. Type B.
    d. All of the above.

6. **Dizygotic twins** are the result of:
    a. two ova being fertilized at the same time.
    b. two sperm fertilizing the same ovum.
    c. a fertilized ovum dividing into two zygotes.
    d. any of the above can produce dizygotic twins.

7. Which of the following does NOT occur during the germinal period?
   a. Implantation of the zygote in the lining of the uterus.
   b. Formation of the blastocyst.
   c. The beginning of mitosis.
   d. Formation of the umbilical cord.

8. **Organogenesis** occurs during:
   a. the embryonic period.
   b. the fetal period.
   c. the germinal period.
   d. conception.

9. The heart and digestive system develop before limb buds, which develop before fingers and toes. This sequence of development illustrates:
   a. organogenesis.
   b. proximodistal development.
   c. cephalocaudal development.
   d. embryonic inductions.

10. The **fetus** differs from the **embryo** in that:
    a. all major organs and body parts have already formed in the fetus.
    b. the fetus is more responsive to stimulation than the embryo.
    c. the fetus is developing regular, integrated behaviors.
    d. all of the above.

11. Most of the neurons that will make up the **cerebral cortex** are formed:
    a. during the germinal period.
    b. during weeks 4-8 of prenatal development.
    c. during weeks 10-20 of prenatal development.
    d. after birth.

12. Morning sickness most often occurs during:
    a. the first trimester of pregnancy.
    b. the second trimester of pregnancy.
    c. the third trimester of pregnancy.
    d. it is equally likely during all three trimesters of pregnancy.

13. For over 40 percent of all birth defects, the cause is:
    a. purely genetic.
    b. purely environmental.
    c. multifactorial.
    d. unknown.

14. Which of the following would be an example of a **single-gene disorder**?
    a. Tay-Sachs disease
    b. Turner syndrome
    c. Down syndrome
    d. all of the above

15. Which of the following is NOT true of Down syndrome?
    a. It results from an extra twenty-first chromosome.
    b. It is caused by recessive genes.
    c. It increases in frequency with maternal age.
    d. Children with Down syndrome show abnormal physical development.

16. Which of the following would be most likely to cause serious negative effects on an unborn child's development?
    a. A mother who contracts rubella early in pregnancy.
    b. Thalidomide taken during the last two months of pregnancy.
    c. Continuous mild emotional stress throughout pregnancy.
    d. All are equally likely to cause serious problems.

17. A baby with unusual facial features who shows a pattern of poor growth, mental retardation, irritability, and hyperactivity is most likely to have been suffered heavy prenatal exposure to:
    a. cocaine.
    b. tobacco.
    c. heroin.
    d. alcohol.

18. **Ultrasound** can be used for:
    a. detecting structural defects in a developing fetus.
    b. monitoring fetal growth.
    c. guiding instruments for obtaining samples of amniotic fluid.
    d. all of the above.

19. The baby moves through the cervix into the vagina during the:
    a. first stage of labor.
    b. second stage of labor.
    c. third stage of labor.
    d. fourth stage of labor.

20. The purpose of the **Apgar scale** is to:
    a. detect fetal abnormalities early in pregnancy.
    b. determine whether a baby is ready to be born.
    c. monitor how much oxygen a baby is getting during delivery.
    d. assess a baby's condition immediately after birth.

21. Babies born less than ____ weeks after conception are considered **premature**; those weighing less than ____ pounds at birth are considered **low birth weight**.
    a. 30; 4.5
    b. 33; 5.0
    c. 35; 5.5
    d. 39; 6.0

22. Current childbirth-related issues of concern in the United States include:
    a. widespread use of general anesthetics.
    b. a high rate of cesarean sections.
    c. exclusion of fathers from the delivery room.
    d. all of the above.

23. In the vignette, Delores Williams expressed concern about having a baby at age 36. Which of the following problems are more likely in a mother of her age, compared to younger mothers?
    a. Birth defects due to recessive genes.
    b. Birth defects due to exposure to teratogens during pregnancy.
    c. Birth defects due to chromosomal damage.
    d. All of the above.

24. From the description of Christine Gordon's labor and delivery, it appears that she had:
    a. a cesarean section.
    b. instruction in the Lamaze method.
    c. an unusually difficult delivery.
    d. anesthesia during delivery.

25. Statistically, which of the following risks are heightened for Karen Polonius and her baby?
    a. Miscarriage.
    b. Stillbirth.
    c. Low birth weight.
    d. All of the above.

MATCHING QUESTIONS:
Match the following key terms with their definitions:

1. ___ Mitosis
2. ___ Meiosis
3. ___ Germ cells
4. ___ Trophoblast
5. ___ Teratogen
6. ___ Fetus
7. ___ Zygote
8. ___ Ectoderm
9. ___ Embryonic induction
10. ___ Anoxia
11. ___ Genotype
12. ___ Polygenic
13. ___ Gamete
14. ___ Heterozygous
15. ___ Organogenesis
16. ___ Allele
17. ___ Embryo
18. ___ Endoderm
19. ___ Homologues
20. ___ Gonads

A. A person's genetic makeup.

B. The sex glands--the ovaries and testes.

C. A mature reproductive cell (egg or sperm).

D. Influenced by multiple gene pairs.

E. The cell resulting from the union of a sperm cell with an ovum.

F. A disruption in the baby's oxygen supply during or just after birth.

G. One of several alternate forms of a particular gene.

H. The cells in the blastocyst that form the basis of the embryo's life-support system.

I. The process of cell division by which the body grows and repairs itself, in which the genetic material from the parent cell is duplicated in each daughter cell.

J. Cells that develop into internal organs such as the stomach, liver, and lungs.

K. The term applied to the developing organism during weeks 3 through 8 of prenatal development.

L. The formation of organs and other major body structures.

M. The cells from which eggs and sperm are produced.

N. Cells that form the central nervous system, sensory organs, and skin.

O. Carrying two different alleles for a particular trait.

P. Two chromosomes that form one of the 23 pairs of human chromosomes and resemble each other in size, shape, and the type of genes they carry.

Q. A chemical interaction between the cells of different tissues that triggers developmental changes.

R. The term applied to the developing organism during weeks 9 through 38 of prenatal development.

S. A substance in the environment that can cause abnormalities during prenatal development.

T. The process of cell division by which egg and sperm cells are formed.

SHORT-ANSWER QUESTIONS:

1. Give three examples of qualitative change during prenatal development.
    (a)

    (b)

    (c)

2. A segment of DNA that contains the code for producing a particular protein is called a

    _____.

3. Name the two processes during **meiosis** that make it possible for each child to inherit a unique combination of genes.
    (a)

    (b)

4. A person's genetic makeup is his or her _____; a person's observable traits constitute his or her _____.

5. Explain the difference between **monozygotic** and **dizygotic twins**.

6. The three stages of prenatal development are:
    (a)

    (b)

    (c)

7. Implantation of the zygote in the lining of the uterus is complete by the end of week ___ of prenatal development.

8. List the three major structures in the embryo's life-support system.
    (a)

    (b)

    (c)

9. The brain and spinal cord, as well as the lens of the eye, form as a result of

    _____.

10. The two major types of genetic defects are:
    (a)

    (b)

11. Explain how **sex chromosome abnormalities** occur.

12. During which period of prenatal development is the developing organism most susceptible to damage from **teratogens**?

13. List three ways maternal diseases can affect an unborn child.
   (a)

   (b)

   (c)

14. A pregnant woman first feels her baby move during the _____ trimester.

15. Which **low-birth-weight** babies are at greatest risk for later developmental problems?

ESSAY QUESTIONS:

1. Explain how the processes of **mitosis** and **meiosis** differ.

2. Explain the difference between the **trimesters** of pregnancy and the three stages of prenatal development.

3. Explain the concept of **critical periods** during prenatal development and describe the effects of a **teratogen** that illustrates this concept.

4. Based on the information in Chapter 3, discuss what could be done to reduce the infant mortality rate and the incidence of **birth defects** in your nation.

5. One of the themes of Chapter 3 is that prenatal development involves the interaction of various elements in a complex system. Discuss three examples of these interactions.

6. Using Bronfenbrenner's model of developmental contexts, discuss the hereditary and environmental contexts of prenatal development.

7. Suggest five practical implications of the information about genetics and prenatal development in Chapter 3 for parents-to-be.

ANSWER KEY

MULTIPLE-CHOICE QUESTIONS:

1. b   See the definition of **differentiation**.

2. c   See the definition of **chromosome**.

3. b   During meiosis, each parent cell produces four daughter cells. In sperm formation, all four become mature sperm cells; in egg formation, only one becomes a mature egg cell.

4. c   Female sex hormones need not be present for a female reproductive system to develop in a XX embryo; the critical factor is the *absence* of male sex hormones.

5. a   Because the gene for Type O blood is recessive, parents with Type O carry alleles only for Type O; thus, their offspring will all have Type O blood.

6. a   See the definition of **dizygotic twins**.

7. d   Formation of the umbilical cord occurs during the first week of the embryonic period.

8. a   All major organs and body structures form during the embryonic period.

9. b   See definition of **proximodistal development**.

10. d   Answers *a*, *b*, and *c* are all major characteristics of the fetal period.

11. c   See the box on prenatal brain development.

12. a   Some women have nausea in all three trimesters, but it is most common in the first.

13. d   About 25 percent of birth defects have purely genetic causes, about 3 percent purely environmental causes, and about 25 percent a combination of genetic and environmental causes; in the remainder of cases--over 40 percent--the cause is unknown.

14. a   Both Turner syndrome and Down syndrome are caused by chromosomal abnormalities.

15. b   It is caused by a chromosomal abnormality, an extra 21st chromosome.

16. a   Rubella early in pregnancy increases the risk of major birth defects. After the eighth week, thalidomide is not likely to produce birth defects. High levels of stress have been linked to low birth weight, prematurity, and newborn irritability, but there is no evidence of serious problems from mild stress.

17. d   These are the symptoms of fetal alcohol syndrome; this combination of problems is not associated with exposure to cocaine, tobacco, or heroin.

18. d   Answers *a*, *b*, and *c* are all common uses of ultrasound.

19. b   There are only three stages of labor; the second stage begins when the baby's head moves through the cervix into the vagina and ends when the baby is delivered.

20. d   See the definition of the **Apgar scale**.

21. c   See the criteria for considering a baby **premature** and of **low birth weight**.

22. b   General anesthetics are rarely used during childbirth in the United States, and fathers are generally allowed in the delivery room.

23. c   Only birth defects caused by chromosomal abnormalities increase with maternal age.

24. b   The mention of breathing exercises during labor suggests Christine used Lamaze or a similar method of childbirth preparation.

25. d   The risks of miscarriage, stillbirth, and low birth weight are all greater for babies of adolescent mothers than for babies of older mothers.

MATCHING QUESTIONS:

1. I	5. S	9. Q	13. C	17. K
2. T	6. R	10. F	14. O	18. J
3. M	7. E	11. A	15. L	19. P
4. H	8. N	12. D	16. G	20. B

SHORT-ANSWER QUESTIONS:

1. Correct answers would involve fundamental transformations in the developing organism. Examples include the process of cell differentiation, the change from the self-contained zygote to the embryo implanted in the wall of the uterus and dependent on the mother's body for nourishment, and the various embryonic inductions.

2. gene

3. crossing over and random assortment

4. genotype; phenotype

5. Monozygotic twins occur when a single fertilized divides into two separate organisms; dizygotic twins occur when two separate eggs are fertilized simultaneously.

6. (a) the germinal period; (b) the embryonic period; (c) the fetal period

7. 2

8. (a) placenta; (b) umbilical cord; (c) amniotic sac

9. embryonic inductions

10. (a) single-gene or Mendelian disorders; (b) chromosomal abnormalities.

11. Sex chromosome abnormalities occur when a baby receives an abnormal number of sex chromosomes (either extra or missing chromosomes), due to an error in meiosis when the father's sperm or the mother's egg was produced.

12. the embryonic period

13. Maternal diseases can affect an unborn child by: (a) directly affecting development of the embryo or fetus; (b) being transmitted from mother to child during pregnancy or delivery; (c) changing the mother's body chemistry.

14. second

15. Babies born small for gestational age, who have usually been affected by other risk factors during prenatal development, such as malnutrition, maternal illness, smoking, or drugs.

ESSAY QUESTIONS:
1. Your answer should include the following key points: Mitosis is the process of cell division by which the body grows and repairs itself throughout life, whereas meiosis is the process of cell division by which egg and sperm cells are formed. Mitosis involves only one cell division; meiosis involves two cell divisions. In both processes, the DNA in the original cell duplicates itself, producing double-stranded chromosomes. In mitosis, these split into single-stranded chromosomes and move

to opposite ends of the cell. The cell then divides, resulting in two new cells that are exact copies of the original, each containing 46 chromosomes. In meiosis, the first meiotic division occurs before the double-stranded chromosomes split, but after maternal and paternal genetic material has been exchanged and shuffled by means of crossing over and random assortment. The second meiotic division occurs after the double-stranded chromosomes split, resulting in four new cells, each containing 23 chromosomes.

2. The trimesters of pregnancy reflect the mother's experiences, such as morning sickness in the first trimester, quickening in the second, and physical strain in the third. Each is three months long. The stages of prenatal development reflect developmental changes in the unborn child, from a zygote in the first two weeks (germinal period), to an embryo in the next six weeks (embryonic period), to a fetus for the remaining 30 weeks or so of pregnancy (fetal period).

3. A critical period is a limited time when a particular organ or structure is especially susceptible to environmental influence, usually a period of exceptionally rapid differentiation and development. The effects of thalidomide clearly demonstrate critical periods in embryonic development. Depending on when a woman took thalidomide, her child might suffer widely varying birth defects. Thalidomide taken about 3 weeks after conception often produced a baby without ears. If it was taken a week later, the defects were usually in the baby's legs. If it was taken more than 8 weeks after conception, there usually were no birth defects at all.

4. Answers should focus on problems in prenatal development highlighted in Chapter 3. Specific proposals for reducing infant mortality and birth defects will vary from country to country. In the United States, examples of possible suggestions include: (a) reducing the number of adolescent pregnancies, which carry a heightened risk of stillbirth, low birth weight, and other problems; (b) making prenatal care more available to women with low incomes, which would increase the chances of identifying and treating problems early, would tend to improve maternal nutrition, would provide a source of social and emotional support to pregnant women, and would reduce the risk of premature delivery and low birth weight; (c) educating young women about the negative impacts of alcohol and tobacco on prenatal development, since exposure to these substances is much more common than exposure to illicit drugs and probably accounts for more infant mortality and birth defects.

5. Three possible answers to this question are: a) Interactions among dominant and recessive genes. Genes do not operate in isolation; the influence of each allele in a pair depends in part on the other member of the pair. Thus, inheriting a recessive gene for blue eyes or for Type O blood does not necessarily mean a child will develop that characteristic; the outcome depends on whether the corresponding

allele is also recessive. b) Embryonic inductions, in which interactions among various tissues in the developing embryo give rise to important developmental changes. For example, early in the embryonic period cells in the mesoderm induce neighboring cells in the ectoderm to differentiate into a brain and spinal cord. c) The development of sex organs in the embryo. The sex chromosomes in the embryo initially determine whether testes or ovaries will develop, but continued development of a male or female reproductive tract depends on hormonal influences. In genetically male embryos, the Y chromosome causes testes to form; the developing testes soon begin to produce androgens, which cause continued formation of the male reproductive tract. In genetically female embryos, the absence of a Y chromosome allows ovaries to form instead of testes. Ovaries do not produce androgens prenatally, and the absence of androgens allows the development of female reproductive organs to continue. This process can be disrupted if the embryo is exposed to abnormal levels of androgens or reacts to them in an abnormal way.

6. Factors that could be mentioned include: *Child's biological makeup*--the baby's genetic makeup (both normal traits and genetic abnormalities), plus all environmental factors that have a biological influence prenatally (drugs, disease, nutrition, hormones, etc.). *Immediate environment*--the day-to-day setting in which the baby's mother lives during her pregnancy, including the comfort and safety of her home and work environment and the state of her interpersonal relationships. These factors may affect the baby directly or indirectly, through their impact on the mother. *Social and economic level*--the mother's income and education level, health policies and political conditions in her country, etc.; these can affect the baby by influencing the mother's access to medical care, good nutrition, etc. *Cultural level*--cultural attitudes toward pregnancy and childbirth (and toward the mother's particular situation--being married or unmarried, old or young, etc.) influence the mother's activities during pregnancy and her feelings about the experience, which may in turn have an impact on the baby.

7. The information about genetics and prenatal development in Chapter 3 has many practical implications for parents-to-be. Here are five examples: (a) Understanding how dominant, recessive, and sex-linked genes interact can help parents-to-be estimate their likelihood of passing on some traits to their children; (b) understanding the mechanics of conception can help prospective parents increase their chances of achieving a pregnancy; (c) understanding the complexity of interactions between genes and environment can help parents appreciate the need to provide a healthy and stimulating environment for their children, rather than assuming genes by themselves are destiny; (d) knowing about the timetable for embryonic development can make mothers-to-be more aware of the importance of avoiding harmful substances early in pregnancy; (e) knowing the risks associated with maternal age can be useful to couples over 35 interesting in having a baby.

CHAPTER 4
FIRST ADAPTATIONS
CHAPTER REVIEW

As you read the chapter, construct your own chapter outline by answering the following review questions and defining the *Key Terms*.

I. INTRODUCTION
   Key Term: **preadapted, neonate**
   A. What are some capacities that make infants **preadapted** to learn about the world and form relationships with people?

   B. What are five major characteristics of infants' early competencies?

   C. What are the major themes of the chapter?

II. EARLY BRAIN DEVELOPMENT
   Key Terms: **brainstem, cerebellum, thalamus, limbic system, hypothalamus, hippocampus, amygdala, synaptogenesis, glial cells, myelination, plasticity, dendrites, axons, experience-expectant synaptogenesis, experience-dependent synaptogenesis**
   A. What research methods are used to study early brain development?

B. Summarize the brain growth that occurs in the first year of life.

C. Summarize the timetable and processes involved in brain development during infancy.

D. How do experience and developmental context influence early brain development?

E. BOX: Summarize practical implications of current knowledge about brain development.

III. INFANT STATES
A. List the six states that constitute the rest-activity cycle of infants and explain why infant states and the transitions between them are significant.

B. Describe and explain changes in sleep patterns over the first months of life.

C. What proportion of a newborn's time is spent crying? How does that change over the first months of life? Explain why babies cry. Describe the three distinct crying patterns that have been reported and factors involved in adults' ability to distinguish among them.

D. How do crying infants soothe themselves? How can caregivers soothe them?

E. How do infant transitions between states change with age? What individual differences in state transitions have been observed?

IV. REFLEXES IN THE NEWBORN
    Key Term: **reflex**
    A. List and describe the major reflexes present at birth.

B.   What is a survival reflex? Give examples of some that remain present throughout life and some that disappear during infancy, and explain why not all survival reflexes endure.

C.   List some reflexes that have no current survival value, but may once have had survival value for our ancestors.

D.   List two reflexes that disappear in the early months of life, but produce behaviors that later become part of voluntary actions. Explain why this shift occurs.

V.   INFANT LEARNING
     Key Terms: **habituation, orienting response, dishabituation, associative learning, classical conditioning, instrumental or operant conditioning, reinforcement, contingencies, shaping, imitative learning, preparedness**
     A.   Describe the process of **habituation** and **dishabituation**. Explain what it reveals about newborns' learning abilities and how it is used in research.

B.   Explain the processes of **classical** and **instrumental/operant conditioning**. When do infants become susceptible to each? What roles do they play in development?

C.   Explain how **imitative learning** differs from associative learning. Summarize Piaget's ideas about the development of imitation. Describe Meltzoff and Moore's findings on newborn imitation and how these findings have been criticized.

D.   Explain the concept of **preparedness** and how it influences infant learning.

E.   BOX: What basic problem do researchers studying infants' early behavior share? Describe the techniques they have developed to address this problem and summarize their uses and limitations.

VI. INFANT MOTOR SKILLS
   Key Terms: **saccadic eye movements, pursuit eye movements, prereaching, stereotypic leg movements**
   A. List and give ages for the major motor milestones in the first two years of life.

   B. List and explain four major principles involved in the development of motor skills.

   C. Summarize the development of infants' eye movement and explain how it is significant for infants' experience of the world around them.

   D. Describe the development of reaching and grasping in infants. Explain how the transfer from reflexive to voluntary action is made.

E. Explain the relationship between walking, reflexive stepping, and stereotypic leg movements. Explain the role of maturation and practice in the development of walking.

VII. SENSING AND PERCEIVING THE WORLD

Key Terms: **visual acuity, retina, fovea, categorical perception, perception, kinetic depth cues, binocular depth cues, strabismus, pictorial depth cues, size constancy, shape constancy**

A. Describe the techniques that have been used to test infants' **visual acuity**. Summarize what is known about early visual acuity and early color vision.

B. Summarize what is known about infants' early hearing abilities and speech perception. What research techniques are used to study these abilities?

C. Summarize what is known about infants' senses of smell and taste.

D. Summarize what is known about infants' sense of touch

E.   What are some ways infant sensory behavior is organized?

F.   What does visual cliff research tell us about infant depth perception?

G.   Summarize research findings on the development of infants' ability to use **kinetic, binocular,** and **pictorial depth cues**.

H.   Summarize research findings on the development of **size and shape constancy**.

I.   Describe and explain the development of infants' responses to and recognition of faces.

VIII. FIRST ADAPTATIONS IN CONTEXT

How do biology and the environment contribute to the development of infants' early abilities?

SELF-TEST

***After* you have studied the chapter, use the following questions to test your understanding.**

MULTIPLE-CHOICE QUESTIONS:

1. Newborns will turn their heads to a variety of sounds, but they show particular interest in human voices. This is an example of:
   a. preadapted behavior.
   b. reflexive behavior.
   c. categorical perception.
   d. instrumental conditioning.

2. Which process of brain development is most nearly complete at birth?
   a. Myelination of neurons.
   b. Formation of new neurons.
   c. Increase in size of neurons.
   d. Formation of connections between neurons.

3. Cross-cultural research on infant sleep patterns has revealed that:
   a. by 8 weeks of age infants around the world adopt a conventional day-night pattern of sleep and wakefulness.
   b. in many cultures babies continue the pattern of short sleep cycles distributed around the clock much longer than in the U.S.
   c. in many cultures babies sleep through the night much earlier than in the U.S.
   d. culture-specific infant care practices seem to have no effect on infant sleep patterns.

4. Which of the following statements about adults' interpretations of infant cries is TRUE?
   a. Women, but not men, are able to instinctively identify the cause of most infant cries.
   b. Experienced and inexperienced nurses are equally good at recognizing different cries.
   c. Mothers can interpret their own infant's cries better than those of an unfamiliar infant.
   d. Most adults cannot distinguish among different types of infant cries.

5. In the first few months of life, infant states and the transitions between them change in which of the following ways?
   a. The states become more stable and predictable.
   b. State changes become less frequent.
   c. Infants gain increasing control over their states.
   d. All of the above.

6. Stepping and grasping are examples of reflexes that:
   a. appear several weeks after birth.
   b. are seen in some infants but not all.
   c. are present continuously from birth until they are transformed into voluntary actions.
   d. disappear but involve movements that later reappear as part of voluntary actions.

7. Which of the following is a description of the Moro reflex?
   a. Flinging out the arms and then bringing them back together in response to the head suddenly being allowed to drop backwards.
   b. Fanning the toes outward and twisting the foot inward in response to the side of the foot being stroked.
   c. Turning the head to one side, extending the arm and leg on that side, and flexing the other arm and leg in response to being placed on the back.
   d. Turning the head straight ahead, opening the mouth, and closing the eyes in response to pressure applied to the palms of both hands.

8. An infant is presented with a blue and red checkerboard pattern that captures his attention. After 30 seconds of looking at the checkerboard, he loses interest and looks away. This is an example of:
   a. habituation.
   b. conditioning.
   c. associative learning.
   d. preparedness.

9. Before age 3 months, infants show little tendency toward:
   a. habituation.
   b. detecting contingencies.
   c. instrumental conditioning.
   d. classical conditioning.

10. Which of the following statements about the development of imitation would Piaget have agreed with?
    a. Newborns are capable of true imitation of others' actions.
    b. The ability to imitate others develops gradually during the first two years of life.
    c. Imitation is not related to infants' capacity for mental representation.
    d. All of the above.

11. The fact that young infants readily smile, detect contingencies, and orient to faces and voices illustrates the concept of:
    a. classical conditioning.
    b. operant conditioning.
    c. preparedness.
    d. habituation.

12. On average, infants become able to stand alone at about age:
    a. 5-10 months.
    b. 7-13 months.
    c. 10-14 months.
    d. 14-22 months.

13. The fact that reaching and grasping develop before walking illustrates the principle of:
    a. cephalocaudal development.
    b. proximodistal development.
    c. differentiation.
    d. All of the above.

14. Research has demonstrated that the onset of walking depends on:
    a. maturation of the nervous system.
    b. maturation of the muscles.
    c. practice.
    d. all of the above.

15. At 2 weeks, infants see at 20 feet what adults with normal vision can see at 300 feet. Five months later, infants see at 20 feet what adults can see at 100 feet. This reflects improved:
    a. visual acuity.
    b. visual evoked potential.
    c. categorical perception.
    d. preferential looking.

16. Based on current research, when do infants appear to achieve adult-like color vision?
    a. At birth.
    b. By age 2 weeks.
    c. By age 3-4 months.
    d. By age 1 year.

17. Research by Peter Eimas and his colleagues revealed that 1-month-olds are particularly sensitive to changes in:
    a.   loudness.
    b.   pitch.
    c.   speech sounds.
    d.   location of a sound.

18. The lack of precision in newborns' sense of taste probably results from:
    a.   inefficient processing of information from the taste buds.
    b.   immaturity of the taste buds at birth.
    c.   the presence of taste buds throughout the mouth in early infancy.
    d.   all of the above.

19. Recent research on infants' experience of pain indicates that:
    a.   newborns do not experience pain in any real sense.
    b.   the neurological structures involved are not in place until six weeks after birth.
    c.   repeated or intense pain has no negative long-term effects on neonates.
    d.   premature newborns and older fetuses are capable of feeling pain.

20. The visual cliff is a device used by Gibson and Walk to study:
    a.   binocular depth cues.
    b.   depth perception.
    c.   size constancy.
    d.   shape constancy.

21. The first type of cues for depth and distance that infants become able to use are:
    a.   binocular depth cues.
    b.   kinetic depth cues.
    c.   pictorial depth cues.
    d.   categorical depth cues.

22. Research on face perception has revealed that newborns show a preference for:
    a.   static face-like patterns.
    b.   moving face-like patterns.
    c.   photographs of their own mothers' faces.
    d.   all of the above.

23. When 4-month-old Malcolm is excited, he kicks his feet vigorously. This is an example of:
    a.   stereotypic leg movements.
    b.   reflexive behavior.
    c.   the stepping reflex.
    d.   all of the above.

24. Mikey probably *started* to say "beh" to request toast as a result of:
    a. associative learning.
    b. classical conditioning.
    c. shaping.
    d. imitative learning.

25. Compared to other babies her age, Meryl's transitions between states seem to be:
    a. smoother.
    b. more predictable.
    c. more uncontrolled.
    d. pretty much on target.

MATCHING QUESTIONS:
Match the following key terms with their definitions:

1. ___ Reinforcement

2. ___ Cerebellum

3. ___ Classical conditioning

4. ___ Saccadic eye movements

5. ___ Orienting response

6. ___ Brainstem

7. ___ Habituation

8. ___ Prereaching

9. ___ Dendrites

10. ___ Plasticity

11. ___ Axons

12. ___ Strabismus

13. ___ Pursuit eye movements

14. ___ Hippocampus

15. ___ Operant or instrumental
        conditioning

A. A brain structure that integrates sensory information and is essential to memory formation.

B. Smooth, continuous eye motions used to track a moving object.

C. Any event following a behavior that increases the likelihood the behavior will be repeated.

D. The capacity for different areas of the brain to take on new functions.

E. The decrease in attention that occurs when the same stimulus is presented repeatedly.

F. Short, branching neuron structures that receive electrical impulses from other neurons.

G. A condition in which the eyes are misaligned and do not function together.

H. Long neuron structures that branch at the end and relay electrical impulses to other neurons.

I. The response when a stimulus is first presented, involving both behavioral and physiological changes.

J. The rapid, jerky eye movements that occur when the gaze is shifted to a new object.

K. A learning process in which a new stimulus comes to elicit an established reflex response through association with an old stimulus.

L. Early spontaneous arm movements, sometimes made in response to an object.

M. The part of the brain that controls basic reflexes and other body functions.

N. Learning in which behaviors are influenced by their consequences.

O. A brain structure involved in motor control.

SHORT-ANSWER QUESTIONS:

1. List five major characteristics of infants' early competencies.
    (a)

    (b)

    (c)

    (d)

    (e)

2. At birth an infant's brain is about _____ of its adult weight.

3. List four research methods used to study early brain development.
    (a)

    (b)

    (c)

    (d)

4. List the six infant states identified in the textbook.

    (a)

    (b)

    (c)

    (d)

    (e)

    (f)

5. Explain why babies cry.

6. An automatic response to a particular stimulus is called a _____.

7. When a father lightly strokes his newborn son's cheek, the baby turns his head toward the father's hand and opens his mouth. This is an example of the _____ reflex.

8. Give two examples of reflexes that have no current survival value, but may once have had survival value for our ancestors.

    (a)

    (b)

9. Describe the process of **habituation** and **dishabituation**.

10. The genetic predisposition to learn certain behaviors is called _____.

11. What is the basic problem faced by researchers studying infants' early behavior?

12. Infants typically begin to roll over at about _____ months of age.

13. List three responses researchers monitor to measure infants' hearing ability.
    (a)

    (b)

    (c)

14. Convergence and retinal disparity are examples of _____ depth cues.

15. Recognizing that a square table remains square, even though it produces a trapezoidal image on the retina when viewed from certain angles, is an example of _____.

ESSAY QUESTIONS:

1. Explain what it means to say that infants are **preadapted** to learn about the world and form social relationships and give three examples of capacities that demonstrate this.

2. Discuss the six main processes involved in early brain development.

3. Explain the difference between **experience-expectant** and **experience-dependent synaptogenesis**.

4. Explain why infant state is of interest to researchers and how a knowledge of states and a sensitivity to state changes might be useful for parents.

5. Describe the development of reaching and grasping in infants and explain the transition from reflexive to voluntary action.

6. Describe the status of the sense of touch at birth and explain how touch is biologically adaptive for newborns.

7. Summarize the various techniques that have been used to measure young infants' visual acuity and the results that have been obtained from them. Suggest an explanation for the differences in results and discuss what we can conclude about early visual acuity when all the results are taken into consideration.

ANSWER KEY

MULTIPLE-CHOICE QUESTIONS:

1. a   Newborns' interest in human voices is one of the built-in capacities that help them understand the world and form social relationships.

2. b   Nearly all the neurons in the brain are present at birth.

3. b   In cultures where adults are less concerned about time and schedules and where babies sleep with their mothers, babies tend to wake frequently at night to nurse.

4. c   Most adults can distinguish among the three major types of infant cries, but experience with babies and familiarity with a particular baby do make a difference.

5. d   As infants gain increasing control over them, states become more stable and predictable, and state changes less frequent.

6. d   Stepping and grasping reflexes do disappear over time, but the motions involved in both later reappear as part of voluntary actions.

7. a   See description of reflexes in Table 4.1.

8. a   See definition of **habituation**.

9. d   Some researchers have classically conditioned newborns, but the disposition toward this form of conditioning does not become well established until about 3 months of age.

10. b   Piaget believed that a capacity for mental representation had to be present before imitation of others' behavior was possible. According to Piaget, that capacity develops gradually over the first two years of life; because newborns lack mental representation, they are not capable of true imitation.

11. c   Babies are genetically predisposed to learn all of these behaviors.

12. c   See Figure 4.4 for ages at which milestones of motor development are typically reached.

13. a   Reaching and grasping involve upper extremities, walking involves lower extremities; thus, this sequence illustrates top-down or cephalocaudal development

14. d   All three factors contribute to the onset of walking.

15. a   See definition of **visual acuity**.

16. c   There is no evidence that babies can reliably discriminate on the basis of color alone until about 7-8 weeks; by 3-4 months they appear to have adult-like color vision.

17. c   Young infants are sensitive to many sound characteristics, but research by Eimas et al. shows that they are particularly sensitive to changes in speech sounds.

18. a   Taste buds are relatively mature at birth, and they become localized on the tongue around the time of birth, but the nervous system initially processes taste information inefficiently.

19. d   The neurological structures involved in pain are in place by about the 29th week of prenatal development, and it is clear that even premature newborns and older fetuses do feel pain. Repeated or intense pain during the neonatal period does appear to have negative long-term effects on physiological responses to pain and stress and on the immune system.

20. b   The visual cliff was used to study the development of depth perception, but not binocular depth cues.

21. b   Infants begin to use kinetic depth cues at about 3 months of age, binocular depth cues between 3 and 5 months of age, and pictorial depth cues between 5 and 7 months of age.

22. b   Newborns show a preference for moving face-like patterns, but a preference for static face-like patterns does not emerge until 2 to 3 months of age. Preference for photographs of their own mothers appears around 3 months of age.

23. a   Stereotypic leg movements occur automatically when a baby is excited, but they are not considered reflexive because they occur in response to a variety of stimuli.

24. d   "Beh" probably represents an attempt to imitate the word "bread"; Mikey's parents may use shaping to help him produce sounds closer to the actual word.

25. c   All of the descriptions of Meryl in the vignette portray her as a relatively cranky baby whose states and state changes are not well controlled or predictable.

MATCHING QUESTIONS:

1.	C	4.	J	7.	E	10.	D	13.	B
2.	O	5.	I	8.	L	11.	H	14.	A
3.	K	6.	M	9.	F	12.	G	15.	N

SHORT-ANSWER QUESTIONS:

1. (a) They depend on prewired abilities; (b) They often meet survival needs; (c) They involve organized sequences of actions that serve some purpose; (d)They involve selective responses; (e)They allow infants to detect relationships between actions and consequences.

2. one-quarter

3. Six methods are mentioned in Chapter 4: (a) Studying the growth of infants' heads; (b) examining the brains of babies who die (post-mortem examinations); (c) EEGs of normal infants; (d) brain imaging methods (such as MRIs and PET scans), usually involving infants with medical need for them; (d) animal experiments involving enriched or deprived environments; and (e) studies of children who have suffered early deprivation.

4. quiet sleep, active sleep, awake-and-quiet, awake-and-active, fussing, and crying

5. Babies cry whenever their nervous systems are overly excited, regardless of the specific cause; however, the cries vary somewhat depending on what produces them.

6. reflex

7. rooting

8. the Moro reflex and the grasping reflex

9. When an unfamiliar stimulus is presented, infants typically show a set of behavioral and physiological responses called the **orienting response**; they stop other activity, pay attention to the new stimulus, and show pupil dilation and changes in heart rate. If the stimulus is presented repeatedly, **habituation** occurs-- the baby gradually loses interest in it and resumes other activity. If a different stimulus is then presented, the orienting response typically occurs again, demonstrating **dishabituation**.

10. preparedness

11. Because young infants can't talk and don't understand language, they can't follow instructions or tell researchers what they are experiencing.

12. 2 to 5

13. eye blinks, heart rate, and the brain's electrical activity

14. binocular

15. shape constancy

ESSAY QUESTIONS:

1. Saying infants are preadapted to learn about the world and form social relationships means that they come equipped with built-in abilities and predispositions that help them with these tasks. Just about all of the inborn capacities discussed in Chapter 4 are helpful in one or the other of these tasks and could be used as examples. A few examples are the built-in tendency to cry whenever the nervous system is overly stimulated, which elicits care from adults; inborn interest in human faces and voices, which foster the beginnings of social interaction with adults; organized use of sensory abilities, such as turning in the direction of a sound and visually scanning the environment, which help babies begin to learn about the world around them; and the built-in ability to detect contingencies between events and their consequences, which is useful both for establishing social interaction and for understanding the world.

2. The six main processes involved in early brain development are: (a) neurogenesis and neural migration, (b) structural elaboration and differentiation of neurons, (c) synaptogenesis, (d) formation of glial cells and myelination, (e) increasing connections between regions of the brain, and (f) pruning of excess synapses and loss of plasticity. Neurogenesis and neural migration occur mainly before birth, though neurons do continue to form in the cerebellum for the first 18 months of life and there is evidence from animal research of limited neuron formation throughout life in other parts of the brain. Structural elaboration involves the formation of axons and dendrites, beginning during neuron migration. These structures eventually form connections with other neurons. Differentiation involves the development of specific functions for neurons, based partly on when they are formed and partly on where they end up after migration. Synaptogenesis is the formation of connections between neurons, which is made possible by the development of axons and dendrites. It begins before birth, but reaches its peak at various points after birth for various parts of the brain. Glial cells produce a fatty substance called myelin, which forms sheaths around nerve fibers. This process of myelination increases the efficiency of electrical conduction between neurons. It begins in the spinal cord and lower brain regions before birth and continues in

higher brain regions until adolescence. In addition to connections between brain cells, connections between various regions of the brain also increase during infancy. Synaptogenesis produces more connections between neurons than needed. Synapses that are not used are eventually eliminated or pruned, beginning around 1 year of age and continuing into adolescence. Pruning of excess synapses reduces brain plasticity.

3. Experience-expectant synaptogenesis occurs in response to input that can be expected in virtually any environment typical for a particular species. It reflects species-level adaptation to the environment and produces developmental outcomes that are found in all normally developing members of a species, such as binocular vision in humans. It is most prominent in early development and is involved in the development of basic neurological structures, such as the human visual system. There are often specific critical periods for experience-expectant synaptogenesis-- for example, if the brain does not receive input from both eyes during a key period of early brain development, binocular vision does not develop normally. Experience-dependent synaptogenesis occurs in response to input that is specific to the individual. It reflects individuals' adaptation to unique features of their environment and produces individual differences in developmental outcomes, such as individual memories, knowledge, and skills. It occurs throughout life and is involved in refinement of neurological structures. It does not have critical periods.

4. Infant state is of interest to researchers because the infant's learning and ability to attend to the environment are significantly affected by state. Babies are most likely to notice and respond to a stimulus when they are in an awake and quiet state. Infants become increasingly easy to study over the first few months of life, partly because their states become more stable and predictable and they develop greater control over them. A knowledge of states and sensitivity to state changes might help parents understand their baby's behavior better and know when attempts at interaction are most likely to succeed. Such knowledge is also useful because parents initially play a large role in helping infants make transitions from one state to another by soothing them when they are distressed, rocking them to sleep, and rousing them to a more active state. An understanding of states and state changes might also help parents cope with infants who are irritable, lethargic, or have unpredictable state changes.

5. Both reaching and grasping begin with reflexive behaviors that are gradually replaced by voluntary ones. Newborns respond to objects with an increased rate of arm movements in the direction of the object, though they seldom actually make contact; these behaviors are called prereaching. Between 1 and 4 months, there is a decline in the frequency of prereaching behaviors. Intentional reaching emerges around 4 months of age and gradually becomes more refined; by about 15 months, babies can reach for objects smoothly and accurately. Grasping begins with the

newborn grasping reflex, an automatic response to anything placed across the infant's palm. This response weakens after about 3 months and disappears entirely by one year. By 3 to 4 months of age, infants can grasp objects voluntarily, but they have trouble letting go of them until about age 6 months. From the beginning, they adjust their grasping somewhat to the size, shape, and texture of the object, but at first they tend to grasp objects with the whole hand. Gradually their grasping becomes more refined; by about 8 months, they can use the thumb in opposition to the fingers, and by about one year they can use just the thumb and forefinger to pick up small objects. The transition from reflexive to voluntary action reaching and grasping depends partly on physical maturation, as higher areas of the brain become increasingly developed. However, experience, active exploration of the environment, and pursuit of particular goals (reaching for a particular object because it is desired, for example) all contribute to the development and refinement of these abilities.

6. Describe the status of the sense of touch at birth and explain how touch is biologically adaptive for newborns. The sense of touch is more fully developed at birth than the other senses. The neurological structures involved in touch begin to form about 6 weeks after conception and are essentially complete by about the 24th week of prenatal development. Having a well-developed sense of touch is biologically adaptive for newborns because touch is involved in many newborn reflexes, such as rooting and sucking. Touch is important for state regulation from the time of birth; swaddling and contact with caregivers help to soothe a crying baby. Skin-to-skin contact with adults, massage, and other forms of tactile stimulation are all beneficial to low-birth-weight infants. For all infants, touch soon becomes an important means of gathering information about the physical world, as they grasp and manipulate objects and put them into their mouths.

7. The techniques that have been used to measure early visual acuity include preferential looking, and the visual evoked potential. In preferential looking studies, infants are shown two cards, one a solid gray and the other containing black and white stripes. As long as the infant can detect the stripes, he or she will spend more time looking at that card than at the gray card. In visual evoked potential studies, infants' brain waves are monitored as they are shown a series of stimuli. If they are able to detect the difference between two stimuli, there will be a characteristic change in their brain wave pattern when the new stimulus is presented. The studies based on preferential looking and other behavioral measures suggest that a 2-week-old's visual acuity is about 20/300 and a 5-month-old's is about 20/100. The visual evoked potential studies give somewhat higher estimates of infants' visual acuity but the same pattern of improvement across time. One possible explanation of the different estimates is that the visual evoked potential is a more sensitive measure of infants' visual acuity. Another is that some visual information may be transmitted to the brain, but the relative immaturity of

connections within the brain and to other parts of the body may not allow the infant to make much use of it. Whatever the reason for the differing results, based on current research evidence we can conclude that infants' visual acuity is considerably worse than adults' at birth and that it gradually improves over the first few months of life.

CHAPTER 5
INFANT COGNITIVE DEVELOPMENT

CHAPTER REVIEW

As you read the chapter, construct your own chapter outline by answering the following review questions and defining the *Key Terms*.

I. INTRODUCTION
    A. What are the major themes of the chapter?

    B. What are the major cognitive advancements and limitations of infancy?

II. PIAGET'S THEORY OF INFANT COGNITIVE DEVELOPMENT
    Key Terms: **sensorimotor period, adaptation, assimilation, accommodation, schemes, equilibration, circular reaction, primary circular reaction, secondary circular reaction, coordination of schemes, tertiary circular reaction, deferred imitation, symbolic or representational thought**
    A. Why does Piaget's theory provide a good starting point for studying cognitive development?

B. What are Piaget's basic assumptions about the nature of infants?

C. Describe the major processes of change in Piaget's theory and explain how they work together to produce cognitive development.

D. On what did Piaget base his initial description of infant cognitive development?

E. Summarize Piaget's description of infant cognitive development, including the approximate age range and the accomplishments of each stage.

III. CHALLENGES TO PIAGET'S THEORY
   Key Terms: **décalage, neo-nativist, working memory**
   A. How accurate has Piaget's theory of infant cognitive development turned out to be?

B. List and explain the major areas of disagreement surrounding Piaget's ideas.

IV. INFANTS' UNDERSTANDING OF THE PHYSICAL WORLD
    Key Term: **object permanence**
    A. Compare how Piaget and the neo-nativists explain the development of infants' understanding of the physical world.

    B. Summarize Piaget's account of the development of object permanence.

    C. What has more recent research revealed about infants' understanding of object permanence?

D. Summarize the results of research on infants' understanding of causality and other relations between objects.

E. Summarize the results of research on infants' understanding of number.

F. Summarize the results of research on infants' use of categorization.

V. MEMORY DEVELOPMENT IN INFANCY
   Key Terms: **recognition memory, recall, cued recall, explicit or declarative memory, implicit or procedural memory, infantile amnesia, autobiographical memory**
   A. What did Piaget believe about infant memory?

B.   What are the characteristics of memory in the first six months of life?

C.   What improvements in memory occur between six and eighteen months of age?

D.   Explain how brain development is related to infant memory.

E.   BOX: What explanations have been proposed for **infantile amnesia**? What factors are most likely to be involved in this phenomenon?

VI. SOCIAL CONTEXT AND COGNITIVE DEVELOPMENT IN INFANCY
   A.   Compare Piagetian, information-processing theorists, and sociocultural perspectives on the role of the environment in cognitive development.

B. How does the social environment influence infants' cognitive and motor development? What has cross-cultural research on infants' sensorimotor development revealed?

C. List three important observations about cognitive development made from the Vygotskian perspective.

D. BOX: What misconceptions do parents sometimes have about stimulation to enhance infant cognitive development? Under what circumstances are special infant stimulation programs useful? How do they foster cognitive development?

VII. INDIVIDUAL DIFFERENCES IN INFANT COGNITIVE SKILLS
   A. How are individual differences in infant cognitive skills measured?

B. Summarize the research findings on the value of measures of infant cognitive ability for predicting later performance on tests of cognitive skills.

VIII. ADVANCES AND LIMITATIONS: AN OVERVIEW
A. Summarize the major cognitive developments of the first two years of life.

B. What cognitive limitations remain at the end of infancy?

SELF-TEST

***After* you have studied the chapter, use the following questions to test your understanding.**

MULTIPLE-CHOICE QUESTIONS:

1. Which of the following cognitive abilities develops primarily after infancy?
    a.   A basic understanding of object properties.
    b.   The ability to use symbolic thought.
    c.   The ability to use categorization.
    d.   The ability to combine actions into sequences to achieve desired ends.

2. According to Piaget, infants' knowledge of the world is based on:
    a.   emerging language and abstract concepts.
    b.   primarily passive observation.
    c.   active physical exploration alone.
    d.   sensory awareness and motor acts.

3. A baby who tries (often unsuccessfully) to pick up all kinds of objects, from a large teddy bear to a tiny raisin, using the same whole-handed grasp, is demonstrating the principle of:
    a.   décalage.
    b.   assimilation.
    c.   accommodation.
    d.   equilibration.

4. **Tertiary circular reactions** involve:
    a.   trial-and-error experimentation.
    b.   goal-directed chains of behavior.
    c.   objects or events outside the infant's body.
    d.   the infant's own body.

5. An infant repeatedly hits a ball on the side of her crib and squeals in delight. This is an example of:
    a.   object permanence.
    b.   a tertiary circular reaction.
    c.   a primary circular reaction.
    d.   a secondary circular reaction.

6. An infant who opens a cupboard door to get to a favorite toy is probably at or past sensorimotor stage:
    a.   3.
    b.   4.
    c.   5.
    d.   6.

7. Reassessments of Piaget's theory of infant cognitive development have primarily focused on:
    a. inaccuracies in his description of infant behavior.
    b. disagreements about his explanations of infant behavior.
    c. both his description and his explanations of infant behavior.
    d. his definition of infancy.

8. **Décalage** refers to:
    a. variations in different children's rate of development.
    b. inconsistencies between one child's physical, cognitive, and social development.
    c. inconsistencies in one child's cognitive development in different domains.
    d. it can refer to any of the above.

9. Piaget believed that infants came equipped at birth with:
    a. reflexive behaviors and a tendency to actively engage the world.
    b. a primitive concept of objects.
    c. an understanding of many basic properties of the physical world.
    d. fairly specific learning mechanisms.

10. According to Piaget, infants first begin to search for completely hidden objects at about age:
    a. 4-8 months.
    b. 8-12 months.
    c. 12-18 months.
    d. 18-24 months.

11. Piaget argued that 12- to 18-month-olds still have an incomplete understanding of object permanence because:
    a. they will not search for completely hidden objects.
    b. they will not search for partially hidden objects.
    c. they search for objects wherever they last disappeared from sight.
    d. they search for objects only in places where they previously found them.

12. Baillargeon's research on events involving hidden objects suggests that:
    a. 4- to 8-month-olds understand that hidden objects continue to exist and occupy space.
    b. 4- to 8-month-olds do not understand that hidden objects occupy space.
    c. 1- to 4-month-olds understand that hidden objects continue to exist and occupy space.
    d. infants have a basic understanding of the properties of hidden objects soon after birth.

13. Research on infants' understanding of causality and other object relations suggests that:
    a.   infants are born with a basic understanding of these relations.
    b.   infants develop a rudimentary understanding of these relations between 4 and 8 months.
    c.   infants develop a rudimentary understanding of these relations between 12 and 18 months.
    d.   children do not begin to develop an understanding of these relations until after age 2.

14. Which of the following is NOT true of infants' understanding of number?
    a.   Infants as young as 3 months can perceive number in sequences of events.
    b.   4- to 7-month-olds can recognize the difference between sets of 2 and 3 objects.
    c.   5-month-olds are sensitive to changes in the number of objects in a display.
    d.   Infants' understanding of number does not seem to be limited to small quantities.

15. At what age do infants clearly begin to use categories to make generalizations about the world?
    a.   as early as 3 months
    b.   at around 7 months
    c.   by about 14 months
    d.   not until 18 months

16. Piaget believed that infants' memory abilities were limited to:
    a.   recognition memory.
    b.   recall.
    c.   cued recall.
    d.   explicit memory.

17. During the first six months of life, infants' memory appears to be:
    a.   bound to particular contexts.
    b.   dependent on immediate perceptual cues.
    c.   consistent with Piaget's view that infants lack true mental representations.
    d.   all of the above.

18. Which of the following types of memory first develops after 6 months of age?
    a.   implicit memory
    b.   explicit memory
    c.   memory that involves lower brain structures
    d.   memory used in habituation

19. For most people, **autobiographical memory** begins at around:
    a.   age 6 months.
    b.   age 1 year.
    c.   age 32 to 4 years.
    d.   whatever age they begin to talk.

20. Cross-cultural research on sensorimotor development has found:
    a.   great variations across cultures in the age at which infants can do object permanence tasks.
    b.   striking similarities in the processes of sensorimotor development.
    c.   wide variations in how infants from different cultures manipulate objects.
    d.   similarities in behavior only with objects that have no cultural meaning.

21. Successful stimulation programs for premature infants usually provide:
    a.   tactile stimulation in the early weeks of life.
    b.   age-appropriate cognitive stimulation.
    c.   support to parents to foster adult-child interaction.
    d.   all of the above.

22. Which of the following abilities measured in infancy is MOST predictive of IQ later in childhood?
    a.   sensorimotor coordination
    b.   overall motor development
    c.   alertness and activity level
    d.   information-processing skills

23. The vignette describes 4-month-old Malcolm as bringing his fist to his mouth and sucking on all five fingers. If he then pulls his fingers out of his mouth and repeats the whole action, this would be an example of a:
    a.   primary circular reaction.
    b.   secondary circular reaction.
    c.   tertiary circular reaction.
    d.   reflexive behavior.

24. Christine wondered whether the fact that Maggie achieved developmental milestones earlier than Mikey meant that she would later do better in school. Based on the material in Chapter 5, the best answer to her question is:
    a.   Yes, babies who are advanced in motor development tend to be smarter and more academically competent later in childhood.
    b.   No, babies who are advanced in motor development tend to become more athletic, but not more academically competent.
    c.   No, babies who are slower and more deliberate in their motor development tend to be smarter and more academically competent later in childhood.
    d.   It is impossible to say; there is no consistent relationship between the speed with which developmental milestones are reached in infancy and later intelligence.

25. Meryl's move toward the laundry basket as she's playing on the living room floor most likely indicates:
    a.   the active nature of her cognitive development.
    b.   intentional disobedience of her mother's rules.
    c.   her cranky and irritable temperament.
    d.   all of the above.

MATCHING QUESTIONS:
Match the following key terms with their definitions:

1. ___ Primary circular reaction

2. ___ Working memory

3. ___ Scheme

4. ___ Assimilation

5. ___ Neo-nativist

6. ___ Coordination of schemes

7. ___ Recognition memory

8. ___ Equilibration

9. ___ Cued recall

10. ___ Secondary circular reaction

11. ___ Accommodation

12. ___ Implicit or procedural memory

A.   A goal-directed chain of behaviors.

B.   In Piaget's theory, the process of modifying an existing strategy or skill to meet a new demand of the environment.

C.   A contemporary developmental theorist who believes infants have a wide range of innate abilities and knowledge.

D.   A type of memory in which a particular stimulus is perceived as familiar.

E.   A type of memory in which a familiar stimulus triggers recall of stored information.

F.   In Piaget's theory, a self-regulatory process that produces increasingly effective adaptations.

G. Memory that is unconscious, involves memory for procedures or skills, and does not lend itself to explicit statement.

H. A circular reaction involving the effects of an infant's behavior on an external object.

I. In Piaget's theory, a cognitive structure that can be applied to a variety of situations.

J. In Piaget's theory, the process of applying an existing capability without modification to various situations.

K. The information-processing capacity available at any one time.

L. A circular reaction involving an infant's own body.

SHORT-ANSWER QUESTIONS:

1. List four major cognitive advances of infancy.
    (a)

    (b)

    (c)

    (d)

2. Give two reasons why Piaget's theory is a good starting point for studying cognitive development.
    (a)

    (b)

3. Explain how the processes of **assimilation** and **accommodation** work together to produce cognitive development.

4. According to Piaget, children begin to use representational thought during Stage ____ of the sensorimotor period.

5. The understanding that objects continue to exist even when they are out of sight is called _____.

6. What is the A, not-B error?

7. Give three reasons why infants' search for hidden objects lags behind their understanding of object permanence.
   (a)

   (b)

   (c)

8. Explain why categorization is a useful skill for an infant.

9. Explain the difference between **explicit/declarative** and **implicit/procedural** memory.

10. List four improvements in memory abilities that occur between 6 and 18 months of age.
    (a)

    (b)

    (c)

    (d)

11. Adults' inability to remember much about their infancies is known as

    _____.

12. List three ways that social environment can influence cognitive and motor development in infancy.
    (a)

    (b)

    (c)

13. List two misconceptions about stimulation and enhancement of infant cognitive development.

    (a)

    (b)

14. List two variables measured in new infant tests that seem to be particularly important for predicting later IQ.

    (a)

    (b)

15. List three cognitive limitations that remain at the end of infancy.

    (a)

    (b)

    (c)

ESSAY QUESTIONS:

1. List and describe the six stages in Piaget's theory of sensorimotor development.

2. Discuss the four major areas of disagreement with Piaget's ideas about infant cognition.

3. Describe three modifications in research methods that have produced evidence of object permanence understanding earlier in infancy than Piaget proposed.

4. Describe the course of memory development in infancy.

5. Compare the Piagetian and sociocultural perspectives on the role of the social environment in cognitive development.

6. Piaget argued that infants are active participants in their own cognitive development, but that the sensorimotor nature of their intelligence limits what they are able to understand and learn. If Piaget is right in these two assumptions, what can parents do to foster their babies' cognitive development? From the information given in the vignettes, what factors in Malcolm's, Maggie's, Mikey's, and Meryl's family environments might help or hinder their cognitive development?

7. Discuss how infants' increasing cognitive abilities might affect their abilities to interact with others and form social relationships.

ANSWER KEY

MULTIPLE-CHOICE QUESTIONS:

1. b A basic understanding of object properties and the ability to use categorization and to combine actions into sequences are all major cognitive developments of infancy; the ability to use symbolic thought begins to emerge only at the end of infancy.

2. d Piaget believed that infants' knowledge of the world is based on sensory awareness and motor acts and on active physical and mental exploration, not on passive observation and not on language and abstract concepts.

3. b Assimilation involves applying an existing capability (in this case, the whole-handed grasp) to various situations without modification.

4. a See definition of **tertiary circular reaction.**

5. d See definition of **secondary circular reaction.**

6. b Stage 4 is when babies begin to perform one action (opening the cupboard door) in order to do something else (get to the toy); Piaget called this coordination of schemes.

7. b Piaget's *description* of infant behavior has help up well; disagreements have centered on his *explanations* of it.

8. c See definition of **décalage.**

9. a Answers *b*, *c*, and *d* are proposals of various neo-nativists.

10. b Infants first begin to search for completely hidden objects during sensorimotor stage 4, though they do not yet have a mature understanding of object permanence.

11. c Infants in this age group will search for partially and completely hidden objects, and they no longer tend to search only in places where they have previously found an object.

12. a In Baillargeon's studies, 4- to 8-month-olds look longer at events showing one object moving through a location where they have just seen another object than at events showing the first object apparently being stopped by the second object.

13. b A rudimentary understanding of causality and other objects develops between ages 4 and 8 months; the complexity and flexibility of this understanding continues to develop after that.

14. d Infants' understanding of number *does* seem to be limited to small quantities.

15. c Infants form perceptual categories by 3 months and conceptual categories by 7 months, but they do not seem to use them to form generalizations until around 14 months.

16. a Piaget believed that infants were capable of recognition memory because it could be based entirely on sensorimotor information and schemes; he believed they were not capable of any form of recall or explicit memory because they required mental representation.

17. d See summary at end of section on memory in the first six months.

18. b Habituation memory and implicit memory, which depend on lower brain structures such as the cerebellum and the hippocampus, are both present before 6 months; explicit memory, which involves the cerebral cortex, does not appear until after 6 months.

19. c See box on infantile amnesia.

20. b Cross-cultural research has found only slight variation in ages at which infants can do object permanence tasks and great similarity in how infants from different cultures manipulate objects, regardless of their cultural meaning.

21. d See box on stimulation to enhance development.

22. d Performance on tasks measuring sensorimotor coordination, motor development, and general alertness or activity level shows little correlation with later IQ.

23. a See definition of **primary circular reaction.**

24. d How fast babies reach developmental milestones, especially motor milestones, does not have any consistent correlation with later intelligence or academic performance.

25. a Crankiness and irritability usually do not lead to exploration of the environment; the active nature of cognitive development does. At 11 months, Meryl is too young to be intentionally disobeying her mother.

MATCHING QUESTIONS:

1.	L	4.	J	7.	D	10.	H
2.	K	5.	C	8.	F	11.	B
3.	I	6.	A	9.	E	12.	G

SHORT-ANSWER QUESTIONS:

1. (a) basic understanding of the physical world; (b) the ability to use basic cognitive tools, such as number and categorization, to understand the world; (c) the ability to combine actions into sequences to achieve desired ends; (d) increasingly powerful and flexible memory abilities.

2. (a) Piaget was the first to propose a comprehensive theory of infant cognitive development based on observation of infants' behavior; (b) Piaget's ideas have set the agenda for research on infant cognition.

3. In assimilation, children apply a capability they already have without modification to new situations. For example, newborns apply their sucking reflex to anything that touches their lips, regardless of whether it provides them with nourishment. When an existing strategy doesn't work in a new situation, accommodation becomes necessary. In accommodation, an existing skill is modified to fit the demands of the situation. For example, infants gradually learn to suck differently on nipples, pacifiers, and their own hands. Assimilation allows children to respond to new situations with existing abilities, while accommodation allows them to change their behavior to meet new demands. In the process, development occurs.

4. 6

5. object permanence

6. The A, not-B error is the tendency for infants in sensorimotor stage 4 to continue searching in one location (location A), where they have found an object in the past, rather than in a second location (location B), where they have just seen it hidden.

7. (a) Difficulty with the means-end behaviors required to search for objects; (b) memory limitations; (c) difficulty inhibiting an established response.

8. Categorization is useful because it allows infants to group things together and treat members of a group similarly. Instead of treating each object, experience, or person as something new, they can apply knowledge from past experience with members of the same category.

9. Explicit or declarative memory is conscious, involves mental representation of images or ideas, and can be explicitly stated or declared. Implicit or procedural

memory is unconscious, involves memory for procedures or skills, and does not lend itself to explicit statement.

10. (a) Emergence of working memory; (b) increases in how long memories are retained; (c) ability to remember and reproduce increasingly complex action sequences; (d) increased ability to engage in cued and spontaneous recall.

11. infantile amnesia

12. (a) The pace of cognitive development is affected by the amount and type of stimulation provided in an infant's home; (b) differences in infant care practices (such as how much "floor freedom" a baby is given) produce differences in motor and cognitive development; (c) with help from adults, infants can learn specialized motor skills at earlier than typical ages.

13. (a) Stimulation that works at one age must be good at other ages; (b) accelerating cognitive development leads to higher academic performance and IQ.

14. (a) Speed of information processing; (b) capacity of working memory.

15. (a) Knowledge and cognitive skills are fragile and not widely generalizable; (b) capacity for long-term memory remains limited; (c) acquisition of language and symbolic abilities is just beginning.

ESSAY QUESTIONS:

1. Your answer should include the name and approximate age range of each of Piaget's sensorimotor stages, along with a brief description of infants' abilities during that stage. The following points should be included in your answer:
Stage 1: Reflexes (birth-1 month). Infants use built-in reflexes to interact with the world. No truly new behaviors emerge; development consists of refinements to the reflexes.
Stage 2: Primary Circular Reactions (1-4 months). New behaviors begin to emerge as infants discover by accident that reflexive behaviors, such as sucking on a thumb that happens to brush their lips, sometimes produce interesting sensory experiences. These behaviors are then repeated for their own sake and become primary circular reactions.
Stage 3: Secondary Circular Reactions (4-8 months). Infants begin to actively experience the effects of their behaviors on external objects. These behaviors are then repeated for the sake of these effects and become secondary circular reactions.
Stage 4: Coordination of Schemes (8-12 months). Infants begin to put actions together into goal-directed chains of behavior, which Piaget called coordination of schemes. They can now do one thing in order to do something else.
Stage 5: Tertiary Circular Reactions (12-18 months). Infants begin to use trial-and-

error experimentation in their actions. They modify behaviors that produce interesting results by chance, producing tertiary circular reactions.
Stage 6: Beginnings of Representational Thought (18-24 months). Infants show the first signs that they can use mental representation, in such behaviors as deferred imitation.

2. First, researchers have disagreed with Piaget's timetable for infant development. Piaget appears to have underestimated the skills of infants at various ages, perhaps because he may have missed the earliest signs of skills in his observations of his own children. Some of the differences are due to the fact that Piaget credited infants with a skill only when it was well developed and widely generalizable, whereas many recent researchers have credited infants with a skill when it was just emerging. Second, infants' cognitive development does not always proceed in the clear stages described by Piaget. Instead, most infants show varying levels of development in different areas of cognitive development. This problem was first documented by Uzgiris and Hunt, using Piagetian tasks. Third, neo-nativists argue that babies have a wider range of inborn abilities and knowledge than Piaget thought. Piaget believed that babies came equipped only with reflexive behaviors and a tendency for active exploration; everything else had to be constructed through experience. Neo-nativists argue that newborns have a much wider range of abilities, including a basic understanding of many aspects of the physical world and a set of specific learning mechanisms. Fourth, some researchers have argued that babies' cognitive limitations are due to constraints on information-processing capacity rather than the cognitive structures proposed by Piaget. Tasks such as searching for hidden objects and imitating others' behavior tax the limits of infants' working memory; expanding working memory makes cognitive development possible.

3. First, researchers have used methods that require less active responses from infants, such as habituation. Second, researchers interested in babies' search behavior during Piaget's object permanence tasks have reduced the memory demands of the tasks by allowing babies to search immediately after an object was hidden. Third, many of the studies of younger infants have used a looser criterion than Piaget did for estimating the age at which object permanence appears. Recent studies have attributed understanding of object permanence to infants of a particular age if a sizable minority of infants that age show understanding, rather than requiring understanding from most or all of them.

4. Infants have some memory abilities at birth, as demonstrated by their habituation to repeated sights and sounds. Within a few days, infants show signs of recognizing newly experienced stimuli for 24 to 48 hours. By about 3 months, they are able to remember relationships between stimuli as well as individual stimuli. Over the first 6 months of life, the length of time they can retain a memory increases, especially

for memories of their own actions. However, their memories remain context-bound, and they seem able to retrieve memories only in response to external cues. In the second 6 months of life, babies show clear signs of being able to hold information in working memory for a short time before using it. Long-term memory and spontaneous recall also emerge during these months. Between 6 and 18 months, babies also become able to remember and reproduce increasingly complex action sequences.

5. Piaget believed that active exploration of the environment produced cognitive growth by allowing infants to construct their own understanding of reality; thus, the role of the environment in cognitive development was to provide an overall context for exploration. The social environment could influence cognitive development by determining what sort of physical environment a child lived in and what opportunities for exploration were provided. Sociocultural theorists argue that adults actively structure the environment to foster the kind of learning they consider most important for their children. Because infants are learning things that adults already know, they do not have to construct their own knowledge entirely on their own; instead, they can learn many things more rapidly with help from adults. In fact, some things they can only learn with help from adults, including specialized motor skills such as swimming and cross-country skiing. Piagetians would argue that the results of such training do not represent true development.

6. Parents should provide opportunities for infants to explore their environment and experiment with it--while ensuring their babies' safety, of course. Baby-proofing the house so that the baby is free to roam would be a better approach to safety than keeping the baby confined to a crib or playpen, if parents are interested in fostering cognitive development. Parents should also realize that explicit teaching, particularly verbal instruction, plays very little role in infants' cognitive development, because of their limited abilities for mental representation. Babies are not primarily learning information at this stage of development; instead, they are figuring out how the world around them works and how they can influence it. This kind of knowledge is not explicitly taught, but is discovered through active engagement with the environment. Providing interesting things for babies to look at and manipulate is more important than trying to teach them.

There is much in Malcolm's environment that should help his cognitive development. The members of his family do not seem to interfere with his very active exploration and manipulation of his world, but often observe it with delight. They respond to his inquisitive nature by talking to him and bringing him toys to look at. The only potential negative factor might be that he has little opportunity to explore things on his own because he seems to be constantly held and entertained by other people. Maggie and Mikey also seem to have freedom to experiment, as when Maggie throws objects down the stairs, and their father enjoys playing games with Mikey that could be helpful in his cognitive development. However, both of them seem to receive less attention than Malcolm does because of the tension between their parents and the lack of other adults or much older children in the family. Their father also tends to be rather didactic in their interactions, as when he tries to teach Mikey to say "bread." Meryl has the least positive environment for cognitive development. Her mother often restricts her exploration because she wants to make her behave, and she does not seem very sensitive to Meryl's state when she tries to play with her. Since there are usually no other adults or children present, Meryl also has a less interesting environment to explore than the other babies do.

7. Cognitive abilities affect not only how infants understand and deal with the physical world, but also how they understand and deal with the people around them in the social world. There are many abilities discussed in both Chapter 4 and Chapter 5 that you could draw on in this essay. For example, as mentioned in Chapter 5, infants' increasing capacity for long-term memory during the second six months of life forms a foundation for specific emotional attachments to parents, as babies begin to form a concept of mother and father as specific, continuing individuals. Understanding of object permanence and causality, as well as the ability to form and use categories, also contribute to infants' social interaction abilities. In addition, many of the perceptual abilities covered in Chapter 4, especially face perception, could be discussed in answering this question.

CHAPTER 6
INFANT SOCIAL AND EMOTIONAL DEVELOPMENT
CHAPTER REVIEW

As you read the chapter, construct your own chapter outline by answering the following review questions and defining the *Key Terms*.

I. INTRODUCTION
    How are cognitive and emotional development related to infants' early social development?

II. DEVELOPMENT IN THE FIRST SIX MONTHS
    Key Terms: **reciprocity, attunement, sensitive care, recognitory assimilation, emotion**
    A. Identify the two extreme views on newborn competencies and explain why neither one is satisfactory.

    B. BOX: Give examples of apparently advanced abilities in very young infants, along with alternative explanations for them. Explain why it is beneficial for infants when caregivers interpret their early behavior as social.

    C. What predispositions make an infant preadapted for social interaction? What is needed for infants' social potential to unfold?

D. What developmental changes in the infant make the emergence of **reciprocity** possible? What does the caregiver contribute to the development of reciprocity?

E. Summarize the course of development of social smiling.

F. What are the two major aspects of emotional development?

G. Describe the development of forerunners of basic emotions during the first six months of life. How are these responses different from full-blown emotions?

H. Describe the development of emotional regulation and coping during the first six months of life.

III. DEVELOPMENT IN THE SECOND SIX MONTHS
Key Terms: **stranger distress, attachment, separation distress, greeting reactions, secure-base behavior, bonding**

A. Explain why social and emotional development in the second six months of life can be considered qualitative change.

B. How do emotional responses change in the second six months of life?

C. Describe and explain the development of stranger distress. What evidence is there that it is not simply wariness toward the unfamiliar? What factors influence infants' reactions to strangers?

D. How do infants' techniques for coping with emotional arousal change over the second six months of life?

E. What are three major hallmarks of attachment? When does **separation distress** appear? How does this vary across cultures?

F. When do infants develop specific attachment relationships? Explain the difference between **attachment** and **bonding**. Explain the process by which infant-caregiver attachments form.

G. Explain how infants are able to form multiple attachments and why they are usually organized into a hierarchy.

H. How did early psychoanalytic theory and traditional learning theory explain attachment formation? How did Erikson and Bowlby explain it? What did the results of Harlow's monkey studies contribute to this debate?

IV. EXPLAINING INDIVIDUAL DIFFERENCES IN EARLY SOCIAL AND EMOTIONAL DEVELOPMENT
    Key Terms: **secure attachment, anxious attachment, anxious-resistant attachment, anxious-avoidant attachment, disorganized-disoriented attachment, internal working model, temperament**
    A. Under what circumstances do infants fail to become attached to a caregiver? How did Bowlby explain differences in attachment quality?

B. Describe Ainsworth's *Strange Situation* and the three patterns of attachment she identified. Describe the fourth attachment pattern identified by Main.

C. Summarize the research findings on connections between quality of attachment and quality of care received by infants. Explain why sensitive care seems to reduce the amount an infant cries rather than increasing it.

D. What factors in parents' own lives seem to influence the security of their infants' attachment? How do these factors produce their effects?

E. What connections have been found between infant attachment and later development? Explain how Bowlby's concept of **internal working models** is involved.

F. What **temperament** categories did Thomas and Chess identify in their research? How has the concept of temperament changed in recent research?

G. Summarize research findings on the stability of temperament over time.

H. List three physiological factors that have been found to be related to infant temperament. Explain why the causal relationship between physiology and temperament is not clear.

I. What have twin studies and animal studies revealed about a possible genetic basis for temperament?

J. Summarize the research findings on temperament and attachment. List four ways temperament and attachment may be related.

V. THE IMPORTANCE OF EARLY CARE
    Key term: **sensitive period hypothesis**
    A. Summarize the research evidence for a sensitive period for attachment formation.

B. What cross-cultural differences and similarities have been found in care of young infants? What cultural differences in attachment patterns have been found?

C. BOX: Why is day care considered potentially risky for infants? Summarize the research evidence on the effects of infant day care on attachment relationships.

D. Explain how early experience has special significance for later development. Under what circumstances can normal development occur in spite of early deprivation?

SELF-TEST

After **you have studied the chapter, use the following questions to test your understanding.**

MULTIPLE-CHOICE QUESTIONS:

1. What does it mean to say that humans are preadapted to become social?
    a. Infants are born with well-developed social skills that allow them to interact with others.
    b. Infants have predispositions that allow them to participate in early social exchanges.
    c. Infants are born with an ability to seek out and recognize their parents.
    d. Infants can imitate complex behaviors and have social expectations from birth.

2. Infants' potential for social interaction will unfold fully only if they receive:
    a. Appropriate stimulation and responsiveness from caregivers.
    b. Any sort of social interaction from caregivers.
    c. Opportunities to interact with a variety of other people.
    d. Nothing specific is needed from the environment; the ability for social interaction comes from genetic characteristics.

3. Predispositions that help newborns become social include:
    a. an ability to signal psychological and physiological needs.
    b. an ability to detect contingencies in the environment.
    c. a tendency to fall in step with caregivers' behavior.
    d. all of the above.

4. Which of the following is NOT true of newborns' cries?
    a. They can serve as a form of social communication.
    b. They are the product of overexcitement of the nervous system.
    c. They are intentional signals of needs and desires.
    d. They are a reflexive response to a variety of sources of stimulation.

5. True social interactions involving mutual exchanges between partners are examples of:
    a. recognitory assimilation.
    b. bonding.
    c. reflexive behavior.
    d. reciprocity.

6. **Sensitive care** of an infant includes:
    a. awareness of the infant's needs and prompt response to them.
    b. continued stimulation of an infant who seems unresponsive.
    c. instinctive understanding of the infant's needs from birth.
    d. all of the above.

116

7. Smiling in a 2-month-old is most likely the result of:
    a. spontaneous brain activity.
    b. recognitory assimilation.
    c. a specific reaction to a particular person.
    d. an attempt to initiate social interaction.

8. Which of the following does NOT occur during the first six months of life?
    a. Infants begin to smile in response to the meaning of an event.
    b. Infants begin to experience the joy of intentional mastery.
    c. Infants' reflexive responses to stimulation become forerunners of basic emotions.
    d. Infants begin to show culturally universal facial expressions of emotion.

9. An infant's reaction to a stranger depends on:
    a. how the stranger behaves.
    b. how familiar the surroundings are.
    c. how the infant's caregiver responds to the stranger.
    d. all of the above.

10. During the second six months of life, infants add which of the following skills to their repertoire for coping with emotionally arousing situations?
    a. Crying.
    b. Moving to the caregiver when threatened.
    c. Turning away from the source of stimulation.
    d. All of the above.

11. Which of the following infants would you expect to develop **separation distress** at the youngest age?
    a. A middle-class American infant who is cared for in a family day care home every day while her mother works.
    b. A middle-class American infant whose mother stays at home to care for him but who is left with babysitters for several hours at a time two or three times a week.
    c. A Japanese infant who is cared for primarily by her mother, sleeps with her parents, and is never left with a babysitter.
    d. An infant on a traditional Israeli kibbutz who lives in a communal nursery, has a regular substitute caregiver, and is visited by his mother several times a day.

12. **Attachment** differs from **bonding** in that:
    a. attachment develops in the first few hours of life, while bonding takes months.
    b. bonding refers only to the parents' tie to their infant, attachment to the mutual relationship between parent and infant.
    c. bonding refers only to the infant's tie to the parents, attachment to the mutual relationship between parent and infant.
    d. none of the above; attachment and bonding are basically the same thing.

13. Infants apparently develop attachments to their parents mainly because:
    a.   their parents feed them.
    b.   their parents are biologically related to them.
    c.   their parents become familiar.
    d.   their parents engage them in repeated interaction.

14. Bowlby hypothesized that individual differences in quality of attachment were based on differences in:
    a.   infants' genetic tendency to become attached.
    b.   infants' overall temperaments.
    c.   the quality of care infants received.
    d.   all of the above.

15. Which pattern of attachment is associated with reluctance to separate from the mother, even when there are interesting toys around?
    a.   secure
    b.   anxious-avoidant
    c.   anxious-resistant
    d.   disorganized-disoriented

16. Infants whose caregivers are emotionally unavailable or actively reject attempts to seek physical closeness are likely to form:
    a.   secure attachments.
    b.   anxious-avoidant attachments.
    c.   anxious-resistant attachments.
    d.   disorganized-disoriented attachments.

17. When caregivers respond promptly to their infants' cries, by the time the infants are a year old they tend to:
    a.   cry a great deal because crying has been reinforced as a way of getting attention.
    b.   cry less than other babies because they have learned that their needs will be met when they do cry.
    c.   show a great deal of variability in their crying because they often test their caregivers' responsiveness.
    d.   use crying as a way of manipulating their caregivers because the caregivers' response to crying is so consistent.

18. A **temperament** researcher would be likely to assume that:
    a.   individual differences in response to novelty are biologically based.
    b.   an infant's activity level varies greatly across situations.
    c.   infants' irritability at birth would not predict their irritability at age 1.
    d.   there is little relationship between infant temperament and later personality.

19. Some researchers have found that infants who are wary in new situations have higher or more variable heart rates than infants who are less wary. This means that:
    a. differences in wariness are caused by underlying physiological differences.
    b. differences in heart rate reflect underlying differences in wariness.
    c. some unknown third factor influences both heart rate and wariness.
    d. all of the above are possible.

20. Studies on connections between temperament and attachment classification have found that:
    a. attachment classification seems to be based almost entirely on temperament.
    b. temperament seems to be based almost entirely on attachment classification.
    c. measures of attachment and temperament are measuring the same thing.
    d. temperament is related to some Strange Situation behavior but not to attachment classification.

21. Which of the following philosophies about infant day care would reflect a **sensitive period hypothesis** about the development of parent-infant attachments?
    a. Infants should not be placed in day care before age 1 because substitute care always interferes with the formation of secure parent-infant attachments.
    b. Infants should be placed in day care as early as possible because it will foster the development of multiple attachments and increase the child's later social adaptability.
    c. Infants in day care before age 1 may be at risk for attachment difficulties, since they may receive less consistent care at the age when attachments are most likely to be forming.
    d. There should be little risk in placing infants in day care, since research with older children indicates that day care may actually be beneficial.

22. Current research on the effects of day care in infancy suggests that:
    a. Day care before age one almost always leads to attachment problems.
    b. Extensive early day care is a developmental risk factor.
    c. Quality of early day care does not make much difference.
    d. Day care poses no risks for infants.

23. From birth Malcolm showed a high level of activity and vigorous response to his environment. These are examples of:
    a. temperamental characteristics.
    b. typical responses to sensitive care.
    c. universal predispositions that aid in social interaction.
    d. typical behaviors of at-risk infants.

24. Mikey's father devotes a great deal of time and attention to him, though his mother is his primary caregiver during the day. Mikey is likely to become attached to:
    a. his mother only, since she feeds him and does most of the routine caregiving.
    b. his father only, since he devotes more intensive attention to Mikey than his mother does.
    c. both parents, with his mother being the person he turns to first when stressed.
    d. both parents, with his father being the person he turns to first when stressed.

25. When Karen showed Meryl the Oscar the Grouch toy and she reacted by crying, Karen's response to Meryl's distress was an example of:
    a. sensitive care.
    b. overstimulation.
    c. emotional unavailability.
    d. attunement.

MATCHING QUESTIONS:
Match the following key terms with their definitions:

1. ___ Internal working model

2. ___ Emotion

3. ___ Anxious-resistant attachment

4. ___ Bonding

5. ___ Attunement

6. ___ Temperament

7. ___ Sensitive period hypothesis

8. ___ Sensitive care

9. ___ Anxious-avoidant attachment

10. ___ Attachment

A. An attachment pattern in which the infant readily separates from the caregiver but avoids contact after a separation.

B. Caregivers' adjustment of the stimulation they provide in response to signs from the infant.

C. An individual infant's general style of behavior across contexts.

D. An enduring emotional tie between infant and caregiver.

E. An infant's generalized expectations about the social world, including caregiver responsiveness, the infant's own ability to obtain care, and the nature of social relationships.

F. The parent's initial emotional tie to the newborn.

G. The idea that certain kinds of experience are especially important at particular points in development.

H. A state of feeling that arises when a person evaluates an event in a particular way.

I. An attachment pattern in which the infant separates from the caregiver reluctantly but shows ambivalence toward the caregiver after a separation.

J. A caregiving style in which the caregiver attends to the infant's needs and responds to them promptly and effectively.

SHORT-ANSWER QUESTIONS:

1. Why is it unlikely that newborns have social expectations and purpose?

2. List three developmental changes in the infant that make social **reciprocity** with caregivers possible.

(a)

(b)

(c)

3. By 8 to 10 weeks, infants smile in response to familiar stimuli, a form of visual mastery known as _____ _____.

4. List the two major aspects of emotional development.

(a)

(b)

5. List three ways emotional responses during the first six months of life differ from later full-blown emotions.

(a)

(b)

(c)

6. List three techniques for coping with emotional stimulation that are present in the first six months of life.

   (a)

   (b)

   (c)

7. How can we tell that **stranger distress** is not simply wariness toward unfamiliarity?

8. The enduring emotional tie between infant and caregiver that is established through repeated interaction over time is called _____.

9. List three hallmarks of **attachment**.

   (a)

   (b)

   (c)

10. Explain the difference between **attachment** and **bonding**.

11. A type of **anxious attachment** in which the infant shows contradictory features of several patterns of anxious attachment is known as _____-_____ _____.

12. Explain the difference between early psychoanalytic explanations of attachment formation and Bowlby's explanation.

13. Under what circumstances do infants fail to become attached to a caregiver?

14. List three factors that influence the quality of caregiving a parent provides and affect the quality of parent-infant attachment.

    (a)

    (b)

    (c)

15. List the three temperament categories identified by Thomas and Chess.

    (a)

    (b)

    (c)

ESSAY QUESTIONS:

1. Discuss how cognitive development facilitates social development during infancy.

2. Explain what is meant by the idea that newborns are preadapted to participate in a social world and give three examples.

3. Discuss the relationship between infant **temperament** and **attachment**.

4. Summarize the connections that have been found between infant attachment and later development and explain how **internal working models** are involved in these connections.

5. Using the results of research on infant day care and other information about early social and emotional development, argue for or against the following statement: "Babies should not be put in day care until they are at least one year old."

6. Meryl would be considered at risk for developmental problems because she was born to a single adolescent mother. Various factors in Meryl and Karen's situation made her infancy a difficult time for both of them. Suggest two factors that could have improved the situation (other than changing Karen's age and marital status) and explain why they would have helped.

7. Imagine that you have been asked to talk to a group of expectant parents on fostering healthy emotional and social development in infancy. What would you recommend parents do to provide the best possible environment for their babies' early emotional and social development?

ANSWER KEY

MULTIPLE-CHOICE QUESTIONS:

1. b Infants are not born with well-developed social skills, but with predispositions that allow them to participate in social exchanges with a supportive caregiver.

2. a Genetic characteristics underlie newborns' potential for social interaction, but an appropriate environment is necessary for them to unfold completely.

3. d Answers *a*, *b*, and *c* are all part of newborns' predispositions toward social behavior.

4. c Newborns' cries can serve as a form of social communication because of the interpretations of them by caregivers, but they are not *intentional* signals.

5. d See definition of reciprocity.

6. a Sensitive care does not include continued stimulation of an unresponsive infant. It is not based on instinctive understanding but develops gradually through day-to-day care.

7. b At 8-10 weeks, infants smile when they recognize a person, object, or event; they do not smile in response to a *particular* person or to initiate social interaction until later.

8. b Infants do not show the joy of intentional mastery until the second six months of life, when their cognitive abilities allow them to anticipate consequences of their actions.

9. d Answers *a*, *b*, and *c* all influence how an infant responds to a stranger.

10. b Crying and turning away are both used as coping skills during the first six months of life.

11. c Separation distress appears earlier in cultures in which infants remain in constant contact with their mothers, as in Japan.

12. b Attachment is the mutual parent-infant relationship that develops over a period of months; bonding is the parent's tie to the infant that develops in the first hours of life.

13. d Early explanations focused on feeding, but research shows parent-infant interaction is more important. Neither familiarity nor biological relatedness alone produce attachment.

14. c   Bowlby focused on quality of care rather than infants' characteristics.

15. c   Infants with anxious-resistant attachment seek a great deal of contact with caregivers, even though they have trouble being comforted by them.

16. b   Anxious-avoidant attachment goes with emotionally unavailable or rejecting caregivers, anxious-resistant with inconsistent care, disorganized-disoriented with frightening or confusing caregiver behavior, and secure attachment with consistent, responsive care.

17. b   Prompt response to infant cries results in *less* crying over time. There is no evidence that infants less than a year old intentionally cry to manipulate or test their caregivers.

18. a   Temperament researchers generally assume individual differences in behavior are biologically based and infant behavior is relatively stable across situations, predicts later behavior, and is related to later personality.

19. d   Associations between biological indicators and behavior do not automatically imply any particular causal relationship.

20. d   Attachment and temperament measures are not consistently related, but temperament does predict some behaviors in the Strange Situation, such as distress during separation.

21. c   Answer *a* is wrong because sensitive period hypotheses do not imply that factors *always* produce particular results. Answer *b* does not focus on parent-child attachment. Answer *d* does not recognize the uniqueness of infancy as a sensitive period.

22. b   Extensive early day care is a risk factor for later developmental problems. Infant day care by itself does not usually lead to attachment problems, unless it is combined with other risk factors, such as insensitive maternal care. Quality of early care does seem to make a difference in later outcomes.

23. a   See definition of temperament.

24. c   Given his father's involvement with him, Mikey will become attached to both parents, but he will turn to his mother first when stressed because she is his primary caregiver.

25. b   Karen's continued attempts to interest Meryl in the toy are likely to
        overstimulate her. She is not emotionally unavailable, but her interactions with
        Meryl show a lack of attunement and sensitive care.

MATCHING QUESTIONS:

1.	E	4.	F	7.	G	10.	D
2.	H	5.	B	8.	J		
3.	I	6.	C	9.	A		

SHORT-ANSWER QUESTIONS:

1. The cerebral cortex, which controls higher cognitive functions, is not yet fully
    functional.

2. Possible answers include developing abilities to stay alert and engaged with the
    environment, to control attention, to coordinate looking and reaching, to turn
    toward or away from stimulation voluntarily, and to produce smiles, coos, and
    actions during attentive looking.

3. recognitory assimilation

4. emergence of various emotions and development of emotional regulation

5. (a) They often require time to build up; (b) the meanings attached to events are very
    general; (c) emotional responses are somewhat global and not well differentiated.

6. falling asleep, turning away, and crying

7. Because babies in the age range when stranger distress appears respond differently
    to unfamiliar events depending on their context.

8. attachment

9. separation distress, greeting reactions, and secure-base behavior

10. Attachment is a mutual parent-infant tie that develops over months of interaction;
    bonding is a parent's emotional tie to an infant that develops in the first hours of
    life. Attachment has a strong impact on later development, but there is no evidence
    that bonding does.

11. disorganized-disoriented attachment

12. Early psychoanalytic explanations of attachment focused on the importance of the parent as a food source; Bowlby emphasized the importance of repeated parent-infant interactions.

13. Infants fail to become attached only if they have no opportunity for repeated interaction with a specific caregiver. Even abused infants and infants who experience negative interactions with caregivers become attached to them.

14. the parent's life stress, social support, and developmental history

15. easy, difficult, and slow-to-warm-up

ESSAY QUESTIONS:
1. Possible answers include: (a) understanding of object permanence contributes to the ability to differentiate caregivers from other people, (b) attentional skills increase infants' ability to engage in social interaction, (c) memory skills influence the development of attachment and expectations about caregivers, and (d) understanding of cause-and-effect relationships and various object properties contribute to the emergence of emotions such as surprise.

2. Being preadapted means infants come equipped with abilities and tendencies that enable them to take part in social exchanges with adults. These exchanges occur mainly because adults assign meaning to infant's social signals. For instance, because newborns are predisposed to pay attention to light-dark contrasts and movement, they tend to stare at faces. Adults often interpret this as a sign of interest and affection and respond by returning the gaze and talking to the infant. Newborns are also predisposed to attend to human voices and turn their heads toward sounds. Adults find this attention rewarding and respond by talking to babies and even carrying on one-sided conversations. Finally, newborns can signal physical and psychological needs by crying. Crying is not intentional behavior, but it is a very effective means of communication, since adults find an infant's cry very aversive and respond by trying to meet the infant's needs.

3. It is important to recognize that attachment and temperament are different aspects of development. Quality of attachment refers to patterns of infant behavior with one particular partner, while temperament involves aspects of behavior that occur across situations without regard to partner. Temperament by itself does not determine quality of attachment, nor does quality of attachment produce temperament. Temperament predicts certain behaviors in the Strange Situation, such as crying during separation, but not overall attachment security. However, the *combination* of temperament and caregiver characteristics seems to have an influence on attachment. The degree of match or mismatch between infant temperament and caregiver personality may predict security of attachment. Exactly

what constitutes sensitive care may vary depending on an infant's temperament. In addition, certain temperamental characteristics, such as irritability, may indirectly contribute to insecure attachment by affecting the quality of care a caregiver is able to provide to an infant.

4. Quality of parent-infant attachment is associated with children's later curiosity, enthusiasm in solving problems, self-esteem, and relationships with teachers and peers. Internal working models are expectations an infant develops about the social world, including the caregiver's availability, the infant's worthiness and ability to obtain care, and social relationships in general. Infants carry these expectations forward as they develop, and the expectations influence later behavior and relationships by coloring interpretations of events and influencing the kinds of experiences they seek or avoid. Internal working models are thus an important mechanism by which parent-infant attachment influences children's later development.

5. The second six months of life are a sensitive period for development of parent-infant attachment; anything that disrupts or diminishes parent-infant interaction could affect attachment security. The type of care a baby receives during the first year also has considerable impact on emotional development and the baby's overall style of responding to the environment, or temperament. Consistent, sensitive care fosters healthy emotional development, can moderate difficult temperament, and can help babies develop skills for coping with emotional arousal. Day care, especially with frequent caregiver changes, can make these developments more difficult. Researchers have found that infant day care does not prevent the formation of parent-infant attachments, nor does day care by itself increase the risk of insecure attachment. However, extensive day care in the first year of life seems to be a developmental risk factor--that is, it increases the chances of later problems in development, especially when combined with other risk factors, such as insensitive maternal care. Quality of day care is also important, probably because it contributes to the overall consistency of care a baby receives. A case could be made that, because infant day care is a risk factor for developmental problems, it is best to avoid extensive day care during the first year of life, if at all possible. However, a case could also be made that parents should not worry unduly about the effects of infant day care because by itself it does not produce developmental problems. Limiting the number of hours a baby is in day care, making sure the day care is of high quality, and providing sensitive, responsive care when the baby is at home all help to reduce the developmental risk associated with early day care.

6. Their situation could have been easier if Karen had had more social support from her boyfriend and mother. Greater social support would have helped her cope more effectively with the sudden responsibility of caring for a baby and would have given her more resources for dealing with her own needs and feelings. Things

might also have been easier if Meryl had been a less irritable, colicky baby. The mismatch between a difficult infant and a lonely, inexperienced mother made it hard for Karen and Meryl to establish a regular rhythm in their interactions. An easier baby would have placed less strain on Karen's overtaxed caregiving abilities and resources.

7. Some possible recommendations based on material in Chapter 6 include: (1) responding promptly to the baby's cries, which will increase the baby's confidence in parents' availability and reduce the amount of crying over time; (2) providing frequent social stimulation and opportunities for interaction from early in life, even before the baby is an active participant; (3) being sensitive to babies' individual differences in irritability, ability to cope with novelty, etc., and responding accordingly (for example, learning when to continue trying to get a response from a baby and when to back off), and (4) not worrying about being perfect parents, but simply providing a reasonably responsive, sensitive, stimulating environment.

CHAPTER 7
TODDLER LANGUAGE AND THINKING
CHAPTER REVIEW

As you read the chapter, construct your own chapter outline by answering the following review questions and defining the *Key Terms*.

I. INTRODUCTION
    Key Terms: **symbolic representation, language**
    A. Why is the transition from infancy to childhood called the toddler period? What age range does it cover?

    B. How is **language** different from speech?

II. THE COMPONENTS OF LANGUAGE
    Key Terms: **phonology, phonemes, semantics, morphology, morphemes, syntax, pragmatics, productive skills, receptive skills**
    A. What are the five major subsystems of language?

B. Explain the difference between *productive* and *receptive* language skills. In what order do productive and receptive skills generally develop?

III. MAJOR TASKS IN EARLY LANGUAGE LEARNING
    Key Terms: **prelinguistic vocalization, crying, cooing, vocal play, canonical babbling, conversational babbling/jargon, protowords, referential style, expressive style, vocabulary spurt, segmentation errors, fast mapping, joint attention, whole-object assumption, lexical contrast, underextensions, overextensions, grammatical morpheme, overregularizations, form class, holophrase, telegraphic speech, communicative competence**
    A. List and describe the five stages in the development of **prelinguistic vocalization**. Explain how physical development and the linguistic environment are involved in this development.

    B. What happens during the transition from babbling to true speech?

    C. BOX: Compare the language development of deaf and hearing children. What difference does early exposure to sign language make?

D. When do children's first identifiable words usually appear? What kinds of words are most frequently found in children's early vocabularies?

E. Summarize the differences between **expressive** and **referential** children and their language environments.

F. Describe how children's productive and receptive vocabularies develop.

G. Describe the processes and assumptions involved in children's early vocabulary development. Explain the errors common in early word learning.

H. Describe the usual course of children's acquisition of English **grammatical morphemes**. What factors seem to influence the order in which grammatical morphemes are acquired? Why are developmentalists interested in children's acquisition of grammatical morphemes?

I. When do **overregularizations** usually appear in children's speech? How common are they? When do they disappear? What do they tell us about children's language learning?

J. Why are syntactic rules difficult to learn? Why are they important?

K. What is children's language like during the one-word stage?

L. At what age do toddlers start to put two words together? Explain why toddlers' first two-word combinations should probably not be considered true sentences. What meanings do toddlers typically express in these first sentences?

M. Summarize Brown's five stages of early syntactic development.

N. Explain the difference between linguistic competence and **communicative competence**. Describe how communicative competence develops and how adults are involved in the process.

IV. THE CHILD AND THE ENVIRONMENT IN LANGUAGE DEVELOPMENT
   Key Terms: **environmentalist theories, nativist theories, language acquisition device (LAD), child-directed speech (CDS)/motherese**

A. Summarize Skinner's and Chomsky's explanations of language acquisition and the criticisms that have been made of each of them. What is the current state of the environmentalist-nativist debate on language acquisition?

B. What evidence is there for a general biological basis for language learning? What are some ways the human brain might be prewired for language learning?

C. BOX: What is language development like for children who grow up as native bilinguals? What effect does bilingualism have on children's linguistic and cognitive development? Under what conditions are children likely to successfully learn a second language in school?

D. How does **child-directed speech** differ from speech to adults? How does fathers' speech to young children compare to mothers'? How does siblings' speech to toddlers compare to adults'?

E. What roles does child-directed speech seem to play in language development and in early parent-child interactions? What cross-cultural differences have been found in child-directed speech?

V. NONLINGUISTIC ASPECTS OF SYMBOLIC REPRESENTATION
A. Summarize Piaget's ideas about the development of symbolic representation.

B. Summarize the development of pretend play during toddlerhood. How does social context affect toddlers' pretend play?

C. Summarize the development of gestures during infancy and toddlerhood. How is the development of gestures related to the development of language and general symbolic abilities?

D. Summarize the development of toddlers' understanding of iconic symbols.

VI. ADVANCES AND LIMITATIONS OF TODDLERHOOD: AN OVERVIEW
Summarize the cognitive advances and limitations of toddlerhood and explain how they build on earlier development and lay the foundation for later development.

SELF-TEST

***After* you have studied the chapter, use the following questions to test your understanding.**

MULTIPLE-CHOICE QUESTIONS:

1. The general capacity for **symbolic representation** appears during:
   a. the first year of life.
   b. toddlerhood.
   c. the late preschool years.
   d. none of the above; it is present from birth.

2. Which of the following would be an example of **language**?
   a. The babbling of a six-month-old.
   b. A parrot saying "Polly want a cracker."
   c. A deaf person signing.
   d. The hand signals of a traffic policeman.

3. The smallest meaningful unit in a language is a:
   a. phoneme.
   b. morpheme.
   c. holophrase.
   d. coo.

4. A psychologist who studies the development of children's understanding of sentences in the passive voice is interested in:
   a. phonology.
   b. semantics.
   c. morphology.
   d. syntax.

5. The set of rules governing conversation and the social use of language is called:
   a. morphology.
   b. syntax.
   c. semantics.
   d. pragmatics.

6. Your neighbor insists that her 14-month-old son is able to understand when she asks him to bring her items from another room, even though he is just beginning to speak himself. Her assessment of the situation is most likely:
   a. incorrect; toddlers can't understand more than they express linguistically.
   b. incorrect; toddlers only understand isolated words.
   c. correct; toddlers can often understand more than they express linguistically.
   d. correct; her son has probably learned to fetch things the way a dog might, without linguistic understanding.

7. Which of the following statements about canonical babbling is TRUE?
   a. Canonical babbling includes strings of different vowel and consonant combinations.
   b. During the canonical babbling stage, children begin to use adult-like stress and intonation.
   c. A typical child's canonical babbling includes all the sounds found in human speech.
   d. An infant's canonical babbling includes only the phonemes of his or her native language.

8. Differences in deaf and hearing babies' vocalizations first appear during which stage?
   a. crying.
   b. cooing.
   c. vocal play.
   d. canonical babbling.

9. Children's tendency to assume that unfamiliar words do not refer to anything for which they already have a label is called:
   a. lexical contrast.
   b. fast mapping.
   c. underextension.
   d. the novelty principle.

10. A child who calls a cow, a horse, and a fuzzy blanket all "doggie" is demonstrating:
    a. overregularization.
    b. overextension.
    c. underregularization.
    d. underextension.

11. Which of the following factors does NOT seem to influence the order in which grammatical morphemes are acquired?
    a. Phonological factors.
    b. Grammatical complexity.
    c. Semantic complexity.
    d. Frequency of occurrence.

12. After a shopping trip with her mother, Meryl proudly said, "I have new shoes on both my foots." This is an example of:
    a. overregularization.
    b. overextension.
    c. underregularization.
    d. underextension.

13. A word used by a toddler to convey what an adult would say with a phrase or sentence is:
    a.   a protoword.
    b.   a segmentation error.
    c.   a holophrase.
    d.   telegraphic speech.

14. Two-year-olds often try to repair breakdowns in understanding during conversations with adults. The most likely reason they do this is:
    a.   they want to make sure their own goals are met.
    b.   they want to make their parents happy.
    c.   they understand what is needed to make conversations go smoothly.
    d.   they sometimes randomly happen to say the right thing.

15. The language acquisition device (LAD) proposed by Chomsky consists of:
    a.   a specific area in the left hemisphere of the brain.
    b.   children's innate capacities to extract linguistic rules from speech.
    c.   the ways adults structure children's linguistic environments.
    d.   all of the above.

16. Which of the following is NOT a criticism of behaviorist explanations of language learning?
    a.   Parents tend to reinforce correctness, rather than grammaticality, in children's speech.
    b.   Parents in different cultures respond to infants' attempts at speech differently.
    c.   Children constantly produce sentences that they have never heard or spoken before.
    d.   There is no evidence that reinforcement or imitation play *any* role in language learning.

17. Evidence that human language has a biological basis includes:
    a.   language is learned rapidly and with little explicit teaching.
    b.   processes of language acquisition are similar across cultures.
    c.   there seems to be a critical or sensitive period for language acquisition.
    d.   all of the above.

18. The brain might be prewired for language learning in which of the following ways?
    a.   Children may be born with conscious strategies for learning language.
    b.   Children may be predisposed to recognize English nouns.
    c.   Children may be predisposed to break words down into morphemes.
    d.   All of the above.

19. Which of the following is TRUE of children who grow up learning two languages simultaneously?
    a. They often mix their two languages or switch back and forth between them.
    b. They tend to develop metalinguistic awareness earlier than other children.
    c. Their vocabulary growth in each language is slower than average.
    d. All of the above.

20. **Child-directed speech** differs from speech to adults in that:
    a. it has more grammatical errors.
    b. phrase boundaries are less likely to be marked by pauses.
    c. it has higher pitch and more exaggerated intonation.
    d. it tends to focus on objects and events that are not present.

21. Which of the following statements about **child-directed speech** is TRUE?
    a. Children must be exposed to child-directed speech in order to acquire language.
    b. Child-directed speech may help children connect words with the things they refer to.
    c. The more a mother uses child-directed speech, the faster her child will acquire language.
    d. The characteristics of child-directed speech are universal across cultures.

22. Which of the following is the last kind of pretend play to develop?
    a. Double substitutions.
    b. Use of replica objects.
    c. Use of substitute objects.
    d. Combining a series of pretend acts around a theme.

23. When Meryl says "Go work now" and Malcolm says "Malcky two," they are producing examples of:
    a. holophrastic speech.
    b. telegraphic speech.
    c. segmentation errors.
    d. overregularizations.

24. When Mikey puts the vacuum cleaner bag on his head and says "Party hat," his behavior is an example of:
    a. symbolic representation.
    b. lexical contrast.
    c. fast mapping.
    d. wanton disobedience.

25. When Malcolm sings "Happy to you, happy to you," the most likely explanation is:
    a. his family sings the song differently than most people.
    b. he doesn't remember his birthday.
    c. his current cognitive capacity is limited to strings of three words.
    d. he is teasing his grandmother.

MATCHING QUESTIONS:

Match the following key terms with their definitions:

1. ___ Protowords

2. ___ Vocal play

3. ___ Grammatical morpheme

4. ___ Phonology

5. ___ Canonical babbling

6. ___ Overextension

7. ___ Syntax

8. ___ Holophrase

9. ___ Telegraphic speech

10. ___ Phonemes

11. ___ Morphology

12. ___ Underextension

13. ___ Overregularization

14. ___ Conversational babbling/jargon

15. ___ Morphemes

A. Prelinguistic vocalizations in which infants use adult-like stress and intonation.

B. The system of rules for combining morphemes to form words or to modify word meanings.

C. A language error in which the meaning a child attaches to a word is too broad.

D. A language error in which a child applies a morphological rule to a word that is an exception to the rule.

E. Vocalizations that seem to have consistent meanings for a child and are used in attempts to communicate, but do not closely resemble adult words in sound or meaning.

F. Speech sounds that contrast with one another in a particular language and can change the meaning of a word.

G. Prelinguistic vocalizations consisting of strings of syllables that sound increasingly like speech.

H. Prelinguistic vocalizations that vary greatly in pitch and loudness, including occasional simple syllables.

I. The smallest meaningful units in a language.

J. A language error in which the meaning a child attaches to a word is too restricted.

K. A unit of language that carries little meaning by itself, but that changes the meaning of words or sentences in a systematic way.

L. A toddler speech style in which words not essential to the meaning of a sentence are omitted.

M. The system of sounds used in a language, the rules for combining those sounds to make words, and the use of stress and intonation in spoken sentences.

N. A single word that conveys the meaning of a phrase or sentence.

O. The rules for organizing words into phrases and sentences.

SHORT-ANSWER QUESTIONS:

1. Explain how **language** is different from speech.

2. _____ consists of the meanings of words and sentences.

3. At about what age do children's first identifiable words usually appear?

4. A mistake in detecting boundaries between words in a sentence is a _____ _____ _____.

5. List and describe two built-in assumptions children seem to use in learning word meanings.
    (a)

    (b)

6. What three factors seem to govern the order of acquisition of **grammatical morphemes**?

   (a)

   (b)

   (c)

7. Why is **overregularization** considered a growth error?

8. Explain why syntactic rules are difficult to learn and why they are important in language acquisition.

9. Why are toddlers' first two-word combinations probably not true sentences?

10. Explain the difference between linguistic competence and **communicative competence**.

11. Theories that stress inborn, biologically based factors in language acquisition are known as
    _____ theories.

12. List three inborn abilities or predispositions that may help infants detect information needed for language learning.

    (a)

    (b)

    (c)

13. Learning a second language while maintaining proficiency in the first language is called _____.

14. How does fathers' speech to young children compare to mothers' speech?

15. List the three major types of gestures children begin to use in the first 18 months of life, in order of their appearance.

(a)

(b)

(c)

ESSAY QUESTIONS:

1. List the five stages in the development of **prelinguistic vocalization**, and explain what is distinctive about each stage.

2. Explain how language development differs for deaf children depending on whether or not they are exposed to sign language from an early age.

3. Explain the differences between a referential style and an expressive style of early word use.

4. Describe the errors commonly seen in early word learning and explain how they change as the child develops.

5. Summarize what takes place during each of Brown's five stages of early syntactic development.

6. Explain why it is difficult to test the notion of a critical period for language development, and give two pieces of evidence for the existence of a critical period.

7. In the vignette discussions, neither Mikey's father nor Meryl's mother seem to use much child-directed speech. Will this have a negative effect on the children's understanding or language development? Suggest some reasons why Mikey's father, in particular, doesn't use much "motherese."

ANSWER KEY

MULTIPLE-CHOICE QUESTIONS:

1. b   The capacity for symbolic representation develops between ages 12 and 30 months.

2. c   See definition of **language**.

3. b   See definition of **morpheme**.

4. d   See definition of **syntax**.

5. d   See definition of **pragmatics**.

6. c   Receptive language skills generally develop more rapidly than productive skills.

7. a   Adult-like stress and intonation do not appear until the **conversational babbling** stage; canonical babbling does not include *all* the sounds found in human speech, but it is not limited to the phonemes of the infant's native language.

8. d   Deaf and hearing infants' vocalizations are similar through the vocal play stage, but deaf infants are slow to produce the consonant-vowel syllables, typical of canonical babbling.

9. a   See definition of **lexical contrast**.

10. b   This child is *overextending* the meaning of the word *doggie*, or using it too broadly. *Overregularization* refers to use of morphological rules in situations in which they don't apply.

11. d   Roger Brown's research showed that how often children hear grammatical morphemes has nothing to do with how fast they acquire them.

12. a   Meryl is overregularizing *foot*, applying the rule for regular plurals to an irregular noun.

13. c   See definition of **holophrase**.

14. a   Two-year-olds do not yet seem to understand others' communication needs, but they do use conversational repairs when their own goals aren't being met.

15. b   Chomsky thought the LAD was innate, but he did not identify its location in the brain.

16. d Reinforcement and imitation do not explain language acquisition in general, but children do use them in learning the specific sounds and words of their native language.

17. d Answers *a-c* all provide evidence for the biological basis of human language.

18. c Infants do not have conscious language-learning strategies or predispositions to recognize specific language forms, but they do seem to be predisposed to break words down into morphemes.

19. d Native bilinguals mix and switch their languages, but they also develop metalinguistic awareness early. They show slower vocabulary growth in each language than monolingual children, but their combined vocabulary in both languages is larger.

20. c Child-directed speech has *fewer* grammatical errors, phrase boundaries that are *more* likely to be marked by pauses, and a focus on objects and events that *are* present.

21. b Child-directed speech may make connections between words and things they refer to more obvious, but there is no evidence it speeds up overall language acquisition. Its characteristics are not culturally universal, and it is not essential to language acquisition.

22. a Use of replica and substitute objects and combining a series of pretend acts around a theme appear in toddlerhood; double substitutions appear later in the preschool period.

23. b In both examples, words not essential to the meaning of the sentence have been left out.

24. a Mikey is using the vacuum cleaner bag to represent a party hat.

25. c Limited cognitive capacity is the most likely explanation for toddlers' shortened imitations.

MATCHING QUESTIONS:

1. E	4. M	7. O	10. F	13. D
2. H	5. G	8. N	11. B	14. A
3. K	6. C	9. L	12. J	15. I

SHORT-ANSWER QUESTIONS:

1. Language is an abstract, rule-governed system of arbitrary symbols that can be

combined in endless ways to communicate information. It need not be spoken; in fact, some languages, such as sign language used by deaf people, cannot be spoken.

2. semantics

3. At about age one, although there is considerable individual variation.

4. segmentation error

5. (a) The whole-object assumption, the assumption that unfamiliar words refer to objects rather than attributes or actions; (b) lexical contrast, the assumption that no two words have the same meaning and unfamiliar words must refer to things that do not already have labels.

6. grammatical complexity, semantic complexity, and phonological characteristics

7. Overregularization is considered a growth error because it indicates a child has learned a morphological rule and thus is developing a more advanced way of thinking.

8. Syntactic rules are difficult because they involve highly abstract categories and cannot be learned simply by observing how specific words are used in sentences. They are important because they are productive; they allow the formation of countless new sentences.

9. Because they often seem to express two separate ideas; there is often a pause between them, and word order does not seem to matter.

10. Linguistic competence involves correct semantics and syntax. Communicative competence also involves being able to carry on conversations, recognize and repair breakdowns in communication, and use language in a socially appropriate way.

11. nativist

12. Possibilities include detecting regularities in word sequences, segmenting words from a stream of speech, breaking down speech into phrases and clauses, and paying attention to perceptually salient stretches of speech.

13. additive bilingualism

14. Fathers make many of the same speech modifications as mothers, but fathers who are secondary caregivers ask children for more labels, explanations, repetitions, and clarifications, use more advanced vocabulary, and are more likely to ignore

children's utterances or respond to an utterance with a non-specific request for clarification.

15. communicative gestures, conventional social gestures, and symbolic gestures

ESSAY QUESTIONS:
1. The five stages of infant vocalization are crying, cooing, vocal play, canonical babbling, and conversational babbling or jargon. During the crying stage, infants vocalize to express discomfort. They cry reflexively whenever they are overly aroused, but their cries vary depending on cause of discomfort. Cooing, which begins at about 2 months, consists of vowel sounds (especially /u/) and a few consonants. During this stage, infants vocalize to express pleasure as well as discomfort. In the vocal play stage, beginning at about 4 months, infants produce sounds varying greatly in pitch and loudness, including simple consonant-vowel combinations. Canonical babbling, starting at about 6 months, sounds increasingly like speech. Vocalizations consist mostly of strings of syllables--initially repetition of the same syllable, but later combinations of different syllables. Babies do not yet imitate the particular sounds of their native language. During the conversational babbling stage, infants start to use adult-like stress and intonation, and their sounds begin to differ, depending on the language they are acquiring.

2. The language development of deaf babies exposed to sign language is similar to that of hearing infants. They engage in manual babbling, produce single signs and two-sign combinations, and begin to use grammatical morphemes and complex syntax at about the same ages as hearing infants. Deaf infants who are not exposed to sign language do not reach these milestones at the usual ages because they have not received linguistic input from the environment. They often create their own system of signs for communication. These homesign systems include a variety of gestures combined in structured ways similar to more formal languages, with distinctions between nouns and verbs, morphological functions marked by variations in hand shape and motion, and ordering preferences. However, they are not as complex as formal sign language.

3. Children with a referential style use words mainly to refer to objects and events; their early vocabulary consists mostly of nouns, with a few verbs and adjectives. Children with an expressive style use words mainly to express social routines; their first words are mostly pronouns and set formulas. Referential children initially show faster vocabulary growth than expressive children, but there is no difference in how grammatical their speech is. Expressive children are more likely to be second-borns and to come from less educated families. Mothers of expressive children use language mainly to direct their children's behavior, while mothers of referential children encourage labeling by asking their children many questions.

4. Segmentation errors occur when children make mistakes in boundaries between words in a sentence. They are fairly common in early speech, especially when word boundaries are marked by unstressed syllables, but they are usually corrected quickly. The most common word learning errors are underextensions, which involve overly restrictive word meanings, and overextensions, which involve overly broad meanings. Overextensions are seen more often, partly because they are more obvious. Underextensions are especially common when words are first learned; children initially tend to use words only in contexts in which they originally heard them. Overextensions occur as children explore the limits of word meanings; sometimes they knowingly overextend a word if it is the closest word available to express a desired meaning. As children's vocabularies expand, overextensions decline.

5. Brown's stages of early syntactic development reflect increases in the length and grammatical complexity of children's utterances. In Stage I, children express simple semantic and syntactic relationships by combining words into two-word utterances. In Stage II, they begin to use basic grammatical morphemes. In Stage III, they produce variations on simple sentences, such as questions. In Stage IV, they begin to embed one sentence in another, producing subordinate clauses. In Stage V, they join simple sentences to form compound sentences.

6. It is hard to test the notion of a critical period for language development because it is unusual to find children who receive no language input early in life. The idea of a critical period is supported by research on second language acquisition and on deaf people who learn sign language after early childhood. The second language acquisition research suggests that people who start to learn English before age 7 understand English grammar as well as native speakers; beyond this point, the older people are when they start learning English, the lower their eventual competence with English grammar. The sign language research suggests that the earlier children learn sign language, the more fluent they become.

7. The relative lack of child-directed speech in their environments is not likely to have a lasting effect on Meryl's or Mikey's language development. Child-directed speech simplifies language for children who are just starting to learn it, and it is useful for attracting and directing children's attention. However, it is not *necessary* for children to hear child-directed speech to learn language, since it is not used in all cultures. Children whose caregivers don't use child-directed speech may have fewer opportunities to participate in conversation early in language development. Their development of certain specific syntactic forms, such as auxiliary verbs, may be slightly slower than for children who hear a great deal of child-directed speech. These effects might be more apparent for Meryl than for Mikey, since Mikey's mother does use child-directed speech. In any case, their ultimate language competence is not likely to be affected; every healthy child eventually learns to speak

his or her native language almost flawlessly.

There are probably several reasons Mikey's father doesn't use motherese much. Like many fathers who are not primary caregivers, he may not be aware of Mikey's communication needs and ways to use language to attract his attention. His background may not have given him many chances to observe adults adjusting speech to match children's understanding. Because of his view of gender roles, he may feel motherese is only appropriate for women. He may use motherese with Mikey when they are alone, expressing affection in a way he is not comfortable doing in public. He may also think that using child-directed speech will make Mikey act like a baby longer or will encourage him to talk in a babyish way. Because he wants Mikey to act like a "big boy," he may feel it is more appropriate to talk to him as if he *were* a big boy.

CHAPTER 8

TODDLER SOCIAL AND EMOTIONAL DEVELOPMENT

CHAPTER REVIEW

As you read the chapter, construct your own chapter outline by answering the following review questions and defining the *Key Terms*.

I. INTRODUCTION
    Key Term: socialization
    A. What does **socialization** involve during the toddler period? What is added to the process later in the preschool years?

    B. What two important tasks do toddlers face? How do they vary across cultures?

II. TWO VIEWS OF SOCIALIZATION
    Key Terms: appropriation, sublimation
    A. What is the difference between socialization from the outside and from the inside?

    B. Describe the views of Freud and the early social learning theorists on how socialization occurs. How has the social learning view changed?

C. Explain Ainsworth's argument for socialization from the inside. How can this be reconciled with the fact that most toddlers display negativism?

III. MAJOR DEVELOPMENTS IN THE TODDLER PERIOD
Key Terms: **executive competence, social referencing, affective sharing, internalization, committed compliance, deviation anxiety, shame, positive self-evaluation, self-conscious emotions**
A. In addition to starting to acquire society's rules and values, what are the other important social and emotional developments of toddlerhood?

B. Describe how psychological contact comes to replace physical contact in support of toddlers' exploration of the environment. Summarize some research findings that illustrate this development.

C. BOX: Explain how toddlers' behavior can be better understood by considering how it is organized.

D. How does **executive competence** develop in toddlerhood? How is it related to the use of other people as resources?

E.   How is toddlers' self-awareness related to their cognitive development? What evidence is there for their emerging self-awareness?

F.   How are self-awareness and understanding of others related? What are the major steps in toddlers' developing concept of others? How does a growing understanding of others influence toddlers' interactions with parents and with peers?

G.   For what purposes and under what circumstances do toddlers use **social referencing**?

H.   What do toddlers' communication of discoveries and **affective sharing** with their caregivers demonstrate about their development?

I.   Summarize the development of toddlers' interactions with other young children. How do they differ from later peer relationships?

J.   Describe developments during toddlerhood that pave the way for the later development of true self-control and self-regulation.

K.   Describe developments during toddlerhood related to sensitivity to social standards and the beginnings of morality.

L.   How do previously existing emotions change during toddlerhood? What new emotions appear during this period and how are they different from earlier emotions?

IV. PARENT-TODDLER RELATIONS
     Key Terms: **scaffolding, guided self-regulation**
     A.   What are the major tasks for parents during toddlerhood? What impacts do the parents' general approach and specific child-rearing practices have on toddlers' development?

     B.   Across cultures, how does caregiving change during toddlerhood? In Western culture, how do father-child and mother-child interaction differ in infancy and toddlerhood?

V. INDIVIDUAL ADAPTATIONS: THE ROOTS OF PERSONALITY
   Key Terms: **patterns of adaptation, separation-individuation process, situational compliance**
   A. Describe how the **separation-individuation process** occurs and how closeness with the caregiver supports development of autonomy and a sense of self. What factors influence the smoothness of the separation-individuation process? How can toddlers' strivings toward independence be reconciled with their continuing need for closeness and security from their parents?

   B. How is attachment history related to toddlers' performance on problem-solving tasks and to mothers' behavior with their children as toddlers? What causal relationships may be involved here?

   C. How do the child's own characteristics influence development during toddlerhood? How do they interact with attachment history and current parenting?

   D. Explain how the larger social context can influence parent-toddler relationships.

VI. PARENTAL ABUSE AND NEGLECT OF TODDLERS
  Key terms: **physical neglect, physical abuse, emotional unavailability**
  A. How common is child abuse and neglect in the United States? Why are toddlers particularly vulnerable to abuse and neglect?

  B. What are the consequences of chronic maltreatment? What are the major forms of maltreatment? What effects have been associated with each?

  C. How are child characteristics related to abuse? BOX: How can associations between child aggressiveness and maltreatment be explained?

  D. What parental characteristics are *not* good predictors of child abuse? What factors *do* place parents at risk for child abuse?

  E. How is the broader environmental context related to child abuse?

VII. THE IMPORTANCE OF THE EARLY YEARS FOR SOCIAL, EMOTIONAL, AND
   NEUROLOGICAL DEVELOPMENT
   A.   How is toddlerhood particularly significant in children's development?

   B.   How are experience and brain development related during toddlerhood?

SELF-TEST

***After* you have studied the chapter, use the following questions to test your understanding.**

MULTIPLE-CHOICE QUESTIONS:

1. Which of the following is NOT part of **socialization** during toddlerhood?
    a. Responding to expectations of parents and others in authority.
    b. Learning rules within the family.
    c. Starting to acquire the rules, standards, and values of the culture.
    d. Internalizing the standards of society.

2. Which view of socialization emphasizes blocking biological drives in order to redirect a toddler's energy toward more socially desirable goals?
    a. Early social learning theory.
    b. Contemporary social learning theory.
    c. Attachment theory.
    d. Psychoanalytic theory.

3. Mary Ainsworth argued that toddlers comply with their parents' wishes because:
    a. they are responding to their parents' earlier responsiveness.
    b. they want to avoid punishment.
    c. they want to receive reinforcement.
    d. they fear losing their parents' love and nurturance.

4. Which of the following toddlers' behavior is the most typical example of toddler negativism?
    a. Bridget, who almost never opposes her parents' wishes or demands her own way.
    b. Kevin, who opposes his parents' wishes when they interfere with his goals.
    c. Maddie, who is oppositional mainly when she is trying to get her parents to help her.
    d. Danny, who consistently opposes or ignores his parents' requests.

5. Compared to infants, toddlers' relationships with their caregivers show:
    a. less physical contact.
    b. greater willingness to separate from the caregiver to explore.
    c. less distress when the caregiver leaves temporarily.
    d. all of the above.

6. Toddlers' sense of **executive competence** seems to develop as a result of:
    a. trial-and-error experimentation with the environment.
    b. reinforcement and punishment they receive from caregivers.
    c. observational learning.
    d. neurological maturation and muscular development.

7. A toddler's reaction to being placed in front of a mirror with a dab of rouge on her nose demonstrates the presence or absence of:
    a. executive competence.
    b. self-awareness.
    c. social referencing.
    d. affective sharing.

8. In an experiment with the visual cliff, 12-month-olds were more willing to cross over the glass if their mothers smiled and encouraged them. This is an example of:
    a. socialization.
    b. affective sharing.
    c. social referencing.
    d. executive competence.

9. Which of the following is NOT true of toddlers' peer interactions?
    a. They show complementary behavior with a partner.
    b. Their interaction is mostly object-centered.
    c. They differentiate between friends and playmates.
    d. They begin to play games with each other.

10. Which of the following is NOT a self-conscious emotion that develops during toddlerhood?
    a. shame
    b. anger
    c. embarrassment
    d. positive self-evaluation

11. Which of the following aspects of parental care is most important in toddlers' development?
    a. Showing sensitivity in determining when a child should be weaned.
    b. Pursuing toilet training without punitiveness.
    c. Providing consistent limits and guidance.
    d. Punishing the child immediately after misbehavior.

12. Which of the following statements about fathers' interactions with toddlers is most accurate?
    a. Fathers usually become less involved with their children when they reach toddlerhood.
    b. Fathers typically engage in more playful interactions with toddlers than mothers do.
    c. Fathers typically are just as involved in basic care and nurturance as mothers are.
    d. Fathers' and mothers' behavior toward toddlers is usually quite similar.

13. Which of the following best states the relationship between independence and emotional closeness to the caregiver during toddlerhood?
    a. Toddlers must choose between independence and emotional closeness to the caregiver.
    b. Toddlers who are very close to their caregivers have trouble achieving independence.
    c. Emotional closeness to the caregiver fosters toddlers' moves toward independence.
    d. Independence and emotional closeness are unrelated; each develops separately.

14. Which pattern of attachment is typical of mothers who remain uninvolved in their child's efforts on a problem-solving task, even as the problems become increasingly difficult?
    a. Secure.
    b. Anxious-avoidant.
    c. Anxious-resistant.
    d. Disoriented-disorganized.

15. When placed in a problem-solving situation with their toddler children, mothers whose children were securely attached as infants tend to:
    a. allow their children to work on their own until they near the limits of their resources.
    b. provide relatively little assistance to their children, even if the problem is difficult.
    c. wait until their children become frustrated before offering assistance.
    d. direct their children's behavior from the beginning, to keep them from getting frustrated.

16. During the toddler period, individual children's behavior becomes:
    a. increasingly stable and consistent.
    b. less stable and consistent.
    c. harder to predict.
    d. none of the above; there is no general pattern.

17. Toddlers' behavior can best be understood and predicted by considering:
    a. attachment history.
    b. current parenting.
    c. temperament.
    d. a combination of attachment history, current parenting, and child characteristics.

18. Which of the following contextual factors seems of greatest importance in fostering good parent-toddler relationships?
    a. Low economic stress.
    b. The presence of other children for the toddler to play with.
    c. An extensive network of family ties.
    d. Supportive relationships with other adults for the parent.

19. Changes from an insecure to a secure attachment classification during toddlerhood are most often associated with:
    a. a positive change in the primary caregiver's life circumstances.
    b. a change in the toddler's temperamental characteristics.
    c. the addition of another child to the family.
    d. improvement in the toddler's health status.

20. Toddlers are particularly vulnerable to abuse because:
    a. they are constantly testing the limits parents impose.
    b. their assertiveness can be misinterpreted as naughtiness.
    c. they have not yet learned how to avoid parental mistreatment.
    d. all of the above.

21 Children who experience chronic emotional unavailability from their parents are most likely to develop which of the following problems?
    a. Major school achievement problems.
    b. Apathy and a lack of joy or pleasure.
    c. Aggressiveness with peers.
    d. Relatively minor and transitory problems because they aren't being physically harmed.

22. In prospective studies, which of the following has been found to be associated with child abuse?
    a. Infant prematurity.
    b. Early infant irritability.
    c. Mother's thoughts and feelings about child rearing.
    d. Mental disturbance in one or both parents.

23. When Malcolm and Momma Jo were almost robbed, Malcolm looked at Momma Jo and then said to the strangers "Go 'way." What type of behavior was he displaying when he looked at Momma Jo?
    a. Affective sharing.
    b. Social referencing.
    c. Executive competence.
    d. Self-assertion.

24. Frank Gordon's behavior toward Mikey when he returns home from work is:
    a.   unusually detached for the father of a toddler boy.
    b.   unusual because he provides more routine caregiving than most fathers.
    c.   unusual because he plays with him and Mikey seems to like it.
    d.   typical of most fathers of toddler boys.

25. The combination of clinginess and tantrum-proneness that Meryl shows as a toddler is:
    a.   not unusual for securely attached children.
    b.   typical of children with anxious-resistant attachments.
    c.   typical of children with anxious-avoidant attachments.
    d.   probably a result of her irritable temperament rather than her attachment history.

MATCHING QUESTIONS:
Match the following key terms with their definitions:

1.   ___ Executive competence

2.   ___ Shame

3.   ___ Scaffolding

4.   ___ Internalization

5.   ___ Socialization

6.   ___ Appropriation

7.   ___ Pattern of adaptation

8.   ___ Guided self-regulation

9.   ___ Affective sharing

10. ___ Deviation anxiety

A.   Individual styles of responding to others and to the environment that form the roots of personality.

B.   The ability of toddlers to regulate their own behavior with guidance from caregivers.

C.   The toddler's sharing of positive emotions with the caregiver.

D.   The process by which children naturally take on the rules and values of their culture through their participation in relationships with caregivers.

E.   The child's feeling that he or she is an autonomous force in the world, with the ability to influence the outcome of events.

F.   The process by which parents support the child in new tasks by offering developmentally appropriate guidance, hints, and advice.

G.   The distress toddlers experience over doing something forbidden.

H.   An emotion in which the self feels exposed, vulnerable, and bad.

I.   Incorporating the parent's standards of behavior into the self.

J.   The process by which children acquire the rules, standards, and values of a culture.

SHORT-ANSWER QUESTIONS:
1. List the two major tasks faced by toddlers in Western cultures.
    (a)

    (b)

2. Barbara Rogoff's term for the process by which children take on the rules and values of their culture in the context of their relationships with their caregivers is
    _____.

3. Explain the difference between socialization from the outside and socialization from the inside.

4. The toddler's realization that "I" can do things, that "I" can be in charge is called
    _____ _____.

5. How do toddlers' interactions with other children differ from later peer relationships?

6. Explain how cognitive development makes self-awareness possible in toddlerhood.

7. The negative feelings toddlers experience when they are doing something forbidden are known as _____ _____.

8. List two self-conscious emotions that emerge during toddlerhood.
    (a)

    (b)

9. List the two major tasks faced by parents of toddlers.
    (a)

    (b)

10. List two factors that influence the smoothness of the **separation-individuation process**.

    (a)

    (b)

11. What happens to children's individual characteristics and their role in development during toddlerhood?

12. Children's unwilling compliance with parents' directives due to fear or parents' control of the situation is called _____ _____.

13. List three major forms of child maltreatment.

    (a)

    (b)

    (c)

14. List three parental characteristics associated with child maltreatment.

    (a)

    (b)

    (c)

15. List three ways the toddler period is particularly significant in children's development.

    (a)

    (b)

    (c)

ESSAY QUESTIONS:

1. Discuss how considering how behaviors are organized, rather than examining each behavior individually, can help in understanding toddler development.

2. Explain the difference between affective sharing and social referencing and discuss what the development of both abilities demonstrates about toddlers' development.

3. Explain the difference between committed compliance and situational compliance in toddlers.

4. Toddlers with a history of secure attachment in infancy have been found to be more enthusiastic, persistent, and flexible in problem-solving situations than toddlers with a history of anxious attachment. Discuss at least two possible explanations for that finding.

5. Discuss the role played by child characteristics in both normal and abusive parent-toddler interactions.

6. Discuss how the new behaviors and abilities of toddlers change their relationships with parents and with peers.

7. Malcolm was an energetic 2-year-old whose grandmother described him as "a pile of mischief." However, he did not seem to be a really difficult child, and his family did not regard his behavior as a problem. Suggest two factors in his family environment that may have helped Malcolm to successfully walk the fine line between "active" and "difficult."

ANSWER KEY

MULTIPLE-CHOICE QUESTIONS:

1. d Children do not begin to internalize society's standards until later in the preschool years.

2. d This view reflects Freud's concept of sublimation.

3. a This reflects Ainsworth's concept of socialization from the inside.

4. b Negativism when parents' goals conflict with their own reflects toddlers' move toward increasing independence. The other forms of negativism mentioned are atypical.

5. d Answers *a-c* all demonstrate the change from a need for physical contact to an ability to rely on psychological contact that is typical of toddlers.

6. a Active engagement with objects and people in the environment is essential for toddlers to develop a sense that they can influence the outcome of events.

7. b This task indicates whether toddlers recognize themselves, a measure of self-awareness.

8. c This is an example of using social cues to interpret a situation.

9. c Toddlers interact differently with familiar and unfamiliar playmates, but they do not differentiate between friends and playmates until later in the preschool period.

10. b Anger is one of the basic emotions that emerge earlier in infancy. Shame, embarrassment, and positive self-evaluation are all self-conscious emotions that require some objective sense of self and some understanding of standards for behavior.

11. c Specifics of weaning and toilet training have little impact on development. Consistent limit-setting and guidance are more important than immediate punishment for misdeeds because they encourage desirable behavior as well as discouraging undesirable behavior.

12. b Fathers become *more* involved with their children during toddlerhood, but most mothers still spend more time in basic care and nurturance and most fathers more time in play.

13. c Toddlers need *both* increased independence and continued emotional closeness

to caregivers. Emotional closeness gives toddlers more confidence to pursue independence.

14. b   This pattern of behavior reflects the general uninvolvement and rejection typical of mothers whose infants develop anxious-avoidant attachments.

15. a   Mothers of securely attached toddlers encourage them to try to solve problems but provide help when they exhaust their own resources.

16. a   Behavior becomes increasingly stable and consistent and therefore easier to predict.

17. d   A combination provides the most complete picture.

18. d   Low economic stress and family ties are positive influences, but supportive relationships with other adults are particularly important because they help parents cope with stress and provide responsive care to their children.

19. a   Improvements in life circumstances increase the caregiver's ability to be responsive to the child's needs, which can increase attachment security.

20. d   Answers *a* and *b* both make toddlers challenging to care for, which can overwhelm parents with inadequate resources. Answer *c* reflects toddlers' inability to escape abuse.

21. b   Major school achievement problems are associated with physical neglect and aggressiveness with peers with physical abuse. Rather than producing minor problems, emotional unavailability is actually a particularly devastating form of maltreatment.

22. c   Infant characteristics *alone* do not increase risk of abuse. The risk rises when infants with challenging characteristics have parents who are not equipped to cope with them. Parents who abuse their children are usually not mentally disturbed, but they often have unrealistic expectations and negative or ambivalent feelings about having children.

23. b   Malcolm was looking to Momma Jo for cues to help him decide whether the situation was dangerous or not.

24. d   Frank's behavior is fairly typical for a father of a toddler boy, though perhaps at the high end of interest and involvement.

25. b   Meryl's behaviors are typical outgrowths of the difficulty separating seen in

infants with anxious-resistant attachments. Irritable temperament alone does not explain clinginess.

MATCHING QUESTIONS:

1. E   4. I   7. A   10. G
2. H   5. J   8. B
3. F   6. D   9. C

SHORT-ANSWER QUESTIONS:

1. moving toward greater self-reliance and starting to comply with social rules and expectations

2. appropriation

3. Socialization from the outside refers to rules and values imposed on an unwilling child by adults, whereas socialization from the inside refers to children's natural tendency to take on the rules and values of their culture through their participation in relationships with adults.

4. executive competence

5. Toddlers are less capable of coordinated play with other children than older preschoolers are. Toddlers' interactions with each other are often centered around joint play with objects, but joint themes and social pretend play do not become common until the preschool years. Toddlers interact with familiar partners in more complex ways than unfamiliar partners, but they do not yet make a distinction between playmates and friends, as older children do.

6. Mental representation allows toddlers to think about themselves and their actions.

7. deviation anxiety

8. shame and positive self-evaluation (embarrassment is another possible answer)

9. To support their child's exploration of the world and to set appropriate limits for the child.

10. The way parents impose limits and the degree of basic trust developed by the child.

11. Various aspects of children's behavior, such as fearfulness and intensity of response to the environment, become increasingly stable and consistent during toddlerhood. Descriptions of the same child's behavior by different observers also agree better in toddlerhood than in infancy. As a child's behavior becomes more stable, it has

increasing influence on parents and on how the child deals with the world around him or her.

12. situational compliance

13. physical neglect, physical abuse, and emotional unavailability

14. Possible answers include low self-esteem, poor impulse control, doubts about personal power, negative emotions, antisocial behavior, inability to cope with stress of pregnancy and child rearing, limited understanding of child development, and maltreatment as a child.

15. During toddlerhood a sense of self emerges, foundations of self-esteem are established, patterns of emotional expression and regulation develop, the roots of morality are laid down, children are especially open to family and cultural influences, both positive and negative, and neurological development with important implications for cognitive, emotional, and social development occurs.

ESSAY QUESTIONS:
1. By itself, the frequency of individual behaviors reveals little about toddlers' development. Considering the organization of toddlers' behavior is far more informative. Organization of behavior includes such factors as how behaviors are combined and the contexts in which they occur. These factors are important because behaviors that appear similar may mean different things in different circumstances, in different combinations, or at different ages. On the other hand, behaviors that appear different may have similar meanings in different situations or at different ages. How behaviors are organized with regard to a caregiver is especially revealing because it taps into the quality of the attachment relationship between the child and the caregiver. Examples of research findings that take the organization of behavior into account include the finding that toddlers behave differently toward strangers depending on whether their mothers are present and the finding that attachment quality tends to be stable from 12 to 18 months of age, even though specific attachment behaviors change.

2. Affective sharing refers to toddlers' tendency to communicate feelings, especially positive ones, to caregivers as they explore their environments. Social referencing refers to toddlers' tendency to use caregivers' facial expressions and other displays of affect as a guide for interpreting unfamiliar situations, especially when they are ambiguous. The development of both of these abilities demonstrates toddlers' increasing ability to coordinate their behavior with others', interpret social signals, and express closeness to their caregivers from a distance.

3. Committed compliance is enthusiastic compliance with parents' directives. It is most often seen in toddlers who have a history of secure attachment to their parents. Toddlers who show committed compliance are later likely to show evidence that they are beginning to internalize parental standards, beginning at age 3. Situational compliance is unwilling compliance with parents' directives due to fear or parents' control of the situation. It is associated with fearfulness in the child and does not predict later internalization of parents' standards.

4. Children who are securely attached in infancy receive more consistent, responsive care than children who are anxiously attached. As a result, they develop more positive internal working models or expectations about the world and their ability to influence events. One explanation for superior problem-solving behavior in toddlers with a secure attachment history is based on continuity in the children; their positive internal working models, carried into toddlerhood, give them greater resources to apply to problem-solving situations. Another explanation is based on continuity in parents' behavior; parents who provide sensitive care in infancy continue to provide it in toddlerhood, including support and assistance in problem-solving situations. It is likely that continuity in both children's and parents' behavior contributes to the association between attachment history and toddler behavior.

5. By age 1, children have developed consistent individual behavioral styles that endure across situations and become even more consistent during toddlerhood. These differences result in differential treatment from adults, with easy, compliant toddlers receiving more positive responses, less punishment, and fewer limits than more difficult toddlers. Treatment from adults reinforces differences in behavior, setting up the potential for continued positive or negative cycles of interaction. In an abusive interaction, the same processes operate, except that the adult may be dealing with a large number of stresses, including the stress of rearing a cranky, demanding, or difficult child. In both normal and abusive parent-child interactions, relationships develop through a bidirectional process, in which child characteristics interact with caregiver characteristics and both child and caregiver influence each other's behavior.

6. Toddlers' new behaviors and abilities change relationships with parents considerably. Their moves toward independence and increased assertion of desires create increased conflict with parents and inject a note of negativism into the relationship. Parents must adjust expectations and behavior to match the new abilities and behaviors of their toddlers, both providing support for exploration and setting appropriate limits. At the same time, toddlers' new sense of self and increased social skills allow them to be more active in expressing affection and other positive emotions to parents. Toddlers' increasing command of language allows them to communicate more effectively, to carry on genuine conversations,

make demands, and respond to parents' instructions and requests. Toddlers' relationships with peers also change as a result of their new behaviors and abilities. Their growing awareness of self and others leads to increasing interest in other children and understanding of others' behavior and feelings. Expanding cognitive skills allow them to engage other children in play and sustain relatively simple interactions with them, with play centering on objects of common interest.

7. One factor would be Malcolm's secure attachment to his parents and grandmother. These relationships give him a strong sense of self-reliance and self-control, as well as a willingness to obey and be responsive to the adults who have been responsive to him. Another factor would be that his caregivers have set consistent limits for him, as shown in his interactions with Momma Jo--she clearly loves him but does not indulge him. The limits give him a clear range within which he can test his abilities, yet he knows he can trust his caregivers not to allow him to go beyond what he can handle.

CHAPTER 9
COGNITIVE DEVELOPMENT IN EARLY CHILDHOOD
CHAPTER REVIEW

As you read the chapter, construct your own chapter outline by answering the following review questions and defining the *Key Terms*.

I. INTRODUCTION
   Key Terms: **centration, appearance-reality problem, egocentrism**
   A. How are preschoolers' cognitive abilities superior to those of infants and toddlers?

   B. What are three major limitations in preschoolers' thinking?

II. GENERAL CHARACTERISTICS OF PRESCHOOLERS' THOUGHT
   Key Terms: **preoperational period, animism, conservation, classification, seriation, transitive inference, class**
   A. How did Piaget characterize the preschool period?

   B. Describe the four levels Piaget found in children's causal reasoning. What have other researchers discovered about preschoolers' causal reasoning? How do preschoolers use magical explanations and how does that change with age?

C.   What did Piaget claim about children's knowledge of living and nonliving things? What have later researchers found?

D.   List the concepts of **conservation** studied by Piaget. Explain why children do not master all of them at the same time.

E.   BOX: Describe the task used to measure conservation of liquid volume and summarize the development of children's ability on this task. List the justifications used by children with a mature understanding of this form of conservation.

F.   What was Piaget's opinion about the possibility of teaching children concepts of conservation? Summarize the results of conservation training studies.

G.   Describe preschoolers' progress toward understanding the concept of number, including their performance on tasks measuring conservation of number. Summarize the development of children's understanding of the effects of addition and subtraction.

H. List the five principles involved in counting and summarize preschoolers' progress in mastering them.

I. What does research reveal about preschoolers' understanding and use of measurement?

J. Summarize the findings about preschoolers' understanding of quantitative concepts.

K. Describe the **classification** skills of infants and toddlers. Summarize Piaget's findings on preschoolers' classification skills. What have more recent researchers found?

L. What did Piaget discover about preschoolers' **seriation** skills? Why is it easier for them to perform this task with a small set of sticks? How are preschoolers' seriation skills related to the appearance-reality problem and to centration?

M. At what stage of development did Piaget believe children became able to solve **transitive inference** problems? What has more recent research revealed about preschoolers' transitive inference skills? Why are transitive inference problems difficult for preschoolers?

N. Summarize the research on preschoolers' understanding of appearance and reality.

III. PRESCHOOLERS' ATTENTION AND MEMORY ABILITIES:
Key Terms: **sensory register, short-term/working memory, long-term memory, attention skills, memory skills, recognition memory, free recall**
A. Explain the basic information-processing model for attention and memory.

B. Summarize the attentional skills and understanding of preschoolers, compared to those of toddlers and older children.

C. Summarize preschoolers' memory abilities and limitations. How can their performance on memory tasks be explained? What have researchers discovered about their ability to use memory strategies?

D. How are adults involved in children's memory performance? What practical implications does this have for preschoolers' reliability as witnesses?

IV. SOCIAL COGNITION
   Key Terms: **social cognition, theory of mind, competence-performance distinction, script**
   A. Summarize research results on various forms of egocentrism in preschoolers. List the cognitive components needed to overcome egocentrism and take another person's perspective. Explain why early signs of sensitivity to others' feelings do not indicate an absence of egocentrism.

B. Explain why children's understanding of the mind can legitimately be referred to as a theory. What five fundamental principles do children come to understand as they develop a **theory of mind**? At what age do they seem to understand each one?

C. Summarize the results from research on preschoolers' ability to communicate information and to adapt their speech to the needs of a listener. Under what circumstances do they perform best on communication tasks?

D. Explain the **competence-performance distinction**. What approach should researchers take to determine a child's maximum skill at a task? A child's typical performance?

E. Explain how limited cognitive resources may be involved in children's communication problems. How does the acquisition of **scripts** help in the development of communicative abilities? Why is a knowledge of scripts more important in communication with peers than in communication with adults?

F.   BOX: Discuss the elements involved in children's readiness for school. What can parents and schools do to increase children's chances of a successful transition to school?

V.   AN OVERVIEW OF PRESCHOOL COGNITIVE DEVELOPMENT
     Summarize the major cognitive advances of the preschool period.

SELF-TEST

After you have studied the chapter, use the following questions to test your understanding.

MULTIPLE-CHOICE QUESTIONS:

1. Which of the following is NOT one of the limitations characteristic of preschoolers' thought?
   a. Difficulty distinguishing between appearance and reality.
   b. Difficulty focusing on more than one aspect of a situation.
   c. Difficulty using mental representation and combining symbols.
   d. Difficulty using memory strategies.

2. At Piaget's Level 1, children's explanations of causal relationships are based on:
   a. the superficial appearance of things.
   b. all-powerful forces, such as God or parents.
   c. improbable natural forces.
   d. factors similar to those cited by adults.

3. In contrast to Piaget, recent researchers studying preschoolers' causal reasoning have found:
   a. preschoolers are even less skilled at causal reasoning than Piaget thought.
   b. preschoolers can give good causal explanations for simple, familiar processes.
   c. preschoolers have a general concept of plausible causal explanations, but they have trouble applying it to specific situations.
   d. preschoolers actually have a fairly mature understanding of causal processes.

4. Recent research on preschoolers' understanding of living and nonliving things indicates that:
   a. preschoolers tend to attribute life to anything that moves.
   b. preschoolers often believe nonliving things can grow and reproduce.
   c. preschoolers do not yet understand all the implications of the living/nonliving distinction.
   d. preschoolers understand nearly as much about living and nonliving things as adults do.

5. On Piaget's conservation of liquid volume task, most 3- and 4-year-olds would:
   a. consistently judge the amount of liquid by the height to which it rises.
   b. vacillate between height and width in judging the amount of liquid.
   c. focus on changes in the liquid, rather than its appearance at any one moment.
   d. offer clear and logical justifications for the answers they gave.

6. Researchers who have tried to train children on concepts of conservation have found that:
   a. it is impossible to speed up children's understanding of conservation, regardless of the form of training used.
   b. training usually produces permanent understanding of conservation, even in young preschoolers.
   c. the younger the children are, the more likely it is that training will be successful.
   d. training can often produce understanding of conservation in children who are already close to grasping it.

7. In solving problems involving addition to or subtraction from groups of objects, 4- and 5-year-olds tend to base their answers on:
   a. a *primitive* rule that focuses only on whether objects were added or subtracted.
   b. a *qualitative* rule that ignores the size of differences between groups.
   c. a *quantitative* rule that takes into account the size of differences between groups.
   d. no consistent rule; they seem to answer more or less randomly.

8. Piaget attributed preschoolers' tendency to sort objects along one dimension at a time to:
   a. memory limitations.
   b. a lack of understanding of conservation.
   c. egocentrism.
   d. centration.

9. When Meryl was 5, she received a set of Russian nesting dolls for Christmas. She liked to take the set apart and line them up in order from smallest to largest. This is an example of:
   a. classification.
   b. seriation.
   c. transitive inference.
   d. conservation.

10. Preschoolers have difficulty placing a set of seven sticks in order based on length because:
    a. they do not have an overall understanding of the task of seriation.
    b. they tend to use a trial-and-error strategy.
    c. they cannot picture the relationship among members of a set that is not visually present.
    d. all of the above.

11. Piaget believed that children were unable to solve transitive inference problems until:
    a. the end of the sensorimotor period.
    b. the late preschool years.
    c. middle childhood.
    d. adolescence.

12. Which of the following best describes 3-year-olds' understanding of appearance and reality?
    a. They show no evidence of knowing there is a difference between appearance and reality.
    b. They show a beginning distinction, but their view of reality is dominated by appearance.
    c. With training, they can usually learn the distinction between appearance and reality.
    d. They show a good understanding of the difference between appearance and reality.

13. According to the basic information-processing model, the transfer of information from sensory registers to short-term memory depends on:
    a. neurological maturation.
    b. attentional skills.
    c. memory skills.
    d. sensory alertness.

14. Preschoolers have difficulty with which of the following attentional tasks?
    a. Selecting information to attend to.
    b. Staying focused on information.
    c. Ignoring irrelevant stimuli.
    d. All of the above.

15. In laboratory settings, preschoolers tend to do best on which type of memory task?
    a. Recognition tasks.
    b. Recall of pictures.
    c. Recall of numbers.
    d. Autobiographical memory questions.

16. Preschoolers can do as well as older children on a memory task, provided that:
    a. the material is completely unfamiliar to both age groups.
    b. they are warned in advance of the need to remember the material.
    c. they are not warned in advance of the need to remember the material.
    d. they are coached on strategies for memorizing the material.

17. Research indicates that young children are most likely to give accurate testimony when:
    a. they are asked concrete, open-ended questions that do not suggest a certain answer.
    b. they are repeatedly questioned about their recollections of what happened.
    c. they are told that the adult questioning them knows what happened.
    d. all of the above.

18. One day DeeDee had to work late and called home to talk to Malcolm before he went to bed. When she asked if he'd had supper, he nodded instead of saying "Yes." This is an example of:
    a. collective monologue.
    b. perceptual egocentrism.
    c. social inference.
    d. the appearance-reality problem.

19. According to Flavell, to overcome egocentrism children need:
    a. a knowledge that others can have viewpoints that differ from their own.
    b. an awareness that it can be useful to consider others' perspectives.
    c. skill at interpreting others' behavior and making social inferences.
    d. all of the above.

20. Children's understanding of the mind and the causes of human behavior is referred to as a *theory* of mind because:
    a. children realize that their knowledge of the mind is tentative.
    b. children's understanding of the mind is usually incorrect.
    c. children's knowledge of the mind goes beyond empirical knowledge.
    d. all of the above.

21. Which of the following is TRUE of preschoolers' communicative abilities?
    a. How egocentric their speech is depends on the complexity of the communication task.
    b. They usually do not vary detail in explanations to match particular listeners' knowledge.
    c. They do not spontaneously vary clarifications to fit the age of their listeners.
    d. All of the above.

22. The acquisition of scripts improves preschoolers' communication because:
    a. it gives them something to talk about.
    b. it reduces their egocentrism.
    c. it reduces demands on their cognitive resources.
    d. it helps them understand adults' thoughts and feelings.

23. When Malcolm and April argued over the tricycle, he ended the argument by punching her. This method of settling an argument is:
    a. a typical strategy for preschoolers in natural settings.
    b. unusual by the time children reach kindergarten.
    c. more common in laboratory settings than in natural settings.
    d. an indication that Malcolm's cognitive development is lagging.

24. Mikey's preschool teachers described him as very good at settling arguments between his peers by finding a compromise. This ability indicates that Mikey:
    a. has learned a script for settling arguments.
    b. has developed some ability to take other people's perspectives.
    c. does not yet realize he can settle a fight by using force.
    d. is afraid to stand up to his peers.

25. Meryl's request for coupons when she was playing store indicates an ability to use:
    a. collective monologue.
    b. perspective-taking.
    c. transitive inference.
    d. scripts.

MATCHING QUESTIONS:

Match the following key terms with their definitions:

1. ___ Sensory register

2. ___ Attention skills

3. ___ Centration

4. ___ Script

5. ___ Short-term or working memory

6. ___ Conservation

7. ___ Memory skills

8. ___ Seriation

9. ___ Egocentrism

10. ___ Classification

A. The inability to take the perspective of another person.

B. The ability to group things by shared characteristics, such as size or shape.

C. Processes that retain information in working memory and/or transfer it to long-term memory.

D. The ability to arrange things in a logical progression, such as from oldest to newest.

E. The part of memory where incoming information from one of the five senses is stored very briefly.

F. Processes that control the transfer of information from a sensory register to working memory.

G. An abstract representation of the sequence of actions needed to accomplish some goal.

H. The part of memory where consciously noted information is stored for 10 to 20 seconds.

I. The tendency to consider only one piece of information when multiple pieces are relevant.

J. The idea that the amount of something remains the same despite changes in form, shape, or appearance.

SHORT-ANSWER QUESTIONS:

1. Explain how preschoolers' cognitive abilities differ from those of infants and toddlers.

2. Why did Piaget refer to the preschool years as the **preoperational period**?

3. Describe the four levels of causal reasoning found by Piaget.
   (a)

   (b)

   (c)

   (d)

4. List the three major justifications provided by children who understand **conservation**.
   (a)

   (b)

   (c)

5. List the five principles involved in counting.

    (a)

    (b)

    (c)

    (d)

    (e)

6. List four overall findings about preschoolers' understanding of quantitative concepts.

    (a)

    (b)

    (c)

    (d)

7. The ability to infer the relationship between two objects by knowing their respective relationships to a third is known as _____.

8. Approximately how long does information remain in **short-term memory**?

9. The ability to perceive a particular stimulus as familiar is known as _____ _____.

10. A child's understanding of the social world is referred to as _____ _____.

11. List the three cognitive components needed to overcome egocentrism.

    (a)

    (b)

    (c)

12. Explain why early signs of sensitivity to others' feelings do not indicate an absence of egocentrism.

13. What should a researcher do to (a) determine a child's *maximum* skill at a task and (b) determine a child's *typical* performance on a task?

    (a)

    (b)

14. Explain why a knowledge of scripts is more important in communication with peers than in communication with adults.

15. List three of the major cognitive advances of the preschool period.

    (a)

    (b)

    (c)

ESSAY QUESTIONS:

1. Give three examples of how the appearance-reality problem interferes with preschoolers' performance on cognitive tasks.

2. Discuss the development of classification skills from infancy through the preschool years, drawing on both Piagetian ideas and more recent research.

3. Although preschoolers show clear evidence of both recognition and recall memory, their memory skills are still not on the same level as those of elementary school children. Give three reasons for preschoolers' continuing memory limitations.

4. Trace the development of children's theory of mind, basing your discussion on the five basic principles proposed by Flavell.

5. Suggest three ways that experience with peers might contribute to the gradual decline in egocentrism seen during the preschool years.

6. Malcolm is extremely active at home and at school. Discuss the advantages and disadvantages of his high activity level for his cognitive development.

7. Discuss three ways that cognitive development in early childhood prepares children for the start of formal education.

ANSWER KEY

MULTIPLE-CHOICE QUESTIONS:

1. c   The ability to use mental representation and combine symbols emerges in toddlerhood.

2. a   Level 2 explanations are based on all-powerful forces, Level 3 explanations on improbable natural forces, and Level 4 explanations on factors like those used by adults.

3. b   Recent researchers have found that children are more skilled at causal reasoning than Piaget thought, but lack a general concept of plausible causal explanations.

4. c   Preschoolers make clear distinctions in reasoning about living and nonliving things, but they do not understand all the implications of the living/nonliving distinction.

5. a   Most 3- and 4-year-olds focus on the liquid's height, not how it changes. Vacillation is typical of 5- and 6-year-olds, who are in a transitional stage. Children do not give logical justifications for their answers until they have a mature understanding of conservation.

6. d   Training sometimes works with children who are close to understanding conservation, but not with young preschoolers, who lack a framework for conservation concepts.

7. b   A primitive rule is typical of 2- and 3-year-olds; a quantitative rule is typical of 6- and 7-year-olds. Even very young children seem to use some sort of rule in their reasoning.

8. d   Piaget believed preschoolers became centrated on one dimension and were unable to switch to another, even when it would have been appropriate to do so.

9. b   Seriation involves arranging things in a logical progression, as from smallest to largest.

10. d   Answers *a-c* all contribute to preschoolers' difficulty with seriation.

11. c   Preschoolers typically could not solve Piaget's transitive inference problems; more recent researchers have found they can solve similar problems under certain circumstances.

12. b Three-year-olds have trouble with Flavell's appearance-reality tasks; on other tasks they show signs of *starting* to make the distinction but are still easily fooled by appearances.

13. b Attentional skills are used to transfer information from sensory registers to short-term memory; memory skills are used to retain information in short-term memory and transfer it to long-term memory.

14. d Preschoolers have trouble with virtually all aspects of attention.

15. a In the laboratory, preschoolers still have considerable trouble with free recall tasks. Autobiographical memory is more prominent in everyday life than in the lab.

16. c Preschoolers are on the most equal footing when not warned in advance to remember; advance warning lets older children use superior memory strategies. Totally unfamiliar material puts preschoolers at more of a disadvantage; coaching has limited effectiveness.

17. a Repeated questioning decreases the chances of accurate testimony; being reminded that the adult questioning them *doesn't* know what happened increases the chances of accurate testimony.

18. b Malcolm was not taking into account what his mother could actually see.

19. d Answers *a-c* are all components Flavell believes necessary for overcoming egocentrism.

20. c In a scientific sense, theoretical knowledge consists of explanations based on constructs that cannot be directly observed, such as the mind.

21. a Preschoolers do vary what they say to fit the knowledge and age of their listeners.

22. c Scripts do not reduce egocentrism or help preschoolers understand adults, but they reduce demands on cognitive resources when communicating with other preschoolers.

23. a Malcolm probably knows more appropriate ways to settle a dispute, but the cognitive demands of a natural setting often cause children to resort to less mature strategies.

24. b   Settling arguments by compromise is an advanced social skill that depends on the ability to take others' perspectives; it is too complex to be captured in a script.

25. d   Meryl's behavior reflects a knowledge of a grocery-shopping script.

MATCHING QUESTIONS:
1.	E	4.	G	7.	C	10. B
2.	F	5.	H	8.	D	
3.	I	6.	J	9.	A	

SHORT-ANSWER QUESTIONS:
1. Infants understand the world by perceiving and acting on it. Toddlers add abilities of mental representation and combining symbols in thinking and communicating. Preschoolers build on and surpass these abilities, seeking explanations for how things work and why events occur.

2. Because he believed preschoolers were not yet using logical operations in their reasoning.

3. Level 1: causal explanations based on superficial appearances. Level 2: causal explanations based on an all-powerful force. Level 3: causal explanations based on improbable natural causes. Level 4: causal explanations similar to those given by adults, but still incomplete.

4. compensation, reversibility, and the nothing added or subtracted criterion

5. one-to-one, stable-order, cardinal, abstraction, and order-irrelevant principles

6. (a) Preschoolers do not display understanding of conservation of quantity despite changes in appearance, in part because of centration; (b) teaching can lead to stable acquisition of new cognitive skills, if the child has an appropriate cognitive framework; (c) preschoolers show sophistication in reasoning about small quantities; (d) preschoolers' quantitative reasoning is immature, but it does follow rules, and the nature of the rules changes with development.

7. transitive inference

8. 10 to 20 seconds

9. recognition memory

10. social cognition

11. (a) Knowledge of existence of alternate viewpoints--realizing other people have thoughts, viewpoints, and desires that may differ from a child's own; (b) awareness of need to consider other viewpoints--realizing that considering another's perspective can facilitate social interaction and communication; (c) social inference--the ability to read another person's actions and imagine his or her point of view.

12. Because a true absence of egocentrism requires an ability to make accurate inferences about others' feelings as well as recognizing that others have feelings and being able to assign them to general categories such as "good" and "bad."

13. (a) Limit cognitive demands not directly related to the task as much as possible; (b) observe the child in an environment with the cognitive demands and distractions of a natural setting.

14. Adults usually structure interactions with young children so that they proceed smoothly and communication is clear, making the cognitive load for a child communicating with an adult manageable. Children communicating with peers must structure and monitor their own conversations. A shared script simplifies communication and reduces cognitive demands.

15. Possible answers include emerging understanding of causation, ability to distinguish living and nonliving things, qualitative understanding of quantitative concepts, ability to reason about small numbers, beginning understanding of classification and other logical relations, gradual development of ability to distinguish appearance and reality, expanding attention and memory skills, and steadily increasing understanding of others' perspectives and thoughts.

ESSAY QUESTIONS:

1. Here are some examples; you may be able to think of others. (a) In the conservation of liquid volume task, preschoolers believe that because liquid in a tall, thin glass looks higher than in a short, wide glass, the tall glass actually contains more. (b) In the conservation of number task, preschoolers believe that a spread-out row of objects contains more than one that is bunched together because the spread-out row appears longer. (c) In reasoning about living and nonliving things, preschoolers assume moving things are living because they appear to be alive. (d) In seriation problems, the appearance-reality problem can be seen in a slightly different form in children's difficulty ordering objects by size without seeing the whole set. (e) In tasks measuring egocentrism, such as the three-mountain task, young preschoolers seem to assume that the way the world appears to them reflects reality for everybody else.

2. Infants show primitive classification skills when they treat objects similarly based on shared characteristics. Toddlers begin to develop the ability to sort objects by common properties. During the preschool years, children become able to consistently make simple classifications. Piaget discovered that 3-year-olds can often sort objects along one dimension, such as shape or color, but they often switch dimensions while sorting. For example, if sorting blocks by shape, they suddenly switch to color by placing a blue circle on top of a blue square. By age 5, children in Piaget's studies sorted along one dimension, but they could not sort consistently along two dimensions at once until about age 10. Later researchers found preschoolers could be trained to sort along two dimensions simultaneously but seldom used this strategy spontaneously. More recently, Zelazo and his colleagues have studied children's classification behavior when given explicit sorting rules. They found that 22-year-olds can tell which category a picture belongs to but tend to sort pictures randomly when given a rule. Three-year-olds can consistently follow one sorting rule at a time, such as color or shape, but have trouble switching rules. Four-year-olds can switch from one rule to another without trouble.

3. Preschoolers' memory is limited by inconsistent use of memory strategies. They can use some memory strategies but often fail to recognize things that need to be remembered. Even if they know they need to remember, they often do not use strategies they know and could use. They are more likely to use strategies in situations that suggest strategy use and are like the situations in which they learned the strategies. Preschoolers' memory is also limited by unsophisticated attention and search strategies. Even when they intend to remember and are trying to use a memory strategy, they may not attend well and often scan the material to be learned unsystematically. Finally, preschoolers are less likely than older children to have extensive experience with the things and events they have to remember. Scripts can decrease the load put on working memory, but they have a smaller repertoire of scripts.

4. The first principle children must grasp to develop a theory of mind is that minds exist. Babies do not realize this, but toddlers show they do by talking about mental states such as feelings and desires. The second principle is that minds have connections to the physical world, that thoughts and feelings are linked to objects and events. Children begin to show understanding of this principle between ages 2 and 3, but even 3- and 4-year-olds do not fully understand the exact nature of the connections. The third principle is that minds are separate and different from the physical world. Three-year-olds show a beginning understanding of this in their knowledge that it's possible to think about things that don't really exist. The fourth principle is that minds can represent objects and events accurately or inaccurately. Because this requires children to think about mental representations, it is usually not grasped by 2- and 3-year-olds, but 4- and 5-year-olds show some understanding of it. The fifth principle is that minds actively interpret reality and emotional

experiences. Preschoolers have very limited understanding of this principle; it is not until well into middle childhood that children really grasp that different people may interpret the same experience very differently.

5. Some ways experience with peers might contribute to a decline in egocentrism are: 1) Playing with peers lets children experience others' egocentric behavior, which can help them learn that some messages or replies are inadequate. If children interacted only with adults, no one would ever treat them egocentrically, and they might be slower to figure out the need to give clear messages. 2) Playing with peers leads to punishment of egocentric responses when playmates fail to understand or react with frustration to egocentric behavior. Adults can more easily understand what a child means, and they often respond appropriately to egocentric statements or requests. 3) It may be easier for preschoolers to understand desires and feelings of other children than of adults, since peers' feelings are more likely to resemble their own.

6. On the positive side, his high activity level means he is exposed to a constantly changing array of new and interesting objects and experiences and he is continuously engaged with his environment. He will thus notice and manipulate a wider variety of things than a quieter child would. His activity also elicits attention from parents and teachers, who may spend more time interacting with him than with a quieter child and may also make an effort to keep him busy and out of trouble. On the negative side, his high activity level may mean that he examines a new object only superficially or engages in a new activity only briefly before moving on to something else. He may not take the time to master objects and activities he encounters. His activity level may cause some playmates and adults to avoid him, thus limiting potential cognitive gains from interpersonal interaction. Finally, if he is perceived as not just active but hyperactive, teachers may expect trouble from him and may spend more time trying to control his behavior than trying to engage his interest in cognitively beneficial activities.

7. A good answer should relate research findings about preschoolers' cognitive abilities to demands children face when they start school. For example, progress from a primitive understanding of number to a qualitative understanding and finally a quantitative understanding prepares preschoolers to learn formal arithmetic concepts. Increasing attentional and memory skills and a growing ability to benefit from adults' prompting about memory strategies prepare them for the attentional and learning demands of the classroom. Declining egocentrism and improving communication skills prepare them to follow teachers' directions and deal with other children on a daily basis.

CHAPTER 10
SOCIAL AND EMOTIONAL DEVELOPMENT IN EARLY CHILDHOOD
CHAPTER REVIEW

As you read the chapter, construct your own chapter outline by answering the following review questions and defining the *Key Terms*.

I.   INTRODUCTION
    A. List three major social achievements of early childhood.

    B. What does it mean to say that behavior becomes increasingly organized and coherent during the preschool years?

II. SOME HALLMARKS OF EARLY CHILDHOOD SOCIAL AND EMOTIONAL DEVELOPMENT
    Key Terms: initiative, self-efficacy, instrumental dependency, emotional dependency, effortful control, self-regulation
    A. How do children's social worlds expand during early childhood? How do these new settings affect development?

    B. What capacities support developing self-reliance?

C. What is the difference between **emotional dependency** and **instrumental dependency**?

D. What advances in self-control and **self-regulation** occur during the preschool years?

III. THE DEVELOPING SELF
Key Terms: **self-constancy, self-representation, sex-typed behavior, gender-role concept, gender constancy, gender schema theory**
A. How is the development of the self related to cognitive development? How does children's understanding of the self change from toddlerhood through preschool?

B. Explain the development of **self-constancy** and **self-representation**.

C. What are some ways gender is a central organizing theme in development? What three steps are involved in the development of a gender-based self-concept?

   D.   Describe the development of **sex-typed behavior** and list factors that contribute
        to it.

   E.   How do **gender-role concepts** develop? How do **sex-typed behavior** and **gender-
        role concepts** affect preschoolers' social behavior?

   D.   Summarize the research evidence on the development of **gender constancy**.
        How is it related to an understanding of conservation?

   E.   How do social-learning, cognitive, and psychoanalytic theorists explain the
        development of **sex-typed behavior** and **gender-role concepts**? Explain **gender
        schema theory**.

IV. SOCIAL DEVELOPMENT: THE NEW WORLD OF PEERS
     A.   How do preschoolers' peer interactions differ from those of toddlers?

B.   What is involved in preschoolers' competence with peers? How is it measured?

C.   What are preschoolers' friendships like?

D.   What can children learn from peer relationships?

V. EMOTIONAL DEVELOPMENT
Key Terms: **emotional regulation, delay of gratification, ego resiliency, aggression, prosocial behavior, instrumental aggression, hostile aggression, empathy, altruism**
A.   What major emotional changes occur during the preschool years?

B.   What do preschoolers understand about emotional expression and causes of emotions?

   C.   Summarize preschool developments in the area of **emotional regulation**.

   D.   How are the self-evaluative emotions of preschoolers different from those of toddlers?

   E.   Describe the development of **aggression** through the preschool years and middle childhood. How is its development related to the development of **prosocial behavior**?

   F.   Describe the three phases in the development of **empathy** and **altruism**. How is parental behavior related to their development?

VI. THE ROLE OF PLAY IN PRESCHOOL DEVELOPMENT
   A.   What are the functions of play for preschoolers? How is fantasy play related to the child's developmental history?

B.   What developmental functions are served by preschoolers' playing of fantasy roles? How does it reflect cultural differences? How is fantasy play related to social competence?

VII. THE PARENTS' ROLE IN EARLY CHILDHOOD DEVELOPMENT
Key Terms: **authoritative parenting, permissive parenting, authoritarian parenting, identification**

A.   What qualities of parenting are important during the preschool years?

B.   Summarize the developmental tasks of preschoolers and their parents.

C.   Describe the patterns of care provided by **authoritative, authoritarian,** and **permissive** parents and summarize the effects of parenting style on children's development. What difference does cultural context make?

D.   How do marital conflict and divorce affect preschool children?

E. What is the psychoanalytic explanation for **identification**? What abilities must be present before **identification** can occur? How is internalization of parental rules and values influenced by the quality of the parent-child relationship?

VIII. THE COHERENCE OF BEHAVIOR AND DEVELOPMENT

A. What coherence is seen in preschoolers' individual characteristics? How is parental behavior involved in this coherence?

B. Explain how attachment history influences preschoolers' social behavior.

C. What factors explain coherence in young children's behavior over time?

D. What factors contribute to the development of personality during the preschool years? To what extent is fundamental change possible at various points in development?

E.   BOX: How can the resilience of children who bounce back from adversity best be explained?

F.   BOX: What are the long-term benefits of high-quality preschool intervention programs?

SELF-TEST

***After* you have studied the chapter, use the following questions to test your understanding.**

MULTIPLE-CHOICE QUESTIONS:

1. Which of the following characteristics of young children are related to the quality of day care and relationships with teachers they experience?
    a. Their general adjustment.
    b. Their competence with peers.
    c. The complexity of their play.
    d. All of the above.

2. Every day Jenny spends most of group activity time on her preschool teacher's lap. She is showing:
    a. secure attachment to her teacher.
    b. emotional dependency.
    c. instrumental dependency.
    d. social competence.

3. Research on preschoolers' ability to inhibit an action until given a "go" signal suggests that:
    a. 2-year-olds are already quite skilled at inhibiting actions.
    b. most children cannot reliably inhibit actions until about age 4.
    c. 4-year-olds are better than 2-year-olds on tasks requiring action inhibition, but only because they understand the instructions better.
    d. even 4-year-olds are not very good at inhibiting actions.

4. Limitations in preschoolers' sense of self include:
    a. they experience self only through immediate experiences.
    b. they cannot mentally move back and forth between different experiences.
    c. they have trouble coordinating different aspects of the self.
    d. all of the above.

5. When preschoolers play with gender-inappropriate toys, they typically receive:
    a. equally negative reactions from their fathers and their mothers.
    b. particularly negative reactions from their fathers if they are male.
    c. neutral or positive reactions from peers.
    d. more negative reactions if they are female than if they are male.

6. A 3-year-old who insists that she will be a boy like her older brother when she starts school is demonstrating a lack of understanding of:
    a. gender roles.
    b. gender stereotypes.
    c. gender constancy.
    d. gender schema.

7. During the preschool period, children's behavior toward peers changes in which of the following ways?
    a. They demonstrate sustained interest in peers for the first time.
    b. They begin to engage in social turn-taking with peers.
    c. Their interactions with peers become increasingly object-centered.
    d. They engage in increasingly sustained, coordinated interaction.

8. Which of the following is NOT a good indication of social competence in preschoolers?
    a. Amount of contact with other children.
    b. Ability to lead as well as follow.
    c. Interest and high regard from peers.
    d. Sustaining give-and-take in peer interaction.

9. Preschoolers' behavior with friends differs from their behavior with nonfriends in that:
    a. they have more frequent positive exchanges with friends.
    b. they disagree with friends less often.
    c. they are less cooperative with friends in problem-solving tasks.
    d. all of the above.

10. Peer relationships are a good setting for preschoolers to learn:
    a. fairness and cooperation.
    b. how to manage interpersonal aggression.
    c. cultural norms and values.
    d. all of the above.

11. Preschoolers' understanding of emotions nearly equals that of adults in which of the following areas?
    a. Reading positive emotions in natural settings.
    b. Interpreting expressions of negative emotions.
    c. Distinguishing what people really feel from what they appear to feel.
    d. Integrating situational cues and emotional expressions to interpret people's feelings.

12. Preschoolers are usually able to delay gratification if:
    a. the reward is a large one.
    b. they have adult support.
    c. they are left on their own.
    d. none of the above; preschoolers have very little ability to delay gratification.

13. Guilt in preschoolers differs from earlier reactions of shame in toddlers in that:
    a. it is more often due to what their parents do or say.
    b. it arises mainly from a fear of being punished.
    c. it involves evaluating the self against internalized standards.
    d. it is more likely to be a global, all-encompassing state of anxiety.

14. During the preschool years, children's aggression changes in which of the following ways?
    a. Object-centered aggression appears for the first time.
    b. Interpersonal aggression appears for the first time.
    c. Aggression intended only to cause distress becomes common.
    d. Individual children's levels of aggressiveness become less consistent.

15. Pretend play by preschoolers with nurturant and supportive parents is likely to include:
    a. little or no conflict.
    b. only positive play themes.
    c. successful resolution of negative themes.
    d. repeated reenactment of simple, unelaborated scenarios.

16. High levels of elaborate social fantasy play are related to high levels of:
    a. aggression.
    b. gender-typing.
    c. parental conflict.
    d. social competence.

17. Which of the following parental qualities are MORE important for preschoolers than for younger children?
    a. Consistency in the parents' approach to discipline.
    b. Parental warmth and emotional responsiveness.
    c. Sharing of positive feelings with children.
    d. Parental control and limit setting.

18. According to Baumrind, parents who fail to set firm limits can expect their children to become:
    a. moody and socially withdrawn.
    b. impulsive and low in self-reliance.
    c. energetic and self-reliant.
    d. curious and emotionally responsive.

19. Which of the following statements about identification with parents is TRUE?
    a. Identification usually occurs as soon as parents begin pressing children to obey them.
    b. Identification cannot occur until children can understand parents' attitudes and feelings.
    c. Identification is mainly a matter of imitating parental behavior.
    d. Children usually identify only with their same-sexed parent.

20. Preschoolers with a history of anxious-avoidant attachment in infancy tend to:
    a. show immaturity and low tolerance for stress.
    b. be frequent targets of bullying by peers.
    c. avoid contact with teachers.
    d. show calculated aggression toward peers.

21. When dealing with children with a history of anxious-resistant attachments, preschool teachers tend to:
    a. accept immature behavior.
    b. exercise little control.
    c. show little nurturance.
    d. be controlling and angry.

22. Resilience is probably best characterized as:
    a. a capacity that develops in a supportive environment.
    b. an inborn temperamental characteristic of certain children.
    c. invulnerability to adversity.
    d. a trait of parents, not children.

23. When Malcolm got in trouble for hitting a girl on the playground, his parents dealt with the situation by explaining to him why what he did was wrong and making clear what kind of behavior they expected in the future. This is an example of:
    a. authoritarian parenting.
    b. permissive parenting.
    c. authoritative parenting.
    d. none of the above; it doesn't really fit any of the categories.

24. Mikey's use of fantasy play with his playmates at preschool and by himself at home indicates:
    a. an inability to deal with conflict.
    b. a high level of social competence.
    c. emotional disturbance caused by his parents' fighting.
    d. all of the above.

25. Meryl's clinginess with her mother and her shyness when she started kindergarten suggest a history of which pattern of infant attachment?
   a. Secure.
   b. Anxious-avoidant.
   c. Anxious-resistant.
   d. It is impossible to say; she probably is just temperamentally wary.

MATCHING QUESTIONS:
Match the following key terms with their definitions:

1. ___ Internalization

2. ___ Self-constancy

3. ___ Empathy

4. ___ Sex-typed behavior

5. ___ Self-efficacy

6. ___ Identification

7. ___ Instrumental aggression

8. ___ Gender-role concept

9. ___ Altruism

10. ___ Ego resiliency

11. ___ Initiative

12. ___ Hostile aggression

A. Actions that conform to cultural expectations about what is appropriate for boys and for girls.

B. The incorporation of standards of behavior into the self.

C. A sense that the self endures despite temporary disruptions in relationships.

D. Erikson's term for a child's sense of independent purposefulness.

E. The ability to modify self-restraint to adapt to changing circumstances.

F. The ability to experience the emotions of another person.

G. Acting unselfishly to aid someone else.

H. Aggression aimed solely at hurting someone else.

I. The sense of being able to do things effectively on one's own.

J. Aggression used as a means to get something.

K. The process by which children strive to be like their parents in thoughts and feelings as well as in actions.

L. Knowledge of cultural stereotypes regarding males and females.

SHORT-ANSWER QUESTIONS:

1. List three major social achievements of early childhood.
    (a)

    (b)

    (c)

2. Explain the difference between **instrumental dependency** and **emotional dependency**.

3. List three signs of self-control and self-management that emerge during the preschool period.
    (a)

    (b)

    (c)

4. Thoughts about the self are referred to as _____.

5. List the three steps involved in development of a gender-based self-concept.
    (a)

    (b)

    (c)

6. At what age do children show gender-related preferences in toys?

7. Explain how **gender schema theory** combines social learning and cognitive explanations of the development of **sex-typed behavior** and **gender-role concepts**.

8. List three characteristics of socially competent preschoolers.
    (a)

    (b)

    (c)

9. List three major emotional developments of the preschool years.
    (a)

    (b)

    (c)

10. Explain how the development of **aggression** and **prosocial behavior** are related.

11. Explain how social fantasy play is related to social competence in preschoolers.

12. Parents who are unresponsive to their children's wishes and inflexible and harsh in controlling their children's behavior are described by Baumrind as _____.

13. Parents who fail to set firm limits or to require appropriately mature behavior are described by Baumrind as _____.

14. Parents who are nurturant, responsive, and supportive, yet also set firm limits, are described by Baumrind as _____.

15. List four developmental tasks for preschoolers and the corresponding tasks for their parents.
    (a)

    (b)

    (c)

    (d)

ESSAY QUESTIONS:
1. Discuss how new capacities developed by preschoolers contribute to increasing self-reliance.

2. Describe the three phases in the development of **empathy** and **altruism** and explain how parental behavior is involved in this development.

3. Define the concepts of **self-constancy** and **self-representation** and explain how they are related.

4. Discuss how cultural factors may influence what constitutes effective parenting.

5. Based on the results of the Perry Preschool Project, discuss the long-term benefits of preschool intervention programs.

6. Drawing on material from Chapter 10, suggest three things preschool and day-care teachers can do to foster healthy social and emotional development in early childhood. Be sure to explain why each suggestion would be a useful one.

7. Although they had a very bad start, things seemed to be looking up for Meryl and her mother by the time she turned 4. Identify two factors that could account for the improvement in their situation.

ANSWER KEY

MULTIPLE-CHOICE QUESTIONS:

1. d Better day care quality and relationships with teachers are associated with better general adjustment, greater competence with peers, and more complex play.

2. b Jenny shows an atypical need for continual reassurance and attention from adults.

3. b Although 2-year-olds seem to understand instructions not to do something, they have trouble actually inhibiting an action; 4-year-olds, in contrast, *can* inhibit actions.

4. c Preschoolers are no longer limited to experiencing self through immediate experience, and they can move mentally between experiences.

5. b Mothers often accept play with gender-inappropriate toys, but fathers and peers typically do not. Boys receive particularly negative reactions, especially from their fathers.

6. c She apparently does not yet understand gender is permanent despite changes in age.

7. d Answers *a-c* are all characteristic of toddlers' behavior toward peers.

8. a *Amount* of contact is not a good indicator of social competence; some children who are not socially competent have frequent *negative* contact with other children.

9. a In conflict situations, preschoolers actually disagree *more* with friends than with nonfriends; in problem-solving situations, they are *more* cooperative with friends.

10. d Answers *a-c* are all learned through interaction with peers.

11. a Answers *b-d* are all areas in which preschoolers still have trouble.

12. b Preschoolers have trouble delaying gratification if left on their own, but they often can do so with support from an adult; reward size was not mentioned in the chapter.

13. c Preschoolers' guilt is more specific, more likely to involve self-evaluation against internal standards, and does not arise solely from what parents do or say or a fear of punishment.

14. c Toddlers show interpersonal aggression, including object-centered aggression; among preschoolers, aggression intended only to cause distress becomes common, and individual children's levels of aggressiveness become *more* consistent.

15. c Preschoolers with nurturant, supportive parents tend to engage in flexible, elaborate play that includes conflict and negative themes, but these are usually successfully resolved.

16. d Elaborate social fantasy play is closely related to social competence.

17. a Consistency becomes especially important during the preschool years; the other characteristics are all equally important for younger children.

18. b A lack of parental limit setting makes it hard for children to set their own limits later.

19. b Identification involves trying to be like parents in thoughts and feelings.

20. d Children with an anxious-avoidant attachment history often show calculated aggression toward peers *and* desperately seek contact with teachers. Immaturity, low tolerance for stress, and being a target for bullies are associated with anxious-*resistant* attachment.

21. a Teachers tend to accept immature behavior and to be nurturant and controlling toward timid children, who often have a history of anxious-resistant attachment. They show more anger toward aggressive, hostile children, who usually do not have this attachment history.

22. a Resilience is a trait that results from experience in a supportive environment, not an inborn temperamental characteristic, and it does not reflect absolute invulnerability.

23. c Malcolm's parents responded supportively and responsively, but they also set firm limits.

24. b Mikey's fantasy play is typical of socially competent children; he uses it to interact with his friends at school and also to work through issues that are troubling him at home.

25. c Meryl's behavior is typical of children with a history of anxious-resistant attachment.

MATCHING QUESTIONS:

1.	B	4.	A	7.	J	10.	E
2.	C	5.	I	8.	L	11.	D
3.	F	6.	K	9.	G	12.	H

SHORT-ANSWER QUESTIONS:

1. experiencing a dramatically expanding world; developing self-reliance, self-control and self-regulation; and beginning to explore adult roles

2. Instrumental dependency is a normal need for adult help on complex problems or difficult tasks; emotional dependency is an atypical need for reassurance and attention from adults.

3. Correct answers include weighing consequences; stopping to think of ways around obstacles; controlling emotions when goals are blocked; blocking out irrelevant thoughts and stimuli to focus on achieving an objective; and being able to do more than one thing at a time.

4. self-representation

5. adopting sex-typed behavior, acquiring gender-role concepts, and developing an emotional commitment to one's own gender

6. By age 2.

7. According to gender schema theory, children use cognitive abilities to form schemas of male and female characteristics, but schema content is based on the child's particular social learning history.

8. Socially competent preschoolers engage and respond to peers positively, are interesting to peers and well-liked, can take the lead and follow, can sustain give-and-take interaction, and can form reciprocal friendships.

9. Growing understanding of emotions and their causes, increased ability to regulate emotional experiences, and further development of the self-evaluative emotions.

10. Aggression and prosocial behavior draw on the same underlying abilities and follow parallel developmental courses. Both involve self-management, emotional regulation, and children's understanding that they are responsible for their own actions and their actions can cause feelings in other people different from their own.

11. The amount, elaborateness, and flexibility of social fantasy play are positively related to social competence. Elaborate social fantasy play may provide opportunities to

develop social competence, social competence may facilitate social fantasy play, or the same general social cognitive skills may underlie both social competence and social fantasy play.

12. authoritarian

13 permissive

14. authoritative

15. Developmental tasks for preschoolers include accepting care and developing trust, complying and controlling self, learning, developing a general understanding of the social world, role taking, self-regulation, and developing a sense of right and wrong. The *corresponding* tasks for parents are nurturance, training and channeling of physical needs, teaching and skill training, orienting child to family and peers, promoting interpersonal skills and control of emotion, guiding formation of goals, plans, and aspirations, and transmitting cultural values. (See Table 10.2 and note that the two lists are linked to each other--for example, the parents' task of nurturance corresponds to the child's task of accepting care and developing trust.)

ESSAY QUESTIONS:
1. New capacities in all areas of development contribute to increasing self-reliance. Improved motor skills, such as object manipulation and climbing, increase what preschoolers can do for themselves. More sophisticated language and cognitive skills allow them to plan and solve problems too hard for toddlers. Growing ability to tolerate frustration and stick with tasks increases their chances of solving problems on their own. An emerging capacity for imagination and fantasy play gives them an increased sense of power in a world generally controlled by adults, providing an important foundation for strivings toward independence.

2. During the first phase, infants show a primitive capacity for empathy by crying when others are distressed, but they do not really distinguish between others' distress and their own. In the second phase, toddlers show purposeful helping behaviors when others are distressed but do not really take others' needs into account. Instead, they do things that would make them feel better themselves, such as getting their own mother or giving the other person their favorite toy. In the third phase, preschoolers show increasing capacity to take the role of others and respond to their needs but do not usually offer immediate help in natural settings, perhaps because they assume an adult will handle the situation. Parents can help children develop empathy and altruism by being nurturant, providing a model of empathy and helpfulness toward others, and explaining and showing strong feelings about the need to be kind to others.

3. Self-constancy is the perception of a stable self enduring through temporary disruptions in relationships with others. It is a natural product of interactions between children and parents over time and cognitive development that allows awareness and understanding of self. Children with a sense of self-constancy know what parents expect of them and are aware of their own thoughts and motivations. As children acquire self-constancy, they also develop a self-representation; they start to think of the self as having consistent dispositions over time. All children form self-representations, but not all come to think of the self in the same way. A child's particular view of the self is based on his or her unique experiences. Positive self-representations stem from positive exchanges with others. Thus, children's interactions with parents form the basis for self-constancy *and* self-representation, with the nature of the self-representation determined by the nature of those interactions.

4. What constitutes effective parenting varies across cultural contexts. In traditional Chinese families, many parents show a combination of Baumrind's authoritative and authoritarian parenting styles; they reason with their children about misbehavior, but are more controlling, directive, and strict than most European-American parents. This combination of styles reflects Chinese concepts of training or teaching appropriate behaviors and a combination of governing and caring for children. Children in these families do not generally show the negative impacts of authoritarian parenting often seen in European-American children. In African-American families, nonabusive physical punishment is not associated with increases in child aggressiveness, as in European-American families, perhaps because physical punishment is used differently in African-American families or is associated with different parental behaviors. In addition, different social contexts may call for different styles of parenting. For example, controlling, strict, and even somewhat authoritarian parenting may produce positive outcomes for children living in dangerous inner-city neighborhoods.

5. The most positive lasting benefit of high-quality preschool intervention programs seems to be the empowering of the children who participate in them. These children gain a higher level of self-esteem, more positive attitudes toward education, and a stronger belief in themselves as learners--all of which lead to better overall performance in school. By age 27, participants in the Perry Preschool Program were more likely to have finished high school, to earn a steady income, and to own their own home, and less likely to have needed special education, to be on welfare, or to have been in trouble with the law, compared with a matched control group. Overall savings to society were estimated at $88,000 per child, with only a $12,000 per child cost of the program. Such positive long-term results are only possible, however, if the quality of the intervention program and parent involvement are both high.

6. There are many possible answers to this question. A good answer should clearly tie research about preschoolers' social and emotional development to practical suggestions for preschool teachers. Some things preschool teachers can do to foster healthy social and emotional development include: (a) Encourage social fantasy play by providing opportunities and props in the classroom and responding positively to this type of play. Social fantasy play is associated with social competence in preschoolers and allows children to try on adult roles and work through conflicts and anxieties. (b) Provide warmth, nurturance, and emotional support, combined with clear limit setting, to the children in their classroom--a combination that resembles Baumrind's authoritative style of parenting. Preschoolers' general adjustment, peer competence, and play complexity are all related to the quality of their relationships with teachers or day care providers; children who are well-adjusted and competent probably tend to have better relationships with teachers, but a positive relationship with a teacher can help a child *become* more well-adjusted and competent. One factor that contributes to resilience in children with less than ideal family environments is social support from adults outside the family. (c) Encourage self-efficacy by providing opportunities for children to master new skills and complete tasks on their own. For preschoolers, these can include things as simple as learning to tie shoes or put on their own jackets to go outside. (d) Be sensitive to differences in children's social and emotional needs and strive to be responsive to them. For example, children who are clingy and want to spend most of their time with the teacher may need encouragement and support to join other children in play, even though teachers may be tempted to indulge their immature behavior. Children who are aggressive toward other children and oppositional toward the teacher may need especially consistent limit setting and nurturance, even though the natural tendency may be to respond punitively.

7. One important factor is Karen's relationship with Joe, which provides effective social support and reduces the stress in her life. Both social support and the reduced stress may help Karen become more responsive to Meryl. His financial support also reduces stress on Karen, indirectly benefiting Meryl. Second, Joe's relationship with Meryl may have direct benefits for her. He is a sensitive caregiver who plays with her, reads to her, and sets clear limits. His consistent, firm, and reasonable disciplinary style provides a good model for Karen and also changes Meryl's perception of how to cope with frustration. Eventually, it may change Meryl's internal working model of the world and move her toward a better developmental outcome.

CHAPTER 11
COGNITIVE DEVELOPMENT IN MIDDLE CHILDHOOD

CHAPTER REVIEW

As you read the chapter, construct your own chapter outline by answering the following review questions and defining the *Key Terms*.

I.   INTRODUCTION
     Key Term: **metacognition**
     A.   Why did Piaget see age 7 as a major turning point in cognitive development? What does more recent research suggest?

     B.   Explain the *5 to 7 year shift.*

     C.   What cognitive advances occur between early and middle childhood?

     D.   What cognitive limitations remain?

II. MAJOR COGNITIVE DEVELOPMENTS OF MIDDLE CHILDHOOD
   Key Terms: **contingent truth, necessary truth, hierarchical classification, matrix classification, collection, constructive memory, mnemonic strategies, rehearsal, organization, elaboration, mediation deficiencies, production deficiencies, utilization deficiencies, metamemory**

   A. At what ages do children in Western societies master the various conservation tasks? Why do children master different tasks at different ages?

   B. BOX: What cross-cultural differences have been found in performance on conservation tasks? How can these differences be explained?

   C. Explain the difference between **necessary truth** and **contingent truth**. How do these concepts apply to children's understanding of conservation?

   D. How would an information-processing approach explain children's performance on conservation tasks? What has research using this approach discovered?

   E. Summarize the major findings on children's understanding of conservation concepts.

F. Describe the development of children's ability to solve **hierarchical classification** tasks. Why is it easier for children to reason about naturally occurring **collections** than classes?

G. Describe the development of children's ability to solve **matrix classification** tasks.

H. Summarize the key points in the development of children's classification skills.

I. How do children's attentional skills change from early to middle childhood?

J. How does children's memory capacity change from early to middle childhood?

K. How does existing knowledge affect children's ability to remember new information? Discuss the development of **constructive memory** in childhood.

L.   How does children's use of **mnemonic strategies** change with age? What effect does training have?

M.   How does **metamemory** develop from early to middle childhood?

N.   Summarize improvements in information-processing abilities in middle childhood.

III. SOCIAL INTERACTION AND COGNITIVE DEVELOPMENT
     Key Terms: **didactic learning experience, cooperative learning experience**
     A.   How do **didactic** and **cooperative learning** differ? What influences their effectiveness?

     B.   How is scaffolding involved in didactic learning experiences? How do didactic learning experiences provided by adults and by peers differ?

C. Under what circumstances are cooperative learning experiences likely to facilitate cognitive advancement? How does children's effectiveness at teaching one another change with age?

D. How do Piaget and Vygotsky explain social interaction effects on cognitive development?

IV. INDIVIDUAL DIFFERENCES IN INTELLIGENCE
Key Terms: **mental age, intelligence quotient (IQ), academic intelligence, practical intelligence, culture-free IQ test, culture-fair IQ test**
A. Explain the origins of modern intelligence testing.

B. Explain the concept of *mental age* and how it was used to calculate *intelligence quotients.*

C.   How did Binet's and Spearman's concepts of intelligence differ? How have
     their ideas influenced contemporary intelligence tests?

D.   How are traditional concepts of intelligence limited? How could the definition
     of intelligence be broadened?

E.   Explain Gardner's theory of multiple intelligences.

F.   Explain Sternberg's triarchic theory.

G.   What major limitation remains for new theories of intelligence, such as
     Gardner's and Sternberg's?

H. What is currently known about the contributions of heredity and environment to IQ?

I. How stable are the effects on IQ from changes in a child's environment? How well do children's scores on intelligence tests predict adult IQ?

J. What factors contribute to cultural bias in intelligence testing? How successful have attempts to develop **culture-free** and **culture-fair intelligence tests** been?

K. What can IQ scores predict about a person's later performance in school and on the job?

V. CULTURE AND SCHOOL ACHIEVEMENT
    Key Term: **decontextualized thought**
    A. How are preschoolers' cognitive skills different from skills acquired in school?

B. Why is the transition to school often particularly difficult for children from cultural backgrounds different from the one represented by their school? Summarize research findings about cultural mismatch and its effects on children's school performance.

C. What differences in math achievement have been found between students in the U.S. and in Asia? What factors may account for the differences? What approaches are being tried to reduce the differences?

D. Why have high-stakes testing programs become increasingly common in the United States in recent years? Based on current research evidence, what are their impacts on schools and on students?

VI. AN OVERVIEW OF MIDDLE CHILDHOOD COGNITIVE DEVELOPMENT
Summarize the state of children's cognitive abilities at the end of middle childhood.

SELF-TEST

After you have studied the chapter, use the following questions to test your understanding.

MULTIPLE-CHOICE QUESTIONS:

1. Recent research suggests that cognitive development in middle childhood mostly involves:
    a. a complete revolution in children's thinking compared to early childhood.
    b. emergence of new skills that are qualitatively different from those of early childhood.
    c. very little change from the skills that were present in early childhood.
    d. refinement and wider use of skills that existed in primitive form in early childhood.

2. Cognitive limitations typical of middle childhood include:
    a. inability to think logically using multiple pieces of information.
    b. difficulty perceiving reality underlying superficial appearances.
    c. difficulty reasoning about abstract and hypothetical problems.
    d. all of the above.

3. **Metacognition** is:
    a. the ability to reason abstractly and hypothetically.
    b. the ability to think about thinking.
    c. thinking that is confined to the here-and-now.
    d. an understanding of logical necessity.

4. Which of the following statements about children's understanding of conservation is FALSE?
    a. Children acquire an understanding of all forms of conservation at about the same age.
    b. Preschoolers show the beginnings of the skills needed to solve conservation problems.
    c. A mature understanding of conservation involves an understanding of necessary truth.
    d. School-age children begin to use conservation concepts to reason about concrete events.

5. Research on cultural differences in performance on conservation tasks has revealed that.
    a. across industrialized cultures children master conservation concepts at about the same age.
    b. children in traditional cultures without formal schooling often lag behind Western norms.
    c. cultures without formal schooling do not provide the same opportunities to learn about conservation concepts as industrialized cultures.
    d. all of the above.

6. Taking an information-processing approach to conservation tasks, rules for describing mature performance on any of these tasks entail:
    a. relying on appearance.
    b. counting or measurement.
    c. an understanding of logical necessity.
    d. focusing on contingent truth.

7. Organizing buttons by size and color is an example of:
    a. matrix classification.
    b. hierarchical classification.
    c. hypothesis scanning.
    d. constraint seeking.

8. Children seem to have an easier time reasoning about hierarchical classification when the superordinate term is:
    a. a naturally occurring collection.
    b. an abstract class.
    c. a large group.
    d. a familiar entity.

9. When children who are in the midst of the transition from early to middle childhood are asked to sort objects along two dimensions, they typically respond by:
    a. sorting the objects along only one dimension, demonstrating centration.
    b. switching randomly between the two dimensions as they sort.
    c. sorting first along one dimension and then along the other.
    d. sorting along both dimensions simultaneously.

10. A major reason for improved performance on attentional tasks during middle childhood is:
    a.   increased brain capacity.
    b.   improved strategies for directing and maintaining attention.
    c.   heightened perceptual and sensory abilities, such as sharper vision.
    d.   decreased individual differences in attentional skills.

11. Increases with age in the amount of information transferred from the sensory register to short-term memory after infancy are thought to be produced mainly by increases in:
    a.   metamemory.
    b.   memory capacity.
    c.   constructive memory.
    d.   processing speed.

12. Between the ages of 7 and 10, children's use of mnemonic devices is:
    a.   extremely rare.
    b.   highly dependent on prompting from adults.
    c.   expanding and becoming more consistent.
    d.   already highly consistent and effective.

13. Which of the following statements about **didactic learning experiences** is FALSE?
    a.   They always involve deliberate teaching.
    b.   They always involve an adult teacher and a child learner.
    c.   They always involve a teacher more knowledgeable than the learner.
    d.   They fit Vygotsky's approach to social interaction in cognitive development.

14. Cognitive advancement is more likely to be facilitated by peer interaction if
    a.   the children are working on a concrete task.
    b.   the children see reaching a consensus as a goal of their interaction.
    c.   the information available to the children is somewhat ambiguous.
    d.   all of the above.

15. Tommy answers 21 items correctly on an IQ test. The average age of children who answer 21 items on the test correctly is equal to Tommy's:
    a.   mental age.
    b.   chronological age.
    c.   intelligence quotient.
    d.   practical intelligence.

16. Binet saw intelligence as:
    a. a collection of specific abilities that had to be measured separately.
    b. a general cognitive capability that could be measured by a single IQ score.
    c. a combination of general and specific abilities.
    d. a combination of academic and practical abilities.

17. Sternberg's and Gardner's theories of intelligence both argue for:
    a. focusing on a unitary concept of intelligence.
    b. abandoning the concept of academic intelligence.
    c. broadening the traditional definition of intelligence.
    d. developing culture-free intelligence tests.

18. As children grow older, the ability to predict adult IQ from childhood IQ tests:
    a. increases.
    b. decreases.
    c. stays the same; it is unrelated to the child's age.
    d. stays near zero; adult IQ cannot be predicted from childhood IQ tests.

19. The most important reason attempts to develop a **culture-free IQ test** have been unsuccessful is:
    a. not enough cultures have been studied yet.
    b. most test developers are culturally biased.
    c. it is impossible to test the intelligence of people who can't read.
    d. intelligence always exists in a particular environmental context.

20. Scores on IQ tests in middle childhood and beyond are LEAST able to predict:
    a. success in school.
    b. success in occupations requiring abstract thought.
    c. performance in job training programs.
    d. general on-the-job performance.

21. Which of the following statements best describes the cognitive skills children develop before they start school?
    a. Preschoolers have very few useful skills in the areas of language, number, and logical reasoning.
    b. Preschoolers have considerable informal knowledge of language, number, and logical reasoning.
    c. Preschoolers have well-developed linguistic, quantitative, and logical skills that they can readily apply to school tasks.
    d. Preschoolers these days generally have good familiarity with most school-related cognitive tasks.

22. Math achievement is more likely to be attributed to _____ in Asia than in the U.S.:
    a. natural ability.
    b. effort and work habits
    c. a student's gender.
    d. all of the above.

23. When Maggie sat at the kitchen table memorizing her spelling words with her hands over her ears, her behavior demonstrated:
    a. information-processing strategies typical of middle childhood.
    b. an unusually mature use of attention and memory strategies.
    c. an unusual need to screen out distractions in the environment.
    d. evidence of an attention deficit disorder.

24. The description of Malcolm in middle childhood in the vignette shows particular evidence of which of Gardner's intelligences?
    a. logical-mathematical intelligence.
    b. bodily-kinesthetic intelligence.
    c. interpersonal intelligence.
    d. all of the above.

25. When Meryl, Amy, and Rita worked together on their school project, the resulting learning situation was most likely:
    a. didactic.
    b. cooperative.
    c. heavily scaffolded.
    d. all of the above.

MATCHING QUESTIONS:
Match the following key terms with their definitions:

1. ___ Cooperative learning experience

2. ___ Decontextualized thought

3. ___ Constructive memory

4. ___ Collection

5. ___ Hierarchical classification

6. ___ Mnemonic strategies

7. ___ Didactic learning experience

A. The capacity to think about thinking.

B. A situation in which a knowledgeable teacher who has already mastered a problem teaches a particular solution to a learner.

C. A classification system in which items are categorized simultaneously along two independent dimensions, such as shape and color.

8. ___ Rehearsal

9. ___ Matrix classification

10. ___ Metacognition

11. ___ Elaboration

12. ___ Metamemory

D. The mnemonic strategy of creating a meaningful connection between items to be remembered, either verbally or visually.

E. The mnemonic strategy of repeating information over and over.

F. Inferences drawn in the process of storing and remembering information.

G. Knowledge about memory and memory processes.

H. A naturally occurring entity with subparts that go together because of their proximity.

I. A situation in which learners at approximately the same level of knowledge and skill interact, share ideas, and discover solutions on their own.

J. Intentional, goal-directed behaviors designed to improve memory.

K. A cognitive skill needed to solve problems that are abstract, self-contained, and removed from any immediate context.

L. A classification system in which items are categorized using a hierarchy of subordinate and superordinate classes.

SHORT-ANSWER QUESTIONS:

1. Explain why Piaget saw age 7 as a major cognitive turning point.

2. What is meant by the *5 to 7 year shift?*

3. Explain why children master the various conservation tasks at different ages.

4. Explain the difference between **contingent truth** and **necessary truth.**

5. What task is most often used to measure understanding of **hierarchical classification?**

6. List three major conclusions about classification skills in middle childhood.
    (a)

    (b)

    (c)

7. List three types of deficiencies in children's use of memory strategies.
    (a)

    (b)

    (c)

8. Intellectual capacity as reflected in performance in everyday, nonschool settings is sometimes called _____ _____.

9. How do the **didactic learning experiences** provided by children and adults differ?

10. What was the purpose of Binet and Simon's original intelligence test?

11. List the three factors in Sternberg's triarchic theory of intelligence.
    (a)

    (b)

    (c)

12. An IQ test with no culture-based content is _____-_____; an IQ test that is appropriate for all the cultures in which it is used is _____-_____.

13. What major limitation remains for new theories of intelligence, such as Gardner's and Sternberg's?

14. How early have differences in math performance between Chinese, Japanese, and American children been observed?

15. List three negative consequences of high-stakes testing.
    (a)

    (b)

    (c)

ESSAY QUESTIONS:

1. Describe the major advances and limitations in a child's cognitive abilities during middle childhood.

2. Describe the development of children's use of **mnemonic strategies.**

3. Explain how Piaget's and Vygotsky's theories differ in their explanations of the effects of interaction on cognitive development.

4. Discuss three ways that intelligence tests can be culturally biased.

5. Using the material in the textbook as a starting point, suggest three arguments for and three against Gardner's theory of multiple intelligences.

6. Discuss the differences that have been observed in the teaching of mathematics in American and Asian elementary schools.

7. Even at age 8, Mikey imagines that his parents' marital problems and divorce were partly his fault. Since he has a number of relatively sophisticated cognitive skills by this time, why does he make this mistake?

ANSWER KEY

MULTIPLE-CHOICE QUESTIONS:

1. d   Contrary to Piaget's belief, cognitive development from early to middle childhood seems to involve refinement of existing skills rather than emergence of totally new skills.

2. c   By this age, children understand appearance-reality and can think logically using multiple pieces of information, but still have trouble with abstract and hypothetical problems.

3. b   See definition of **metacognition.**

4. a   Understanding of different forms of conservation develops at different ages.

5. d   Answers *a-c* all reflect results of cross-cultural research on conservation.

6. c   Relying on appearance, counting or measurement, and focusing on contingent truth are all typical of rules that do not reflect mature understanding of conservation.

7. a   Matrix classification involves categorizing items simultaneously along two independent dimensions--size and color in this example.

8. a   The structure of hierarchical categories seems to be clearer to children when the superordinate term is a naturally occurring collection.

9. c   Very young children tend to switch randomly between two dimensions, older preschoolers tend to sort along one dimension at a time, and children do not consistently sort along both dimensions simultaneously until age 8 or 9.

10. b   Improved strategies seem to be the main reason for improved performance on attentional tasks, just as on memory tasks.

11. d   Increased processing speed allows children to transfer more information from the sensory register before it fades.

12. c   The period from age 7 to age 10 is a transitional stage when the use of mnemonic devices expands and becomes more consistent.

13. b   Both adults and children can provide didactic learning experiences.

14. d   Answers *a-c* are all factors that increase the likelihood cooperative learning experiences will facilitate cognitive advancement.

15. a.   See definition of **mental age**.

16. b   Binet saw intelligence as a general cognitive capability and focused on academic abilities; concepts of specific abilities and practical intelligence were developed later.

17. c   Gardner and Sternberg do not want to abandon the concept of academic intelligence, but to broaden the definition of intelligence to take account of other factors and abilities.

18. a   The older children are, the better their IQ scores predict their adult IQs, because their abilities become more stable or because the IQ tests used become more similar.

19. d   Although answers *a-c* are issues, the more fundamental problem is that intelligence always develops in and must be measured in a particular context.

20. d   IQ tests are best at predicting success in school, which was their original purpose. They are also good predictors of success in occupations requiring abstract thought and in job-training programs, perhaps because tasks in these settings resemble school tasks.

21. b   Preschoolers have considerable informal knowledge of language, number, and logical reasoning, but their knowledge does not always transfer well to school-- related tasks.

22. b   In the United States more emphasis is placed on natural ability. Gender is not mentioned as a factor in the chapter, but is used more to explain math ability in the United States.

23. a   Not all 10-year-olds are this skilled at strategy use, but Maggie's behavior is not unusual.

24. c   Malcolm is socially competent and well-liked, and his behavior demonstrates that he is skilled at understanding the feelings and behaviors of others.

25. b   Although children can provide didactic learning experiences for each other, a cooperative learning experience is more likely.

MATCHING QUESTIONS:

1. I	4. H	7. B	10. A
2. K	5. L	8. E	11. D
3. F	6. J	9. C	12. G

SHORT-ANSWER QUESTIONS:

1. He believed that was the approximate age when children made the transition from preoperational to concrete operational thinking.

2. Between the ages of 5 and 7, children begin to be treated differently in cultures around the world. In many cultures, they are considered to be accountable for their actions, and they often receive additional responsibility and begin formal schooling.

3. According to Piaget, children learn characteristics of different kinds of quantities at different ages. Some conservation tasks are also probably more complex than others.

4. Contingent truth depends on empirical observation, information gathered through the senses. Necessary truth is based on logical necessity, apart from what is observed through the senses. In other words, *contingently* true statements must be checked against current *reality; necessarily* true statements are always true and do not need to be checked.

5. class inclusion

6. (a) In middle childhood, children begin to make effective use of classification to organize information. (b) Performance on classification tasks improves because children overcome centration and can focus on more than one dimension or level at a time. (c) Elementary school children do not yet fully grasp the logical necessity of classification structures.

7. mediation deficiencies, production deficiencies, and utilization deficiencies

8. practical intelligence

9. Because children often are not aware of what the learner knows, they may not provide effective scaffolding. They tend to focus on what they are trying to get the learner to do, not on making sure the learner understands what they are teaching or on managing their interactions. Therefore, they are often less effective than adults in didactic learning situations.

10. To differentiate between normally intelligent children and those requiring special help.

11. The componential element, the experiential element, and the contextual element.

12. culture-free; culture-fair

13. There are no methods for assessing nonacademic intelligence as well established as IQ tests.

14. first grade

15. Negative consequences of high-stakes testing include narrowing the curriculum, overemphasizing decontextualized skills, increasing stress for teachers and students, reducing student engagement in school, and a disproportionately negative impact on students at risk.

ESSAY QUESTIONS:
1. Middle childhood is a time of great cognitive advances. During this period, children begin to think systematically and consider multiple pieces of information simultaneously as centration declines. They are no longer fooled by superficial appearance and can reason more maturely about transformations. Their domain-specific knowledge increases. Their information-processing capacity and control over attention and memory increase, in part because of improved attentional and memory strategies. These improved strategies are a result of expanded capacity for metacognition, the ability to think about their own knowledge and thought processes and plan memory and problem-solving strategies. However, their cognitive abilities remain limited in some ways. They do not have the broad knowledge base of adults, which often makes their reasoning immature. Because their thinking skills are not yet well-practiced, they do not always apply them when appropriate. Finally, they cannot yet reason maturely about abstract or hypothetical problems; their reasoning remains concrete.

2. Preschoolers and young elementary schoolers usually do not spontaneously use mnemonic strategies; in one study, only 10% of 5-year-olds used rehearsal to help themselves remember a set of pictures. Between ages 7 and 10, children's use of mnemonic strategies increases, and their strategies become increasingly flexible and effective. Children use mnemonic devices consistently and effectively by about age 10, though they continue to learn new strategies and increase the effectiveness of existing strategies into early adulthood. The types of strategies used change with age. Rehearsal is seen regularly from age 7 or 8. Organization is used increasingly

236

from age 6 to age 11. Elaboration is the last of the major strategies to appear. The problems children have in using strategies also change with age. Mediation deficiencies, in which children are unable to use a strategy even when adults suggest it, occur when a child has not yet acquired the strategy in question. They are most common in preschoolers, but even older elementary schoolers show mediation deficiencies for more complex strategies, such as elaboration. Production deficiencies, in which children do not use a strategy spontaneously but can use it when prompted, occur when a child is in the midst of acquiring a strategy. They are very common in elementary school children but are sometimes seen in adolescents for complex or infrequently used strategies. Utilization deficiencies, in which children use a strategy spontaneously but without benefit to their memory performance, are the most enduring. They occur when a child has acquired a strategy but hasn't had much practice using it; they are seen throughout childhood and adolescence, for simpler strategies at younger ages and for more complex strategies later.

3. Vygotsky saw cognitive development as part of a shared social reality. His theory applies best to didactic learning situations, in which a knowledgeable teacher provides scaffolding within a learner's zone of proximal development. A common frame of reference, which is necessary for successful scaffolding, is provided by the teacher's understanding of the learner's immature viewpoint. Piaget saw cognitive development as a constructive process within each individual. His theory applies best to cooperative learning situations, in which two peers work on a problem together. Piaget also believed a common frame of reference was necessary, but he thought it was provided by the similarity in peers' status and their ability to understand each other's point of view. This understanding prompts children to notice and resolve discrepancies between their ideas, resulting in changes to their cognitive structures.

4. First, an intelligence test can be biased because of its content--test items invariably include information specific to the culture in which the test was created. Second, an intelligence test can be biased because of the particular cognitive skills it is designed to measure. Different cultures value and foster the development of different cognitive skills. Third, an intelligence test can be biased because of the interpersonal situation in which it is given. Children in particular may be uncomfortable being tested by an adult who is a member of a cultural group different from their own, or they may be unfamiliar with the interpersonal format of the test.

5. A variety of arguments can be made both for and against Gardner's theory. Here are a few possible answers. *For:* Traditional theories limited to academic intelligence capture only a small portion of human ability, and traditional IQ tests

assess only a small segment of human competence. Children who do not score well on tests of academic intelligence are often assumed to be generally incompetent and their abilities are often overlooked. Individual children's patterns of abilities and achievements vary; they have different talents to develop, need different kinds of help, and may benefit from different educational experiences.

Against: Gardner's theory waters down the concept of intelligence by including too wide a range of abilities. There are no reliable tests to measure most of the intelligences in his theory. Some of his intelligences are less central to success in school or in a job than others, and there is no research on how childhood abilities in these areas are related to adult behavior.

6. Japanese and Chinese teachers spend more time on math instruction and assign more math homework than American teachers do. The processes used to teach math are different in Asian schools than in American schools. Asian teachers explain math problems in more detail, direct more attention to underlying principles and less to computational procedures, and analyze and correct students' errors more carefully, encouraging them to learn from failures as well as successes. Japanese children spend more time learning math in cooperative learning situations where the primary goal is mastering skills, not outperforming others. They are also encouraged to explore multiple ways to solve a problem, rather than focusing on repeated practice of one strategy. American children spend more time learning math by rote repetition.

7. Because 8-year-olds still have a tendency to think egocentrically in the face of complex problems, Mikey may think of himself as the cause of situations for which he was not responsible. Second, Mikey can only apply his cognitive skills to relatively concrete problems; his parents' problems are too abstract for him to comprehend. Finally, Mikey is handicapped by the fact that his knowledge base regarding such adult problems is very limited. He is more likely to be able to apply his developing cognitive skills to topics he knows a lot about.

CHAPTER 12
SOCIAL AND EMOTIONAL DEVELOPMENT IN MIDDLE CHILDHOOD
CHAPTER REVIEW

As you read the chapter, construct your own chapter outline by answering the following review questions and defining the *Key Terms*.

I. **INTRODUCTION**
    Key Terms: **latency period, sense of industry**
    A. Why was middle childhood once considered an uneventful phase of development?

    B. Why was the lack of attention to middle childhood a problem for developmental psychology?

    C. What are the major developmental tasks of middle childhood, according to Erikson and others?

II. THE INNER WORLD OF THE SELF
    Key Terms: **psychological self, metatheory of the self, social self, social comparison, executive functioning**
    A. How do school-aged children's self-descriptions differ from those of preschoolers? How does their changing concept of themselves relate to their understanding of others?

B. Describe the development of the **social self** and **social comparison** in middle childhood.

C. How does knowledge of gender stereotypes develop in middle childhood? What influence do they have at this age? What factors contribute to flexibility in conforming to gender stereotypes?

D. How does children's sense of personal effectiveness develop during middle childhood? What other capacities develop along with it?

III. PEER RELATIONSHIPS IN MIDDLE CHILDHOOD
   Key Terms: **relational aggression, peer group norms, border work, sociometrics**
   A. Why are peers influential in school-aged children's social development?

B. What advances enable peer relationships to become more complex?

C. What are the major developments in peer relations during middle childhood?

D. How do children's ability to form friendships and understanding of friendship change from early to middle childhood? How does behavior with friends and acquaintances differ?

E. BOX: What does the Sherifs' study tell us about intergroup conflict in middle childhood? How might this be applied to the problem of gang violence?

F. How do peer group concepts change from early to middle childhood? How do girls' and boys' groups differ?

G. How is learning to coordinate friendship and group interaction important in children's development? How is it related to social competence?

H. What **peer group norms** are especially important in middle childhood? How are peer group norms related to the norms of the child's culture and to moral development?

I. How does the peer group maintain the boundary between the sexes during middle childhood? Under what circumstances is contact with the opposite sex permissible? What developmental significance does maintaining gender boundaries have?

J. How is children's peer status measured? Summarize the characteristics of rejected, neglected, and popular children. Why are the differences between these categories of children significant? What can be done to improve the status of unpopular children?

IV. EMOTIONAL DEVELOPMENT IN MIDDLE CHILDHOOD
    A. How does understanding of emotion change during middle childhood?

B. How do cognitive, social, and emotional development contribute to moral development?

V. CONTEXTS OF DEVELOPMENT IN MIDDLE CHILDHOOD
Key Term: **agency**
A. How do children's relationships with their parents change during middle childhood?

B. How are parenting characteristics related to children's behavior? Why is it important to look at clusters of parental characteristics rather than individual traits?

C. What have studies using Baumrind's parenting classifications in middle childhood found? What factors did Maccoby and Martin emphasize in their study of parenting styles? What factors encourage development of harmonious parent-child relationships?

D. BOX: What evidence is there that parenting has an impact on children's development that is not reducible to genetic influence?

E.   Summarize the effects of violence, family conflict, and divorce on children's development. What factors maximize long-term positive outcomes for children of divorce?

F.   How are sibling relationships distinctive? What emotional qualities do they have? What factors contribute to the overall quality of sibling relationships? What developmental impacts do sibling relationships have?

G.   How do children's lives change when they start school? What do children learn in school beyond the curriculum? How do schools reinforce gender roles?

H.   What factors influence school success? How is school success related to later development?

I.   How does after-school care affect children's development?

VI. THE COHERENCE OF DEVELOPMENT IN MIDDLE CHILDHOOD
   A. In what ways is development in middle childhood coherent?

   B. How are the influences of family, peers, and school interrelated in middle
       childhood?

   C. How are individual children's patterns of adaptation coherent?

   D. What does attachment history predict about adjustment during middle
       childhood? How can these connections be explained?

SELF-TEST

After you have studied the chapter, use the following questions to test your understanding.

MULTIPLE-CHOICE QUESTIONS:

1. Erikson proposed that the major task of middle childhood is developing:
    a.   a coherent self-concept.
    b.   close same-sex friendships.
    c.   a sense of industry.
    d.   strong self-esteem.

2. Elementary school children's self-descriptions differ from those of preschoolers in that elementary schoolers:
    a.   describe the self as a concrete, physical entity.
    b.   increasingly describe themselves in terms of psychological traits.
    c.   no longer use physical characteristics in their self-descriptions.
    d.   usually do not compare themselves to others.

3. In middle childhood, flexibility in conforming to gender stereotypes is influenced by:
    a.   the child's sex.
    b.   the child's level of cognitive development.
    c.   whether the child's mother engages in nontraditional roles.
    d.   all of the above.

4. School-aged children are more likely than preschoolers to believe that their _____ accomplishments depend on their own efforts:
    a.   physical
    b.   cognitive
    c.   social
    d.   all of the above

5. By about age ___, time spent with peers usually surpasses time spent with family.
    a.   6
    b.   8
    c.   11
    d.   14

6. Compared to preschoolers, elementary school children are more likely to:
    a.   pay attention to the personal traits of their friends.
    b.   define a friend as "someone I like."
    c.   feel that conflict is not a part of friendship.
    d.   label other children as friends.

7. During middle childhood, girls' peer groups tend to:
   a. be larger than boys' peer groups.
   b. place great emphasis on loyalty and shared activities.
   c. include both boys and girls.
   d. focus on one or two best friends.

8. In Sherif and Sherif's classic study of boys' intergroup conflict, it was found that:
   a. strangers who worked together on tasks requiring cooperation developed a strong sense of group identity.
   b. competitive intergroup games initially produced upheaval within the groups.
   c. "emergencies" requiring cooperation between groups reduced intergroup conflict.
   d. all of the above.

9. Which of the following statements about **peer group norms** is NOT accurate?
   a. Equity is an important peer group norm during middle childhood.
   b. Peer group norms often conflict with the culture's moral values.
   c. Strict adherence to peer group norms is typical in middle childhood.
   d. Children who refuse to follow peer group norms are often ostracized.

10. Which of the following statements about socially rejected children is FALSE?
    a. Aggressive children are especially likely to be rejected by peers.
    b. On the playground, rejected children tend to stay on the sidelines.
    c. Rejected children are those who are actively disliked by their peers.
    d. Rejected children who are aggressive are especially likely to be maladjusted.

11. In North American culture, how is the boundary between the sexes generally maintained in middle childhood?
    a. Boys and girls who interact with the other sex get a negative reaction from both sexes.
    b. Girls are willing to interact with children of either sex, but boys reject their overtures.
    c. Boys are willing to interact with children of either sex, but girls reject their overtures.
    d. Adults discourage boys and girls from interacting with each other.

12. Which of the following aspects of emotional understanding would be *atypical* in middle childhood?
    a. Seeing that different aspects of a situation could make a person happy and sad.
    b. Taking account of particular situations in determining appropriate emotional responses.
    c. Insisting that it's never a good idea to hide one's true feelings about a situation.
    d. Being able to feel true empathy for someone who is hurt, sad, or angry.

13. During middle childhood parent-child relationships change in which of the following ways?
    a. Parents become less inclined to use reasoning in dealing with their children.
    b. Concern about equity and fairness in the parent-child relationship increases.
    c. Parents begin to exert greater control and offer more direction to their children.
    d. All of the above.

14. **Authoritative parenting** is associated with a high degree of _____ in middle childhood.
    a. agency
    b. impulsiveness
    c. passivity
    d. defiance.

15. Divorce seems to have the greatest impact on:
    a. young children.
    b. adolescents.
    c. children who are old enough to understand fully what is happening.
    d. none of the above; age does not seem to matter.

16. Boys' and girls' reactions to parental divorce differ in that:
    a. boys' problems are more immediately evident than girls'.
    b. boys usually are affected more severely than girls are.
    c. boys usually are not affected as severely as girls are.
    d. boys are more likely than girls to react with anxiety and withdrawal.

17. The emotional quality of most sibling relationships can best be described as:
    a. predominantly positive.
    b. predominantly negative.
    c. a mixture of positive and negative.
    d. negative early in life, positive later on.

18. Sibling relationships provide children with good opportunities to learn:
    a. how to deal with conflict.
    b. nurturance and leadership.
    c. accommodation and negotiation.
    d. all of the above.

19. Which of the following statements about teachers' treatment of boys and girls is FALSE?
    a. Teachers tend to assign classroom chores along stereotypically gender-appropriate lines.
    b. Teachers interact more with girls, reinforcing their tendency to be model pupils.
    c. Teachers are more likely to criticize girls, especially high-achieving girls, than boys.
    d. Teachers generally attribute poor performance by boys to insufficient effort, poor performance by girls to low aptitude.

20. By the end of elementary school, children who have been held back a year, compared to low-performing children who were not held back, tend to be:
    a. better off academically and more well-adjusted.
    b. better off academically but less well-adjusted.
    c. no better off academically but more well-adjusted.
    d. no better off academically and less well-adjusted.

21. Research on latchkey children indicates that after-school self-care is associated with:
    a. major academic problems for children at all socioeconomic levels.
    b. many behavior problems for children at all socioeconomic levels.
    c. academic and behavior problems for children from low-income families.
    d. academic and behavior problems for children from middle-class families.

22. In middle childhood, attachment history is related to:
    a. ability to form friendships.
    b. likelihood of being ridiculed or excluded from group activities.
    c. time spent in same-sex peer groups.
    d. all of the above.

23. The behavior of Malcolm and his friends when they meet a group of girls is an example of:
    a. social comparison.
    b. border work.
    c. relational aggression.
    d. gender stereotyping.

24. Mikey's family situation after his parents' divorce, including his relationships with both Christine and Frank, suggests that the long-term outcome for him will probably be:
    a. negative; boys almost always suffer more severe effects from a divorce than girls do.
    b. negative; the loss of a male role model outweighs the ending of his parents' conflicts.
    c. positive; he seems to have a good relationship with both of his parents.
    d. positive; he shows few immediate negative effects.

25. The fact that Meryl and Amy spend so much time together and seem to center their social lives around each other is an example of:
    a. a typical peer relationship for girls their age.
    b. the type of friendship often formed by children with an insecure attachment history.
    c. the type of friendship formed by children who are trying to escape problems at home.
    d. an unusually close friendship for middle childhood.

MATCHING QUESTIONS:
Match the following key terms with their definitions:

1. ___ Psychological self

2. ___ Agency

3. ___ Latency period

4. ___ Social self

5. ___ Sociometrics

6. ___ Metatheory of the self

7. ___ Peer group norms

8. ___ Sense of industry

9. ___ Relational aggression

10. ___ Border work

11. ___ Social comparison

A. Freud's term for middle childhood, the period in which the child's sexual urges lie relatively dormant.

B. A research technique used to measure peer status.

C. Attempts to hurt another person by damaging a relationship.

D. In Erikson's theory, the basic belief in one's own competence.

E. The rituals of teasing and ostracism with which elementary school children maintain the boundary between their gender-segregated peer groups.

F. A concept of the self that is made up of psychological characteristics, such as mental abilities and customary ways of feeling.

G. An awareness that the self is intimately tied to other people.

H. The tendency to use others as a source of information in evaluating the self.

I. The tendency to take initiative, rise to challenges, and try to influence events.

J. Informal rules governing the conduct of children within a peer group.

K. Children's understanding of the nature of selves in general.

SHORT-ANSWER QUESTIONS:

1. Why was middle childhood once considered an uneventful phase of development?

2. Explain the difference between the **psychological self** and the **social self**.

3. List three factors that contribute to the use of **social comparison** in evaluating the self.
    (a)

    (b)

    (c)

4. List three aspects of self-management that develop along with a sense of personal effectiveness:
    (a)

    (b)

    (c)

5. List three factors contributing to increasingly mature peer relationships in middle childhood.

    (a)

    (b)

    (c)

6. Explain the developmental significance of gender boundaries in middle childhood.

7. List the major characteristics of *rejected* and *neglected* children.

8. List three major middle childhood advances in understanding of emotion.

    (a)

    (b)

    (c)

9. What two factors in parent-child relationships did Maccoby and Martin emphasize?

    (a)

    (b)

10. List three factors that contribute to long-term positive outcomes for children of divorce.

    (a)

    (b)

    (c)

11. Explain how sibling relationships are distinctive.

12. What do children learn in the classroom besides the academic subjects being taught?

13. List three factors that influence children's success in school.
    (a)

    (b)

    (c)

14. List three ways that development in middle childhood is coherent.
    (a)

    (b)

    (c)

15. Explain how *internal working models* are involved in the connections between children's early attachment history and functioning in middle childhood.

ESSAY QUESTIONS:
1. Summarize the changes in children's self-description that occur during middle childhood and explain how they are related to cognitive development.

2. List and briefly discuss the five major advances in peer relations during middle childhood.

3. Discuss how learning to coordinate friendship and group interaction are important in children's development and how it is related to social competence.

4. Discuss the evidence that parents' behavior has an impact on their children's behavior beyond their genetic contribution.

5. Discuss the role that children's age and sex play in determining impacts of parental divorce.

6. By third grade, Meryl appeared shy and withdrawn only around strangers and in new situations. She had recently established two important new relationships, one with her baby brother Joey and another with her best friend Amy. Explain how Joey and Amy may have led to improvements in Meryl's social behavior.

7. Discuss three ways social, emotional, and cognitive development are interrelated during middle childhood.

ANSWER KEY

MULTIPLE-CHOICE QUESTIONS:

1. c Developing close same-sex friendships and a coherent self-concept are important middle childhood tasks, but Erikson saw developing a sense of industry as the *central* task of this period.

2. b Elementary school children increasingly use psychological traits to describe themselves, and they frequently compare themselves to others; they no longer describe the self as a concrete, physical entity, but they still use physical characteristics in self-descriptions.

3. d Girls tend to be more flexible about gender stereotypes than boys, and higher levels of cognitive development and having a mother who engages in nontraditional roles are also associated with increased flexibility.

4. c Preschoolers believe that their physical and cognitive accomplishments depend on their own efforts, but not their social accomplishments.

5. c Age 11 is typically when time spent with peers surpasses time spent with family.

6. a Preschoolers label other children as friends, define a friend as "someone I like," and tend to feel conflict is not part of friendship.

7. d Boys' peer groups tend to be larger than girls' and to emphasize loyalty and shared activities; neither gender's peer groups usually include both boys and girls.

8. d Answers *a-c* are all findings of the Sherifs' study.

9. b Peer group norms usually match the culture's moral values.

10. b *Neglected* children tend to stay on the sidelines; rejected children are often involved in negative interactions involving aggression.

11. a Adults are generally not involved in maintaining the boundary; children of both sexes maintain it themselves.

12. c In middle childhood, children typically recognize that sometimes it is better to hide one's true feelings, and they become quite good at doing so.

13. b Parents become increasingly inclined to use reasoning in dealing with children in middle childhood, and the amount of control and direction they provide gradually declines.

14. a Impulsiveness is more likely to be an outcome of permissive parenting; passivity and defiance are both possible outcomes of authoritarian parenting.

15. a Older children are more likely to understand what is happening, to realize it is not their fault, and to have experienced a period of stable parenting before the divorce.

16. a Boys' problems are more immediately evident than girls', but they are probably not affected more severely. Girls are more likely to respond with anxiety and withdrawal.

17. c The emotional quality of sibling relationships varies, but it is generally a mixture of positive and negative.

18. d Both older and younger siblings have opportunities to learn how to deal with conflict; older siblings have chances to develop nurturance and leadership in dealing with their younger siblings, who in turn have chances to learn accommodation and negotiation.

19. b Teachers tend to interact more with boys.

20. d Being held back a year does not benefit most children either academically or socially.

21. c After-school self-care is associated with problems only for children from low-income families.

22. d Children with secure attachment histories tend to be better at forming friendships, they are less likely to be ridiculed or excluded from group activities, and they spend more time in same-sex peer groups than children with anxious attachment histories.

23. b The teasing and denial of interest shown by Malcolm and his friends, typical of boys their age, help maintain boundaries between genders by insuring that boys who want to retain their standing with their peers will not publicly associate too closely with girls.

24. c Despite the immediate negative effects of the divorce on Mikey, his long-term outlook is positive, due to the strong relationships he has with both parents.

25. a   In middle childhood, girls tend to spend much of their time interacting
         intensely with one or two close friends.

MATCHING QUESTIONS:

1. F	4. G	7. J	10. E
2. I	5. B	8. D	11. H
3. A	6. K	9. C	

SHORT-ANSWER QUESTIONS:

1.   Because changes during this period are less dramatic than in infancy and early
     childhood. Freud called middle childhood the latency period, when sexual urges
     were relatively dormant; other researchers assumed this meant that little of social
     or emotional importance happened in middle childhood.

2.   The psychological self is a concept of the self made up of psychological
     characteristics, such as mental abilities and customary feelings; in other words, it
     consists of characteristics *inside* the child. The social self is an awareness that the self
     is intimately tied to other people; it includes defining the self in terms of
     relationships with others and evaluating the self in comparison to others. In other
     words, it draws on factors from *outside* the child.

3.   The decline in centration, a normative understanding of ability, and the cultural
     context.

4.   Capacities for coping with stress and emotionally challenging situations develop
     along with a sense of personal effectiveness. These include being able to tolerate
     aversive emotions, view a stressor in different ways, recruit social support, and
     delay gratification.

5.   A greater ability to understand perspectives, needs, and feelings of others; an
     ability to grasp more complex rules regarding interpersonal behavior; and a
     growing ability to communicate feelings and wishes with words rather than
     actions.

6.   One function served by maintaining gender boundaries is protection from
     premature sexual contact. In terms of individual development, children who do not
     maintain gender boundaries are less popular with other children and are seen as
     less socially competent by adults. Following peer group norms about gender
     boundaries is a sign of competence and adjustment in middle childhood and
     predicts successful functioning in mixed-gender peer groups during adolescence.

7.   *Rejected* children are consistently named as disliked by other children. They are
     often viewed as aggressive or mean, and the combination of rejection and

aggressiveness is a sign of maladjustment. On the playground, rejected children spend much of their time in isolation or negative behavior. *Neglected* children are rarely named as liked or disliked and seem to be of little interest to other children. They tend to be ineffective with peers and dependent on teachers, but generally not hostile. If they are submissive and low in assertiveness, they can become chronic victims of aggressive children. On the playground, they tend to stand on the sidelines and watch others play.

8. The ability to understand the complexity of emotion-arousing situations, the ability to take particular situations into account when determining appropriate emotional responses, and a knowledge of display rules for emotions.

9. The frequency of conflict over goals between child and parent and the degree of balance in resolution of parent-child disagreements.

10. Correct answers include ongoing contact with both parents, an end to parental conflict, cooperation between parents concerning child care, emotional well-being of the custodial parent, and good relationships in any stepfamilies created after the divorce.

11. They continue through life and are often deeply emotional, like parent-child relationships. Because siblings are closer in status to each other than parents and children, the relationship is also somewhat like a peer relationship. However, there is usually a greater age disparity between siblings than between peers, and sibling relationships often cross gender boundaries, unlike most middle childhood peer relationships.

12. Overall, they learn mainstream cultural norms and values, including gender roles. More specifically, in the United States these include hard work, achievement motivation, respect for private property, obedience to authority, punctuality, neatness, compliance with rules, competition, and the idea that girls have less math and science ability than boys.

13. Correct answers include the quality of the school; association with well-adjusted, academically motivated peers; a history of nurturant support from parents; a well-organized home environment; and being praised for effort rather than being smart.

14. Various influences reinforce each other, individual children's characteristics fit together in ways that make sense, and development in middle childhood has continuity with the past.

15. *Internal working models* include feelings and expectations about the self and others that originate in early attachment relationships. Carried forward by children and

modified in various ways by experience, these working models influence children's later interactions and relationships, forming a link between early attachment history and later functioning.

ESSAY QUESTIONS:

1. Elementary school children increasingly describe themselves in terms of psychological traits, thoughts, and feelings; their earlier self-descriptions centered around physical characteristics and activities. School-aged children include physical characteristics in self-descriptions, but usually to indicate things that make them unique. Their self-descriptions include more comparisons with peers and more self-evaluation. Self-descriptions also become increasingly social, as children describe themselves in terms of group membership and their dealings with others. These changes reflect increasing abilities to deal with multiple pieces of information, to make comparisons, to distinguish between appearance and reality, and to understand other people's points of view--in other words, declining centration and egocentrism.

2. First, elementary schoolers form deeper and more loyal friendships than preschoolers. Preschoolers call other children friends, but lack real understanding of what friendship entails. Second, elementary schoolers form networks of friends and develop a sense of group membership. Differences between boys' and girls' groups become more pronounced; girls' groups are smaller and more focused on intimacy, boys' groups larger and more focused on shared activities. Third, elementary schoolers learn to coordinate close friendships and group interactions. Interactions with friends and with groups teach different things, and social competence includes learning to deal with both simultaneously. Fourth, middle childhood is a time of learning to follow peer group norms. Because these norms typically match those of the general culture, the peer group becomes an important agent of socialization. Fifth, elementary schoolers become very concerned with maintaining gender boundaries. Gender segregation is pervasive during middle childhood, and the peer group rigidly enforces norms for acceptable interaction with the opposite sex.

3. Learning to coordinate friendship and group interaction are important because both provide children with experiences that are valuable developmentally. Children learn trust and reciprocity from close friendships; they learn cooperation, coordination of activities, and the need to follow rules and norms from interacting in the larger peer group. Close friendships and peer acceptance are both related to self-worth and lack of loneliness in children. In addition, the two types of involvement with other children feed into each other; friendships promote integration into the peer group and interactions in the group provide a context for sharing between friends. Social competence seems to make it possible for children to coordinate their involvement with a close friend and with a larger group.

Socially competent children are able to preserve their connection to their friend even when interacting with a group of peers, and interaction with other peers does not threaten the friendship. In contrast, less socially competent children have trouble balancing the two; interacting with a group may disrupt their friendship, or they may form an exclusive relationship with each other and avoid interacting with other children. It is as if the demands of the two different types of social relationships are too much for them to handle simultaneously.

4. There are several lines of research that indicate that parents' impact on their children goes beyond their genetic contributions. First, research with monkeys allows researchers to separate the influence of parental genes and parental behavior more clearly than in humans. For example, the amount of time a female vervet monkey is held as an infant is a better predictor of how much she later holds her own babies (a measure of her mother's behavior toward her) than the average amount of time her mother held all of her babies (an estimate of genetic influences). Second, in humans as well, parents' specific behavior toward their children is often a better predictor of the children's behavior than the parents' overall traits. For example, a parent's harsh treatment of a child predicts that child's later aggressiveness better than measures of the parent's overall aggressiveness. Third, changes in parental behavior over time are often associated with changes in children's behaviors. For example, caregiver depression is associated with a number of negative outcomes for children, but children show more problems if the depression occurs during their first year of life than if it occurs earlier or later, even thought the genetic influence should remain similar regardless of timing of depression. If the caregiver's depression improves, the child's behavior also often changes. Fourth, links between parent behavior and child outcomes are not always obvious; the child's behavior does not always resemble the parent's. For example, lack of parental monitoring predicts child aggressiveness, and rejecting behavior from parents is associated with avoidant attachment in their children, who later often show dependency and contact-seeking toward their preschool teachers. Fifth, experiences with parents predict other aspects of children's functioning, such as behavior with peers, in ways that do not seem to be due to straightforward genetic influences.

5. In general, the impact of parental divorce is greatest for children who are very young; older children may be better able to understand what is happening or may have enjoyed a longer period of more stable, responsive parenting before the divorce. Effects are more immediately noticeable for boys than for girls, but probably no more severe. Boys often show aggression and impulse control problems, while girls show anxiety, inhibition, and withdrawal. Since boys' problems are more likely to be disruptive, parents and teachers are more likely to notice and respond to them. Boys growing up with maternal custody may lack the role-modeling, sex-role socialization, and impulse control provided by fathers, and

they may be affected more negatively by living with an opposite-sex parent. Girls' divorce-related problems often do not emerge until adolescence, and girls may react more negatively than boys if their mothers remarry.

6. The birth of Joey allowed Meryl to take on a new role as big sister and to develop more responsible, nurturant behavior, which in turn increased her social competence and sense of self-efficacy. Because her parents apparently prepared her well for his birth, his presence in the family became an asset for Meryl rather than merely a source of potential conflict. Joey's presence also caused changes in Meryl's relationship with her parents, perhaps pushing her toward greater independence as they devoted time to the baby. Meryl's friendship with Amy is a typical elementary school girls' friendship, emphasizing mutual trust, intimacy, and support. This type of relationship would help Meryl increase her understanding of others and of herself, while providing her with an additional source of social support. The experience of being liked probably enhanced her self-esteem, and the continuity in the friendship may have modified Meryl's expectations about social relationships and her own social competence. Finally, the relationship with Amy would have reduced Meryl's focus on her parents and further encouraged her developing independence.

7. One set of connections that is mentioned in the book are those between social, emotional, and cognitive factors in the development of morality. The cognitive advances of middle childhood make possible a deepening of moral concerns, increased understanding of moral issues, and perhaps also increasingly moral behavior. Increased ability to understand others' points of view and feelings leads to the development of true empathy and becomes a major factor in moral growth, as well as changing how children react to others' distress. Increased social comparison and attempts to adhere to group standards in interacting with peers, along with the emergence of such social emotions as true guilt, also contribute to moral development and change children's behavior. Other examples would include connections between cognitive development and the knowledge and use of emotional display rules (overcoming the appearance-reality problem and centration makes it possible for children to understand that people can feel one way but appear to feel another, that it is possible to mask one's feelings; applying this knowledge changes how they interact with others in both positive and negative ways) and between cognitive development and the ability to understand the complexity of emotion-arousing situations (that different features of a situation can make a person happy and sad, or that expectations influence emotional reactions).

CHAPTER 13
PHYSICAL AND COGNITIVE DEVELOPMENT IN ADOLESCENCE
CHAPTER REVIEW

As you read the chapter, construct your own chapter outline by answering the following review questions and defining the *Key Terms*.

I. INTRODUCTION
    A. Approximately what age span does adolescence cover?

    B. How long has adolescence been regarded as a distinctive developmental period? What were G. Stanley Hall's views on adolescence?

    C. Why does adolescence last longer today than it did in Hall's day? What are the age ranges and characteristics of early, middle, and late adolescence?

II. BIOLOGICAL CHANGES DURING ADOLESCENCE
    Key Terms: **puberty, menarche, spermarche, adrenarche, adrenal glands, gonads, gonadarche, pituitary gland, hypothalamus, gonadotropins, secondary sex characteristics, plasticity, hemispheric specialization**
    A. What is the clearest indicator of **puberty** in girls? In boys?

    B. How long does puberty last? What sex difference is there in the timing of puberty?

C. What factors influence individual differences in the timing of puberty? What is the normal range for beginning and completing puberty?

D. How has the timing of puberty changed over the last 100 years? What cross-cultural differences have been found in timing of puberty?

E. Describe the hormonal process that leads to the onset of puberty.

F. Discuss the roles of weight and body fat in the onset of puberty.

G. What **secondary sex characteristics** did Tanner use as markers for his stages of puberty? How does rate of development compare across the various characteristics?

H. Summarize the physical changes associated with puberty for girls and for boys.

I. Describe the changes that occur in the brain around the time of puberty and their possible impacts.

J. BOX: How do sleep patterns change during adolescence? What factors contribute to these changes? What practical implications do they have?

K. What impacts does puberty and its timing have on body image, relations with the opposite sex, parent-child relationships, the prevalence of problem behaviors, and overall adjustment? How can these effects be explained?

III. CHANGES IN THINKING DURING ADOLESCENCE
  Key Terms: hypothetico-deductive reasoning, formal operations, selective attention, divided attention, automatization, cognitive socialization
  A. What three major advances in cognitive abilities occur during adolescence? What implications does each have?

B. How did Piaget explain the new thinking skills that appear during adolescence?

C. Describe Piaget's three experiments that are discussed in the textbook. Explain what general cognitive ability each one is intended to measure and how performance on each one changes with age.

D. What are the current assessments of Piaget's description and explanation of adolescent cognitive abilities? What questions have been raised about Piaget's theory?

E. How does the use of **formal operations** change from early to late adolescence? How commonly are they used by adolescents and adults in our culture? How widely are they used in other cultures? How can these patterns of use be explained?

F.   Under what circumstances can **formal operations** be taught?

G.   How are **formal operations** related to academic performance?

H.   How are adolescents' information-processing abilities superior to those of younger children? What factors explain the advances they have made?

I.   How does the social environment affect the development of cognitive skills during adolescence?

J.   BOX: What is involved in critical thinking? Why do adolescents often fail to think critically? What can be done to foster critical thinking in adolescents?

IV. SOCIAL COGNITIVE CHANGES OF ADOLESCENCE

Key Terms: **adolescent egocentrism, imaginary audience, personal fable, moral realism, autonomous morality, preconventional morality, conventional morality, postconventional/principled morality**

A.   What factors contribute to **adolescent egocentrism** and its eventual disappearance?

B.   Summarize the stages in Piaget's and Kohlberg's models of moral development. How are they related to general cognitive development?

C.   What criticisms have been made of Kohlberg's theory and method?

V. AN OVERVIEW OF ADOLESCENT PHYSICAL AND COGNITIVE DEVELOPMENT

A.   What implications do the physical changes of adolescence have for other areas of development?

B.   Summarize the major cognitive advances that occur during adolescence and the cognitive limitations that remain.

SELF-TEST

After **you have studied the chapter, use the following questions to test your understanding.**

MULTIPLE-CHOICE QUESTIONS:

1. Adolescence has been regarded as a separate developmental period since:
    a. the days of ancient Greece and Rome.
    b. the Renaissance.
    c. the early twentieth century.
    d. the 1960's.

2. The period during which a child changes from a sexually immature person to one who is capable of reproduction is known as:
    a. adolescence.
    b. puberty.
    c. menarche.
    d. the growth spurt.

3. The timing of **puberty** is influenced by:
    a. heredity.
    b. nutrition.
    c. physical exercise.
    d. all of the above.

4. Given the information in your textbook about generational changes in the timing of puberty, which of the following trends would you expect to discover in girls' age at **menarche** in Japan since World War II?
    a. It has increased.
    b. It has decreased.
    c. It has remained unchanged.
    d. It has increased in some families, decreased in others.

5. Evidence AGAINST the critical weight hypothesis includes:
    a. menarche seems unrelated to weight.
    b. the growth spurt seems unrelated to weight.
    c. menarche requires a certain body fat percentage.
    d. all of the above.

6. Which of the following statements about **secondary sex characteristics** is TRUE?
    a. They differentiate males from females but are not essential to reproduction.
    b. They usually appear only after reproductive maturity has been attained.
    c. They are essential to reproduction but are not always visible to observers.
    d. They are considered secondary because they are present in only about half of all normal adults.

7. Which of the following is NOT one of the criteria for Tanner's stages of puberty?
    a. Pubic hair development.
    b. Facial and underarm hair development.
    c. Female breast development.
    d. Male genital development.

8. The decrease in the number of synapses around the time of puberty results in:
    a. increased flexibility in meeting new demands to the brain.
    b. a temporary loss of certain brain functions.
    c. increased ability to recover from brain damage.
    d. increased efficiency for the remaining synapses.

9. In early adolescence, girls with the most positive body image tend to be:
    a. about average in physical development.
    b. well ahead of their peers in physical development.
    c. behind their peers in physical development.
    d. most aware of their own and others' physical development.

10. Young adolescents who have reached puberty tend to have more advanced relationships with the opposite sex than others of their age who have not reached puberty, probably because:
    a. higher androgen levels after puberty lead to increased sexual interest.
    b. the appearance of secondary sex characteristics produce increased sexual attractiveness.
    c. parents perceive physically mature adolescents as more personally responsible.
    d. all of the above.

11. Which of the following is NOT a major cognitive advance of adolescence?
    a. The ability to apply logical thought to the possible as well as to the real.
    b. The ability to think of hypothetical solutions to a problem and deduce which is correct.
    c. The ability to go beyond concrete experience to form abstract concepts.
    d. The ability to think about relationships among mentally constructed concepts.

12. Piaget's theory of adolescent cognitive development included the idea that:
    a. the ability to use formal operations is qualitatively different from the cognitive skills of younger children.
    b. formal operations are produced by different developmental processes than earlier cognitive structures.
    c. formal operations are fundamentally similar to the cognitive skills of middle childhood.
    d. formal operations cannot be discovered by adolescents on their own, but must be taught.

13. Adolescents' performance in the law of floating bodies study demonstrates that:
    a. adolescents are able to reason about ratios.
    b. the cognitive skills of adolescence build upon those of middle childhood.
    c. adolescents are able to think about relationships among mentally constructed concepts.
    d. all of the above.

14. Which of the following statements best represents the current assessment of Piaget's theory of adolescent cognitive development?
    a. His explanation of adolescent cognitive development is accepted, but his description of the changes is flawed.
    b. His description of adolescent cognitive changes is well accepted, but his explanation of them is widely criticized.
    c. Both his explanation and his description of adolescent cognitive development are generally accepted.
    d. Both his explanation and his description of adolescent cognitive development have been generally rejected.

15. Cross-cultural research on formal operations has revealed that:
    a. formal operations are less culture-bound than earlier stages in Piaget's theory.
    b. there is no evidence that formal operations are used in non-industrialized cultures.
    c. formal operations are least valued in cultures with an orientation toward science and technology.
    d. the emergence of formal operations is associated with education at the secondary level.

16. Which of the following people is LEAST likely to benefit from attempts to teach formal operations?
    a. An 8-year-old of above average intelligence.
    b. A typical 9-year-old.
    c. A typical 12-year-old.
    d. A 16-year-old who does not normally use formal operations.

17. Compared to younger children, adolescents are better at:
    a. selective and divided attention.
    b. selective, but not divided attention.
    c. divided, but not selective attention.
    d. none of the above.

18. **Adolescent egocentrism** results from teenagers':
    a. inability to imagine others' thoughts.
    b. assumption that others' thoughts are identical to their own.
    c. increased ability to think about thinking.
    d. all of the above.

19. In the example in your textbook when Mike worried about other people noticing his skinny arms, he was showing the effects of:
    a. an imaginary audience.
    b. moral realism.
    c. a personal fable.
    d. autonomous morality.

20. According to Piaget's theory, children in the stage of **moral realism** would be likely to:
    a. consider intentions in judging the morality of an action.
    b. ignore consequences in judging the morality of an action.
    c. see behavior as either totally right or totally wrong.
    d. see morality as relative to the situation.

21. In Kohlberg's theory, moral judgments based on obedience and punishment are typical of:
    a. the preconventional period.
    b. the conventional period.
    c. the postconventional period.
    d. autonomous morality.

22. Which of the following is the best overall conclusion from studies examining gender differences in moral reasoning?
    a. Men consistently score higher on Kohlberg's tasks than women do.
    b. Women consistently score higher on Kohlberg's tasks than men do.
    c. Both men and women use both caring- and justice-related issues in moral reasoning.
    d. There are no gender differences in moral reasoning.

23. At the community action meeting, Malcolm argued against a redevelopment plan on the grounds that it would be unfair to low-income residents and that it would disrupt neighborhood harmony. This is an example of:
    a. preconventional moral reasoning.
    b. conventional moral reasoning.
    c. postconventional moral reasoning.
    d. moral realism.

24. Mike's systematic questioning about his mother's car trouble is an example of:
    a. cognitive competence.
    b. hypothetico-deductive reasoning.
    c. moral reasoning.
    d. metacognition.

25. When Meryl described her feelings after breaking up with Jim as the deepest state of depression ever experienced, she was showing the effects of:
    a. an imaginary audience.
    b. hypothetico-deductive reasoning.
    c. childhood egocentrism.
    d. a personal fable.

MATCHING QUESTIONS:
Match the following key terms with their definitions:

1. ___ Puberty

2. ___ Cognitive socialization

3. ___ Formal operations

4. ___ Hypothalamus

5. ___ Moral realism

6. ___ Preconventional morality

7. ___ Hypothetico-deductive reasoning

8. ___ Pituitary gland

9. ___ Autonomous morality

10. ___ Gonadotropins

11. ___ Secondary sex characteristics

12. ___ Conventional morality

A. In Piaget's theory, a set of principles of formal logic on which the cognitive advances of adolescence are based.

B. The ability to think up hypothetical solutions to a problem and to formulate a systematic plan for deducing which of these solutions is correct.

C. A small gland at the base of the brain that plays a major role in regulating the hormonal output of other glands.

D. In Piaget's theory, the stage in which children see morality as relative to the situation.

E. Physical features that differentiate adult males from adult females but are not directly involved in reproduction.

F. Pituitary hormones that affect hormone output by the gonads.

G. In Kohlberg's theory, moral reasoning based on opinions of others or formal laws.

H. The influence of social environment on the development of cognitive skills.

I. The period during which a child changes from a sexually immature person to one who is capable of reproduction.

J. In Piaget's theory, the stage in which children treat morality as absolute and moral constraints as unalterable.

K. In Kohlberg's theory, moral reasoning based on fear of punishment or desire for reward.

L. A part of the brain that regulates many body functions, including the production of pituitary hormones.

SHORT-ANSWER QUESTIONS:

1. Give the approximate age ranges for early, middle, and late adolescence.

2. Explain why adolescence lasts longer today than it did in the early twentieth century.

3. What is the clearest indicator of puberty in girls?

4. The sex glands--ovaries in women and testes in men--are known as the _____.

5. During adolescence, girls who mature _____ than average seem to be at a disadvantage, while boys who mature _____ than average tend to have more problems.

6. Explain how weight and body fat seem to be involved in the onset of puberty.

7. What two major changes occur in the brain between childhood and adulthood?
   (a)

   (b)

8. List the three major advances in cognitive abilities that occur during adolescence.
   (a)

   (b)

   (c)

9. What was Piaget's pendulum study designed to measure?

10. How does the use of formal operations change from early to late adolescence?

11. The tendency for basic cognitive processes to require less effort with practice is called _____.

12. List four important factors in encouraging critical thinking in adolescents.
    (a)

    (b)

    (c)

    (d)

13. Elkind's terms for teenagers' exaggerated belief in their own uniqueness is the _____ _____.

14. List three criticisms that have been made of Kohlberg's theory of moral reasoning.
    (a)

    (b)

    (c)

15. List four cognitive limitations that remain in adolescence.
    (a)

    (b)

    (c)

    (d)

ESSAY QUESTIONS:

1. Discuss impacts from the timing of puberty on three domains of adolescent girls' development.

2. Describe the changes in sleep patterns typical of adolescence and explain why they occur.

3. Discuss the prevalence of formal operations among adolescents and adults in our own and other cultures. What factors increase the likelihood that formal operations will be used?

4. Discuss four factors that contribute to the improvements in memory and attentional skills seen during adolescence.

5. Summarize the stages in Kohlberg's theory of moral development and explain how they are related to general cognitive development.

6. Discuss three ways that the schools in your home town meet the developmental needs of adolescents and three ways that they do not.

7. In the vignettes, Malcolm, Meryl, and Mike all show a tendency toward passionate belief in certain principles and some disgust at what they see as hypocrisy in their parents and the rest of the adult world. Given what you have learned about adolescent cognitive development, how would you explain the emergence of this combination of idealism and self-righteousness during adolescence?

ANSWER KEY

MULTIPLE-CHOICE QUESTIONS:

1. c Before the early twentieth century, reproductive maturity marked entry into adulthood; there was no transitional phase between childhood and adulthood.

2. b See definition of **puberty**.

3. d Answers *a-c* all influence the timing of puberty.

4. b Japan has become more industrialized since World War II, resulting in improved overall nutrition and health, which has led to an earlier average age at menarche.

5. c Menarche and the growth spurt are both related to weight. Because menarche requires a certain body fat percentage, the timing of puberty depends on more than weight alone.

6. a Secondary sex characteristics are not essential to reproduction, are visible to observers, and begin to appear before reproductive maturity is reached.

7. b In girls, Tanner's stages are based on pubic hair development and breast development; in boys they are based on pubic hair development and genital development.

8. d The decreased number of synapses results in a more efficient network of synapses, at the cost of decreased flexibility and decreased ability to recover from brain damage.

9. a Being out of step with peers in physical development seems to have a negative effect on girls' body image. Because of the increase in body fat at puberty, this effect is greater for girls who are ahead of their peers in physical development.

10. d Answers *a-c* all contribute to more advanced relationships with the opposite sex.

11. c The ability to form abstract concepts is already present in middle childhood.

12. a Piaget believed that the ability to use formal operations was qualitatively different from the cognitive skills of younger children, but that they were produced by the same developmental processes as earlier cognitive structures and thus could not be taught.

13. d Answers *a-c* are all demonstrated in the law of floating bodies study.

14. b   As with earlier stages of development, Piaget's description of adolescent cognitive skills is generally accurate, but his explanation for them has been widely criticized.

15. d   Cross-cultural research indicates formal operations are *more* culture-bound than earlier Piagetian stages. They are most valued in scientific and technological cultures and are associated with secondary education, but formal operational thought is used by people from non-industrialized cultures when they are engaged in tasks with meaning for them.

16. b   Training is most likely to work for people who are on the brink of discovering formal operations or who may not be displaying their true competency in using them. This would include unusually bright 8-year-olds, typical 12-year-olds, and 16-year-olds who don't normally use formal operations, but not typical 9-year-olds.

17. a   Adolescents are superior at both selective and divided attention tasks, mostly because of improved attentional strategies.

18. c   Due to increased ability to think about thinking, adolescents *are* able to imagine others' thoughts, but they tend to assume that their own thoughts and feelings are unique.

19. a   Mike was unduly concerned that everyone at the party would focus attention on him.

20. c   Children in Piaget's stage of moral realism would be likely to judge the morality of an action on the basis of consequences, not intentions, and they would see behavior as either totally right or totally wrong, not relative to the situation.

21. a   The obedience and punishment orientation is typical of Stage 1 in Kohlberg's theory, one of two stages in the Preconventional Period.

22. c   Although women often give priority to caring-based issues and men often give priority to justice-based issues, both sexes use both types of issues in moral reasoning.

23. c   Malcolm's arguments are typical of the Social Contract Orientation of Stage 5, the first stage in the Postconventional Period.

24. b   See the definition of hypothetico-deductive reasoning. Mike's approach is to think of a series of hypothetical reasons his mother's car might not be starting and form a systematic plan for figuring out which of them is most likely to be correct.

25. d   Meryl's description of her feelings reflects an exaggerated belief in her own uniqueness, that no one could possibly have had the same feelings she was having.

MATCHING QUESTIONS:

1. I	4. L	7. B	10. F
2. H	5. J	8. C	11. E
3. A	6. K	9. D	12. G

SHORT-ANSWER QUESTIONS:

1. Early adolescence: the beginning of puberty to about age 13; middle adolescence: ages 14 to 16; late adolescence: age 17 to early adulthood.

2. Because puberty occurs earlier and people need more years of education to prepare for most adult occupations.

3. menarche

4. gonads

5. earlier, later

6. Menarche occurs at a relatively constant weight, and the adolescent growth spurt in both sexes is weight-related. However, weight alone does not trigger the changes of puberty; instead, factors related to weight, such as girls' body fat ratio, appear to be involved. For example, for menstruation to begin or continue, a girl's body mass must be at least 17% fat.

7. A decline in plasticity and an increase in the efficiency of brain functioning.

8. (a) Adolescents become able to apply logical thinking to the possible as well as the real; (b) adolescents become able to think about relationships among mentally constructed concepts; (c) adolescents' thinking becomes even more logical and systematic than in childhood.

9. The ability to investigate the effects of a single variable while holding other factors constant.

10. Young adolescents often use formal reasoning in some situations but not others; this type of thinking is known as *emergent* formal operations. By middle or late adolescence, the use of formal operations often becomes more consistent and mature, a type of thinking referred to as *consolidated* formal operations.

11. automatization

12. (a) The process of critical thinking should be embedded in the teaching of content; (b) adolescents must be convinced of the value of critical thinking; (c) adolescents need opportunities to practice critical thinking; (d) adolescents need to be encouraged to explore subjects in depth over time.

13. personal fable

14. Criticisms that have been made include: measures of moral reasoning are not necessarily related to actual moral behavior, the form of moral reasoning should not be separated from the content of moral judgments, Kohlberg's method of assessing moral reasoning--especially his scoring system--may lack reliability, Kohlberg's model may be biased against women, and Kohlberg's theory is too culture-specific.

15. (a) Not all adolescents show evidence of logical, systematic, abstract thinking abilities; (b) adolescents who do have such abilities do not always use them; (c) adolescents do not always apply their memory strategies effectively; (d) adolescents' knowledge base is still not as broad as it will be in adulthood.

ESSAY QUESTIONS:

1. Three domains of adolescent girls' development that are affected by the timing of puberty are body image, relationships with the opposite sex, and problem behaviors. (Note: You could also choose to discuss parent-child relationships.) Early-maturing girls tend to have a more negative body image than average or late-maturing girls, beginning early in adolescence and continuing at least through tenth grade. Specifically, early-maturing girls tend to be more dissatisfied with their height, weight, and overall figure. There are also differences between early- and late-maturing girls in their relationships with the opposite sex. Interest in the opposite sex, dating, and sexual activity all become more likely after puberty; compared to late-maturing girls, by mid-adolescence early-maturing girls have more dating experience and are more likely to have a steady boyfriend, to be sexually experienced, and to have had an unwanted pregnancy. Early-maturing girls are more likely than late-maturing girls to show an increase at puberty in problem behaviors, including school behavior problems, decreased academic performance, truancy, drug and alcohol use, running away, and shoplifting.

2. The overall amount of sleep *needed* does not seem to decline from middle childhood to adolescence, but the amount of sleep adolescents actually *get* does decline, along with the proportion of deep sleep. At the same time, adolescents typically show a shift in the *timing* of their sleep, staying up later at night and sleeping later in the morning than they did in middle childhood. There is evidence that this shift in timing is not due to bad habits or a desire to stay up late; instead, it seems to have a biological basis. The shift in the timing of sleep is related to physical indicators of puberty, rather than to chronological age. In addition, during puberty a shift occurs in the timing of daily secretion of melatonin, a hormone associated with onset of sleep. In contrast, the decline in the amount of sleep adolescents get does not seem to be biologically based, but instead related to factors in their daily schedules, including early starting times for school, after-school and evening jobs, homework, and family routines.

3. Even in our own culture, many adolescents and adults do not regularly use formal operations in solving problems; in many studies only about 1/3 of the adolescent and adult subjects show mature use of formal operations. Use of formal operations tends to be positively associated with intelligence and years of schooling. People are most likely to use formal operations in domains where they have high interest and expertise. Cross-cultural studies have found that formal operations are most prevalent in cultures that emphasize science and technology; within a culture, they are associated with the achievement of secondary level education. Although studies using traditional Piagetian measures found little evidence of formal operations in non-industrialized cultures, people in such cultures show evidence of formal operational thought when they do in complex tasks that are meaningful to them.

4. First, increased efficiency of brain functioning during adolescence may result in improved attention and memory skills by producing a modest increase in memory capacity. Second, increased sophistication in the use of mnemonic strategies, both internal and external, seems to result in improved memory processes. Third, the process of automatization, in which basic cognitive processes become less effortful with practice, produces an increase in available cognitive processing capacity. Fourth, adolescents' expanding store of both general and specialized knowledge leads to improvements in memory.

5. Kohlberg's theory of moral development includes three periods of moral reasoning --preconventional, conventional, and postconventional or principled morality--that can be further subdivided into six stages. During the period of preconventional morality, moral judgments are not based on social conventions, rules, or laws. During this period moral reasoning is based first on an obedience and punishment orientation (stage 1), and then on a hedonistic and instrumental orientation (stage 2). At stage 1, good behavior is based on a desire to avoid punishment; at stage 2, good behavior is based on a desire for reward or benefit. During the period of

conventional morality, moral judgments are based on internalized standards arising from concrete experience in the social world. Reasoning at this stages focuses either on opinions of others or on formal laws. At stage 3 (the good-boy, nice-girl orientation), good behavior is motivated by a desire to avoid disapproval; at stage 4 (the authority or law-and-order orientation), good behavior is based on doing one's duty as prescribed by society's laws. Finally, during the period of postconventional or principled morality, moral reasoning focuses on abstract principles underlying right and wrong. At stage 5 (the social contract orientation), good behavior is motivated by an obligation to keep society running smoothly and to maintain self-respect and the respect of peers. At stage 6 (the hierarchy of principles orientation), the goal is to make decisions based on the highest relevant moral principle, and good behavior is motivated by a desire to avoid self-condemnation for violating one's own principles. Although Kohlberg's three periods of moral reasoning seem to correspond to Piaget's preoperational, concrete operational, and formal operational stages of cognitive development, the emergence of each level of moral reasoning seems to lag behind the development of the corresponding cognitive skills.

6. Obviously, your answers to this question will depend in part on what the schools are like in your home town. Good answers will clearly relate characteristics of local schools to developmental needs of adolescence drawn from research results discussed in the textbook. For example, the increased emphasis on science and advanced mathematics in many high schools matches the increased capacity for abstract and hypothetical reasoning that develops during adolescence. In contrast, the early starting times of many high schools do not mesh well with the shift in sleep patterns that typically come with puberty. Remember to consider in your answer not only whether the curriculum and practices of local schools match the current abilities of adolescents, but also whether they provide challenges to help adolescents overcome their current limitations. For example, you could use the material in the box on encouraging critical thinking to assess whether or not your local schools provide adequate encouragement and challenge to foster the development of adolescents' critical thinking skills, or whether sufficient opportunities are offered for the use of formal operations.

7. The emergence of idealism may be a result of adolescents' increased sophistication in thinking about abstract concepts and their growing metacognitive abilities. As they become more able to reflect on their own thoughts, they may also devote more time and energy to thinking about and developing their own system of beliefs. Because they see the resulting belief system as something they have built themselves, they may be particularly passionate in expressing and defending it. The self-righteousness may be explained as part of adolescents' personal fables; they may believe that no one has ever felt as strongly as they do about a particular issue and that they are therefore morally superior to their elders.

CHAPTER 14
SOCIAL AND EMOTIONAL DEVELOPMENT IN ADOLESCENCE
CHAPTER REVIEW

As you read the chapter, construct your own chapter outline by answering the following review questions and defining the *Key Terms*.

I. INTRODUCTION
    Key Term: **identity**
    What are the major developmental tasks of adolescence?

II. THE SOCIAL WORLD OF ADOLESCENCE: AN OVERVIEW
    Key Term: **puberty rites/rites of passage**
    A. To what extent and how does adolescence truly seem to be a period of storm and stress?

    B. Why are adolescents in Western cultures particularly prone to stress and conflict? What is adolescence like in non-Western cultures?

III. DEVELOPMENT OF THE SELF
    Key Terms: **identity crisis, identity diffusion, foreclosure, moratorium, identity achievement**
    A. How does self-concept change from middle childhood to adolescence? From early to late adolescence?

B. Why is the sense of self fragile in early adolescence? What factors decrease this fragility?

C. What is involved in the concept of personal **identity**? What did Erikson mean by the term **identity crisis**?

D. Explain Marcia's four categories of identity status.

E. What have researchers discovered about young people in each of Marcia's categories?

F. What two sets of ingredients did Erikson believe were necessary for consolidating an optimal sense of personal identity?

G. What group differences in identity development have been found?

IV. PEER RELATIONSHIPS IN ADOLESCENCE

Key Terms: **clique, crowd**

A. How do peer relationships change during adolescence? How are they connected to experiences during middle childhood?

B. How is understanding of others related to self-understanding? Summarize Selman's stages in understanding of self and others.

C. How do friendships change from middle childhood to adolescence? How do they continue to change over the course of adolescence?

D. How do adolescent boys' and girls' friendships differ?

E. Explain the differences between **cliques** and **crowds**. Describe the course of their development during adolescence.

F.   When do dating and sexual activity typically begin? When does opposite-sex intimacy become comparable to same-sex intimacy? What developmental functions do intimate relationships with the opposite sex serve?

G.   How has adolescent sexual activity changed in the last few decades? What age, gender, and ethnic differences are there in adolescent sexual activity?

H.   How do peers influence adolescents' behavior? How does conformity to the peer group change over the course of adolescence? How do teenagers vary in their level of conformity? How does the influence of peers compare to the influence of parents during adolescence?

I.   BOX: Summarize recent trends in adolescent alcohol and drug use and attitudes.

V. FAMILY RELATIONSHIPS IN ADOLESCENCE
  A. How and why do parent-child relationships typically change during adolescence? What factors contribute to parent-child conflict in early adolescence? What happens to parent-child conflict over the course of adolescence?

  B. How do the tasks of parenting change during adolescence?

  D. What connections are there between parenting style and adolescent development?

  E. What bidirectional influences are seen in parent-adolescent relationships?

  F. How does divorce affect adolescents?

G. How do sibling relationships change during adolescence? What impacts do they have on adolescents' development?

VI. ADOLESCENTS IN THE BROADER WORLD
Key Terms: **internal locus of control, external locus of control**
A. Summarize the positive and negative aspects of secondary schools as a context for development. What are some possible reasons for the drop in grades that typically occurs in adolescence? How is gender involved in school achievement?

B. Describe current patterns in adolescent employment.

C. BOX: Summarize the risks and benefits of employment for adolescents.

VII. THE COHERENCE OF DEVELOPMENT IN ADOLESCENCE
In what ways is development coherent during adolescence?

SELF-TEST

After you have studied the chapter, use the following questions to test your understanding.

MULTIPLE-CHOICE QUESTIONS:

1. Which of the following statements about parent-child conflict during adolescence is FALSE?
    a. Parent-child conflict tends to peak during the early years of adolescence.
    b. The majority of teenagers continue to get along with their parents.
    c. Most parent-child conflicts center around issues of basic values and beliefs.
    d. Families that functioned well before a child reached puberty tend to continue functioning well afterward.

2. Compared to traditional cultures, Western industrialized cultures tend to have a transition to adulthood that is:
    a. earlier.
    b. less stressful.
    c. less clearly marked.
    d. more abrupt.

3. The sense of invulnerability and uniqueness seen in early adolescence probably stems from:
    a. an overestimation of one's abilities that is common at that age.
    b. a cognitive inability to take the perspective of other people.
    c. an underlying fragility of self and uncertainty about one's abilities.
    d. unrealistically high levels of self-esteem.

4. Erikson's concept of **identity crisis** refers to:
    a. an abnormal, obsessive concern with issues of personal identity.
    b. the struggle teenagers encounter in establishing a personal identity.
    c. the general crises and conflicts encountered during adolescence.
    d. a sudden, acute feeling of not knowing who you are.

5. **Identity diffusion** is the developmentally appropriate identity status for:
    a. early adolescence.
    b. middle adolescence.
    c. late adolescence.
    d. early adulthood.

6. The least stable identity status is:
    a. identity diffusion.
    b. foreclosure.
    c. moratorium.
    d. identity achievement.

7. Which identity status is associated with the lowest level of anxiety, based on self-reports?
    a.   identity diffusion.
    b.   foreclosure.
    c.   moratorium.
    d.   identity achievement.

8. Identity development proceeds differently for boys and girls in that:
    a.   boys show more concern about occupational issues.
    b.   girls show more concern about the interpersonal domain.
    c.   identity formation is more complex for boys.
    d.   all of the above.

9. In Selman's theory of self- and social understanding, an adolescent who knows that both self and others can act and reflect on their actions is at the level of:
    a.   self-reflective perspective taking.
    b.   subjective perspective taking.
    c.   in-depth perspective taking.
    d.   mutual perspective taking.

10. Girls who are best friends in junior high may spend all day at school together, visit each other's houses after school, and talk much of the evening on the telephone. The endless conversation that occurs during all this time together reflects a strong desire for:
    a.   social comparison.
    b.   peer group identification.
    c.   self-disclosure.
    d.   an imaginary audience.

11. A qualitative change in the nature of friendship that first appears in late adolescence is:
    a.   the ability to coordinate a broader range of friends.
    b.   the ability to keep confidences.
    c.   increasing intimacy and commitment.
    d.   the capacity for mutual understanding.

12. Teenage boys' friendships differ from those of girls in that:
    a.   boys have more disagreements with their friends.
    b.   negative feelings are more likely to persist after a disagreement between boys.
    c.   boys have more intimate knowledge of their friends.
    d.   boys are more likely to have conflicts over friends pressuring them to do things.

13. Which of the following statements about **crowds** is FALSE?
    a.   Clearly identifiable crowds appear in early adolescence.
    b.   Crowds are identified by characteristics such as attitudes, interests, and reputation.
    c.   Adolescents' descriptions of crowds are generally highly accurate.
    d.   Adolescents are often reluctant to assign themselves to any one crowd.

14. Intimacy in opposite-sex relationships becomes comparable to intimacy in same-sex relationships at about what point in development?
    a.   In early adolescence.
    b.   In middle adolescence.
    c.   In late adolescence.
    d.   Not until adulthood.

15. From the 1960s to the 1980s, adolescent sexual activity in the United States changed in which of the following ways?
    a.   The percentage of sexually active boys doubled.
    b.   The percentage of sexually active girls doubled.
    c.   The percentage of sexually active teenagers of both sexes actually declined.
    d.   The percentage of sexually active teenagers stayed the same, but their willingness to admit to sexual activity increased greatly.

16. Peers seem to have a stronger influence than parents on adolescents' attitudes about:
    a.   smoking cigarettes and marijuana.
    b.   use of illicit drugs other than marijuana.
    c.   education and important life decisions.
    d.   all of the above.

17. In 2000, use of illicit drugs by high school seniors was:
    a.   up sharply after years of decline.
    b.   down slightly after several years of increase.
    c.   about half as high as in 1975.
    d.   at about the same level as in 1975.

18. The most widely used drug among adolescents is:
    a.   marijuana.
    b.   nicotine.
    c.   alcohol.
    d.   all of the above are equally widely used.

19. Adolescent development is best supported by:
    a. a warm, supportive parenting style that provides guidance and feedback.
    b. a firm parenting style that emphasizes limit-setting.
    c. a highly involved parenting style in which the child's behavior is closely monitored.
    d. a parenting style that minimizes parent-child involvement.

20. In her study of adolescent girls who had grown up without fathers, Hetherington found that:
    a. the girls were less strongly sex-typed than girls who had grown up with fathers.
    b. regardless of the reason for their fathers' absence, the girls tended to be shy and hesitant with men.
    c. regardless of the reason for their fathers' absence, the girls tended to be sexually forward.
    d. the girls had trouble with opposite-sex relationships, but the type of trouble depended on whether their mothers were widows or divorcees.

21. After doing well on a geometry test, Maggie attributes her success to luck and the fact that the teacher happened to ask questions she knew. Maggie is demonstrating:
    a. an external locus of control.
    b. an internal locus of control.
    c. a confused locus of control.
    d. no locus of control.

22. Which of the following statements about the effects of adolescent employment is most accurate?
    a. Working has mostly positive effects, regardless of the number of hours worked.
    b. Working has mostly negative effects, regardless of the number of hours worked.
    c. The positive effects of working increase as the number of hours per week increases.
    d. The negative effects of working increase as the number of hours per week increases.

23. Sixteen-year-old Malcolm's involvement with Felicia and his refusal to go with his parents to the church retreat suggest:
    a. an appropriate shift in emphasis on interaction with parents and peers.
    b. an unusual disagreement with his parents about basic values.
    c. early than usual involvement in dating.
    d. rebellion against authoritarian parents.

24. Mike's passionate feelings about the environment and strong commitment to going to college and becoming a marine biologist suggest that by his senior year in high school he would fit which of Marcia's identity development categories in the area of vocational choice?
    a. Foreclosure.
    b. Moratorium.
    c. Identity diffusion.
    d. Identity achievement.

25. Fourteen-year-old Meryl's conflicts with her parents about their rules for dating are:
    a. more intense than most adolescent-parent conflicts.
    b. unusual because conflicts are more common later in adolescence.
    c. typical in their focus on issues of independence and responsibility.
    d. all of the above.

MATCHING QUESTIONS:
Match the following key terms with their definitions:

1. __ Moratorium
2. __ Identity crisis
3. __ Crowd
4. __ External locus of control
5. __ Identity
6. __ Clique
7. __ Internal locus of control
8. __ Puberty rites/rites of passage
9. __ Identity achievement
10. __ Foreclosure
11. __ Identity diffusion

A. A sense of an integrated, coherent, and goal-directed self.

B. A close-knit group of a few friends who are intimately involved with each other.

C. Identity status in which there has been no active exploration of roles and values and no commitment to an adult identity.

D. Identity status in which a person has committed to a set of roles and values following a period of active exploration.

E. Ceremonies that mark the transition from childhood to adulthood.

F. A larger, less exclusive group; more loosely organized than a clique.

G. The belief that success depends on factors outside one's control.

H. Identity status in which commitment has been made to a set of roles and values without a period of exploration.

I. Identity status in which a person is in the midst of exploring options for a personal identity, but has not yet committed to any of them.

J. The belief that success depends on one's own efforts.

K. In Erikson's theory, the struggle that teenagers experience when trying to establish their personal identities.

SHORT-ANSWER QUESTIONS:

1. List the four major developmental tasks of adolescence.

    (a)

    (b)

    (c)

    (d)

2. Explain why young adolescents' sense of self tends to be relatively fragile.

3. List the two sets of ingredients Erikson saw as critical to optimal identity development.

    (a)

    (b)

4. The developmentally appropriate identity status for middle adolescence is

    _____.

5. What gender differences in identity development have been found?

6. List four ways in which peer relationships change during adolescence.
   (a)

   (b)

   (c)

   (d)

7. In Selman's system, recognizing that persons are unique, complex combinations of their own histories and that they may not always understand their own motivations is characteristic of _____ perspective taking.

8. List three important characteristics of adolescent friendships.
   (a)

   (b)

   (c)

9. By age _____, 90 percent of adolescents are dating.

10. Approximately what percentage of 12th graders in the United States report that they have had sexual intercourse?

11. Conformity is highest among teenagers who have a _____ level of status with their peers.

12. Based on nationwide student surveys, which ethnic group has the lowest rate of drug, alcohol, and tobacco use in the United States?

13. Explain how the tasks of parenting change when children reach adolescence.

14. List three major research findings concerning adolescents and divorce.

(a)

(b)

(c)

15. Explain why grades tend to decline during adolescence.

ESSAY QUESTIONS:

1. Discuss evidence for and against the idea that adolescence is a stormy and stressful period.

2. Discuss how adolescence in Western industrialized societies differs from adolescence in more traditional cultures.

3. Discuss how the self-concept changes from middle childhood to adolescence and how it continues to change from early to late adolescence.

4. Discuss the positive and negative impacts of employment on adolescents.

5. Discuss two domains in which gender seems to make a difference in adolescent development.

6. Discuss three ways that the individual functioning of adolescents is related to their earlier developmental history.

7. In spite of some adolescent rebellion, Mike Gordon's developmental path took a definite positive turn while he was in high school. Suggest two factors that may have contributed to this change.

ANSWER KEY

MULTIPLE-CHOICE QUESTIONS:

1. c   Most parent-child conflicts center around mundane matters such as appearance, household chores, homework, and phone or stereo use.

2. c   In traditional cultures, transitions to adulthood tend to be earlier, less stressful, and more clearly marked than in Western cultures. Abruptness of the transition varies.

3. c   Adolescents are more likely to be uncertain about their abilities than to overestimate them or have unrealistically high self-esteem, and they *can* take others' perspectives, even though they don't always do so.

4. b   See definition of **identity crisis**.

5. a   Identity diffusion only becomes a problem in later adolescence and adulthood.

6. c   Moratorium is least stable because it involves an ongoing exploration of options.

7. b   Self-reported anxiety is lower in identity achievement than in diffusion or moratorium, but it is lowest in foreclosure.

8. b   Boys and girls show equal concern about occupational issues, but girls show more concern about balancing career and family, which makes the process of identity formation somewhat more complex for girls.

9. d   See Table 14.3 for descriptions of each level in Selman's theory.

10. c   Self-disclosure is a major feature of adolescent friendships, especially for girls.

11. a   The ability to keep confidences, increases in intimacy and commitment, and the capacity for mutual understanding all begin to appear in early adolescence.

12. d   Girls actually have more disagreements with friends, and negative feelings are more likely to persist afterwards. Girls also have more intimate knowledge of their friends.

13. c   Adolescents' descriptions of crowds usually turn out not to be particularly accurate reflections of reality; they seem to be based more on reputation than on actual behavior.

14. c   Earlier in adolescence couples tend to operate in a parallel manner--together, but not mutually involved on an emotional level.

15. a   The percentage of sexually active girls quadrupled. Some but not all of the
          reported increase was probably due to increased willingness to admit to sexual
          activity.

16. a   Parents have a greater influence with regard to education, important life
          decisions, and illicit drugs other than marijuana.

17. d   See box on adolescent drug and alcohol use for drug use levels since 1975.

18. c   About half of high school seniors said they had used alcohol in the last 30 days,
          whereas only about 31% said they had used tobacco and 22% said they had used
          marijuana.

19. a   Parents' tasks change in response to adolescents' new abilities, but many of the
          same parenting qualities continue to be important in adolescence.

20. d   Girls from father-absent homes were not less strongly sex-typed, but they had
          trouble in relationships with men. If their fathers had died, they tended to be shy
          and hesitant; if their parents had divorced, they tended to be sexually forward.

21. a   Maggie is demonstrating a belief that success depends on factors outside her
          control.

22. d   Working has both positive and negative impacts on adolescents. The negative
          effects tend to increase as the number of hours worked goes up, but the positive
          effects do not.

23. a   Ninety percent of 16-year-olds have started to date. Malcolm's preference for
          spending time with his girlfriend is normal for his age. There is no evidence that
          he and his parents disagree about basic values or that his parents have been
          authoritarian.

24. d   Mike appears to have explored options and developed a strong commitment to
          marine biology as a career, reaching identity achievement in the area of vocational
          choice. He may still be in diffusion, foreclosure, or moratorium in other areas.

25. c   Meryl's conflicts with her parents are typical in issues, intensity, and timing.

MATCHING QUESTIONS:

1.	I	4.	G	7.	J	10.	H
2.	K	5.	A	8.	E	11.	C
3.	F	6.	B	9.	D		

SHORT-ANSWER QUESTIONS:

1.   Establishing a personal identity, achieving greater closeness and trust with peers, gaining a new status in the family, and moving toward more autonomy in the larger world.

2.   At first teenagers are unsure how valid the new self is, and other people can easily challenge it.

3.   (a) Successful resolution of issues from earlier developmental periods--from middle childhood, inner confidence about competence and ability to master new tasks, along with basic trust from infancy, autonomy from toddlerhood, and initiative from early childhood; (b) opportunity to experiment with new roles, combined with support from parents and other adults.

4.   moratorium

5.   The interpersonal domain, especially related to marriage and family, is more prominent in girls' identity exploration. Girls and boys show equal concern about occupational issues, but girls show more concern about balancing career and family. Girls may deal with identity and intimacy issues simultaneously instead of sequentially. As a result, the process of identity development seems more complex for girls than for boys.

6.   (a) Cognitive advances of adolescence make possible a deeper, more mature understanding of others; (b) involvement with peers becomes increasingly critical to progress in self-understanding; (c) peer group membership contributes to the development of personal identity; (d) friendships with same-sex peers pave the way for romantic relationships.

7.   in-depth

8.   Correct answers include mutual understanding, self-disclosure, intimacy, and commitment.

9.   16

10. 60 percent

11. medium

12. African Americans

13. Parents must respond to their children's new cognitive abilities and desire for

autonomy, not by letting them do whatever they want, but by staying involved and continuing to set limits. They change from monitoring the child to monitoring the child's self-monitoring. Guidance and feedback replace demands and directives, as parents give the adolescent more responsibility.

14. Major findings include: (a) Adolescents in divorced and remarried families have higher risk of behavior problems, drug and alcohol use, early sexual activity, adolescent pregnancy, and poor school performance; (b) divorce can produce sleeper effects, results that show up years later, often in adolescence; (c) normative tasks of adolescence are especially difficulty for young people from divorced or remarried families; (d) boys and girls continue to show different effects of divorce; (e) although divorce and remarriage doubles the risk of many problems, many adolescents from families that have gone through these processes do well; (f) adolescents in remarried families have a similar risk for problems as those from divorced, single-parent families; and (g) father absence due to divorce has different effects than father absence due to death.

15. The decline in grades may be partly due to harder classes and stricter grading, partly to the changes of adolescence, including transitions to new schools and puberty.

ESSAY QUESTIONS:

1. The level of storm and stress varies from early to later adolescence, across different aspects of behavior, and across different individuals. Evidence for the "storm-and-stress" view: Overall, adolescence is more challenging than other periods of development. Early adolescence is a time of particular stress, turmoil, and conflict for both adolescents and their parents. High levels of stress and conflict are more likely for adolescents with a difficult developmental history. Experiencing multiple changes at the same time (new schools, puberty, etc.) increases stress levels. Inner turmoil seems to peak in adolescence; teenagers report more negative moods and unhappiness than younger children. Evidence against the "storm-and-stress" view: Emotional turmoil and family conflict both diminish in late adolescence. Most teenagers get along well with their parents, and families that functioned well before adolescence continue to function well during adolescence. There is usually little parent-adolescent conflict over basic values and beliefs, and most adolescents continue to have positive feelings toward their parents. Even though some stress is created by adolescents' increasing self-assertion, most teenagers stay emotionally connected to their parents. Adolescents do not break ties to their families; instead, they reorganize them to reflect newfound autonomy and increased maturity.

2. The complexity of life in modern Western societies requires extensive education, leading to a long period of dependency on parents and a delay between puberty and full entry into adult sexual roles. During this time, the sense of being caught between childhood and adulthood can lead to feelings of frustration. In addition, the

boundary between childhood and adulthood is not clearly marked in Western cultures. Young people are allowed to take on various adult privileges and responsibilities, such as driving, drinking, and voting, at varying ages, and receive ambiguous messages about their status. In contrast, the transition from childhood to adulthood in many traditional cultures is clearly marked, often by a specific rite of passage. The transition may be quite abrupt or more gradual, but it often begins at an earlier age than in Western cultures, with responsibility and training in adult tasks beginning in childhood.

3. From middle childhood to adolescence, self-concepts change in five major ways. First, they become more differentiated; teenagers begin to see themselves in more complex ways, taking situations, relationships, and areas of expertise into consideration. Second, they become more individuated; younger children often describe themselves in terms of similarities to other children, but adolescents tend to describe themselves in terms of differences. Third, teenagers' self-concepts begin to focus on how they interact with others, on traits related to how they function in the social network. Fourth, teenagers increasingly view themselves as self-reflective, able to think about and evaluate the self, and to make choices about values and behaviors. Fifth, adolescents increasingly think of the self as a coherent system made up of diverse parts despite seeming contradictions. From early to late adolescence, the self-concept continues to change as teenagers gain an understanding of conscious and unconscious levels of experience and become increasingly able to explain contradictory aspects of the self.

4. Positive impacts include increased self-esteem, a sense of personal identity, increased financial independence, experience managing money, increased maturity, a chance to develop skills, and more continuous employment and higher wages after graduation. Negative impacts include involvement in routine, impersonal jobs with little opportunity to feel close to adult coworkers, fewer close peer relationships, less involvement in school activities, less enjoyment of school, lower grades, less investment in education, more psychological distress, and greater delinquency and drug and alcohol use. Positive impacts are seen in adolescents who work only a few hours a week but do not increase with more hours worked. Negative impacts are seen in adolescents who work as few as 11 hours per week and increase from there.

5. Domains that could be discussed include identity development, friendships, relationships with parents, effects of divorce, and school achievement. Identity development: girls' identity exploration tends to focus more on interpersonal issues, especially future marriage and family roles. Boys and girls are equally concerned about occupational issues, but girls think more about balancing work and family. Young women tend to deal with issues of identity and intimacy simultaneously, while young men deal with them sequentially. All of this makes identity development more complicated for girls. Friendships: girls have more intimate and

intense relationships with friends--they report more frequent intimate interactions, more intimate knowledge of friends, more disagreements, and longer-lasting negative feelings after conflicts with friends. Girls' disagreements with friends tend to be about interpersonal issues, while boys report more conflicts over friends pressuring them to do things. School achievement: girls are often socialized away from feelings of instrumental competence and toward feelings of helplessness. Parents tend to believe boys have more talent for math, and girls have lower expectations for success in math and related areas, even though their grades are higher than boys'. Girls are more likely to attribute failure to factors they cannot change, such as lack of ability. Finally, girls experience less pride in academic success than boys.

6. A number of ways that adolescents' individual functioning is related to their earlier developmental history are mentioned in Chapter 14 and in earlier chapters. Infant attachment security is related to adolescents' later functioning in several areas; adolescents who were securely attached as infants tend to be less dependent, more effective in the peer group, and more able to form intimate relationships than adolescents who were anxiously attached. Adolescents who showed high dependency and difficulty entering the peer group in early childhood often continue to have similar problems. Overall peer functioning in middle childhood is related to success in relationships in adolescence; as mentioned in Chapter 12, children who observe gender boundaries in middle childhood peer interactions later tend to be more successful in establishing relationships with the opposite sex during adolescence.

7. First, Mike's relationship with his biology teacher contributed to his development in several ways. Mr. Yamoto awakened Mike's interest in biology and gave him a concrete reason to work hard in school. By helping Mike get a summer research job, Mr. Yamoto gave Mike added responsibility that increased his self-esteem and also made him aware of broader educational and occupational horizons. In biology Mike found a subject about which he cared intensely and around which he could build his plans for the future. As a college graduate and scientist, Mr. Yamoto also provided a role model for Mike and helped him raise his personal aspirations. Second, his relationship with his stepfather provided him with further practical advice and encouragement. The fact that it came from a male member of his family may have made it even more effective for Mike, whose relationship with his father seems to have become increasingly distant in the years following his parents' divorce and his father's remarriage.

CHAPTER 15
DEVELOPMENTAL PSYCHOPATHOLOGY
CHAPTER REVIEW

As you read the chapter, construct your own chapter outline by answering the following review questions and defining the *Key Terms*.

I. INTRODUCTION
    Key Term: **developmental psychopathology**
    A. What does the field of **developmental psychopathology** include?

    B. How has studying psychopathology from a developmental standpoint enriched our understanding of emotional and behavioral disorders?

II. A DEVELOPMENTAL PERSPECTIVE ON PSYCHOPATHOLOGY
    Key Terms: **risk factor, protective factor**
    A. What are some **risk factors** for child and adult psychiatric disorders?

    B. What does it mean to say that risk is a statistical and not a causal concept? What happens when several risk factors occur together? Explain why the same disorder may be associated with various risks and the same risk factor can predict several disorders.

C. How do **protective factors** influence the development of psychological problems?

D. Why is there a need in developmental psychopathology to consider normal and abnormal behaviors together? How can abnormal behavior be distinguished from normal behavior? What behavior patterns have been most strongly linked to later disorders?

E.. What patterns of change and stability over time did Robins find in her St. Louis study?

III. EXPLAINING PSYCHOPATHOLOGY
   Key Terms: **model**
   A. Explain the assumptions of the traditional medical model of psychopathology. What mental disorders best fit the medical model?

   B. What is the focus of modern neurological and physiological models? What does current research indicate about connections between imbalances in brain chemistry and psychopathology?

C. How are genetic models of psychopathology related to neurological and physiological models? What have researchers discovered about genetic mechanisms for transmitting predispositions toward psychological disorders? How is the environment involved in genetic models?

D. What factors are emphasized by sociological models of psychopathology?

E. What aspects of the environment do behavioral models focus on? How would disorders be treated in these models? How do current behavioral models differ from the earliest versions?

F. What connection does Freud have to psychodynamic models? What assumption do these models make about the causes and treatment of psychopathology?

G. How do family models view psychopathology?

H. How is the developmental perspective related to the various models of psychopathology? How has it been applied to schizophrenia and juvenile depression?

IV. SOME CHILDHOOD DISORDERS

Key Terms: **autism, autistic spectrum disorders, mind blindness, Asperger's syndrome, conduct disorder, life-course-persistent conduct disorder, adolescent-limited conduct disorder, attention deficit/hyperactivity disorder (AD/HD), comorbidity, generalized anxiety disorder, separation anxiety disorder, spontaneous remission, anorexia nervosa, bulimia**

A. What are the major categories of disorders that appear in childhood and adolescence?

B. How common is full-blown **autism**? How common are **autistic spectrum disorders**? What are the core features of autism? What other difficulties do children with autistic spectrum disorders have? What is known about the causes of autistic spectrum disorders? What is the long-term outlook for children with autism?

C. What are the various types of **conduct disorder**? How common and how stable are they? What biological and environmental factors have been proposed as causes? What treatment approaches have been most successful?

D. List the characteristics of children with **attention deficit/hyperactivity disorder**. Summarize the research evidence for biological and environmental factors in AD/HD. How do stimulants such as Ritalin affect children with AD/HD? What are some non-drug treatments for AD/HD? What is the long-term prognosis for children with AD/HD?

E. How do **anxiety disorders** compare to other disorders in prevalence and severity? What are some likely causes of anxiety disorders? What is the long-term outlook for children with anxiety disorders? What treatments seem to be most effective?

F. Why is depression often difficult to diagnose in children? How does it differ from adult depression? How can it be treated?

G. What are the characteristics of a typical person with **anorexia nervosa**? What factors seem to contribute to it? How can it be treated?

H. Why is **comorbidity** so widespread in children's psychological disorders?

V. CHILDHOOD DISORDERS AND DEVELOPMENT
Explain how the study of psychopathology in general and the disorders discussed in this chapter in particular can further the understanding of normal development.

SELF-TEST

After you have studied the chapter, use the following questions to test your understanding.

MULTIPLE-CHOICE QUESTIONS:

1. The field of **developmental psychopathology** is concerned with:
   a. the study of disturbed children.
   b. the developmental roots of adult disorders.
   c. the patterns disorders follow after they emerge.
   d. all of the above.

2. Prematurity, unstable family structure, and parental alcoholism are all **risk factors** for childhood psychiatric disorders. Another way of stating this relationship would be to say:
   a. prematurity, unstable family structure, and parental alcoholism cause childhood psychiatric disorders to develop.
   b. most of the children with a history of prematurity, unstable family structure, or parental alcoholism will develop psychiatric disorders.
   c. children who were premature or have an unstable family or alcoholic parent have an increased likelihood of psychiatric disorders.
   d. children who were not premature and do not have an unstable family or alcoholic parent are not likely to develop psychiatric disorders.

3. When multiple risk factors are considered, adult criminal behavior is most likely for children who have:
   a. more than three total risk factors.
   b. specific individual risk factors.
   c. specific combinations of risk factors.
   d. low IQ in combination with any other risk factor.

4. Which of the following statements about the connections between risk factors and disorders is FALSE?
   a. Different combinations of risk factors can lead to the same disorder.
   b. Different disorders can be associated with the same combination of risk factors.
   c. Even very specific risk factors, such as having a schizophrenic parent, can lead to a variety of disorders.
   d. Most disorders are associated with their own specific set of risk factors.

5. Which of the following childhood symptoms is most likely to predict psychological problems in adulthood?
   a. A high activity level in a preschool boy.
   b. Food finickiness in a 3-year-old girl.
   c. Persistent problems with peers in elementary school.
   d. Disturbing dreams in a child entering adolescence.

6. In her follow-up study of adults who had been seen in a child guidance clinic in St. Louis, Robins found that:
    a. children seen at the clinic did not have a higher than usual rate of serious psychological disorders in adulthood.
    b. depression and schizophrenia in adulthood were both linked with conduct disorders in childhood.
    c. shyness and anxiety in childhood were associated with psychological problems in adulthood.
    d. most of those who showed sociopathic behavior as adults had not shown such behavior as children.

7. Modern neurological and physiological models suggest that the cause of psychological problems is:
    a. structural brain damage.
    b. chemical imbalances in the brain.
    c. recessive single-gene traits.
    d. neurological impacts of the environment.

8. From the perspective of a psychodynamic model of psychopathology, which of the following forms of treatment would be most appropriate?
    a. Psychotherapy to address the underlying causes of a problem.
    b. Drug treatment to correct chemical imbalances in the brain.
    c. Behavior therapy to eliminate reinforcement of disturbed behavior.
    d. Changing the environment to increase support to the patient.

9. In the developmental perspective, which of the following factors are assumed to influence the development of emotional and behavioral problems?
    a. Genetic and other biological influences.
    b. Socioeconomic and cultural contexts.
    c. Past developmental history.
    d. All of the above.

10. Core features of **autism** include:
    a. an insistence on constant variety in the environment.
    b. extreme social isolation.
    c. uncontrollable aggressiveness.
    d. all of the above.

11. Which of the following is NOT likely to be a cause of **autistic spectrum disorders**?
    a. Genetic factors, probably involving multiple genes.
    b. Neurological abnormalities.
    c. Childhood immunizations.
    d. Prenatal complications.

12. Compared to other psychological disorders, **conduct disorders** are:
    a.   very common and very persistent.
    b.   very common, but not very persistent.
    c.   rather uncommon, but very persistent.
    d.   rather uncommon and not very persistent.

13. A critical element in treating conduct disorders appears to be:
    a.   brief but intensive therapy.
    b.   early detection and intervention.
    c.   drug therapy to correct chemical imbalances.
    d.   focusing on the child's problems, not the family environment.

14. Which of the following statements about children with **AD/HD** is FALSE?
    a.   They typically have attention-related difficulties.
    b.   They usually do not have symptoms of other psychological disorders.
    c.   They often have problems with peers.
    d.   They do not represent a single type.

15. When stimulants such as Ritalin are used to treat children with AD/HD, the drugs typically:
    a.   reduce their overall level of activity.
    b.   enhance their ability to concentrate.
    c.   remain effective indefinitely.
    d.   all of the above.

16. Compared to conduct disorders and hyperactivity, anxiety disorders are:
    a.   more likely to recede without professional treatment.
    b.   more likely to lead to serious adjustment problems in adulthood.
    c.   more frequently seen at clinics.
    d.   more difficult to treat.

17. The type of model that seems to offer the best explanation of anxiety disorders is:
    a.   the traditional medical model.
    b.   a neurological/physiological model.
    c.   a behavioral model.
    d.   a family model.

18. Evidence that childhood depression may be distinct from adult depression includes:
    a.   childhood depression is more strongly associated with psychosocial adversity.
    b.   there is more evidence for a genetic factor in childhood depression.
    c.   there is a clear biochemical marker for childhood depression, but not adult depression.
    d.   childhood depression can be treated more readily with antidepressants.

19. Which of the following factors is probably LEAST responsible for **anorexia nervosa?**
    a. A tendency toward perfectionism.
    b. Overinvolved parents.
    c. A dysfunctional hypothalamus.
    d. Cultural emphasis on thinness.

20. Successful long-term treatment of anorexia nervosa is most likely to be achieved by means of:
    a. behavioral therapy.
    b. family therapy.
    c. drug therapy.
    d. none of the above.

21. Which childhood disorder represents the most profound deviation from normal development?
    a. Conduct disorder.
    b. Depression.
    c. Anxiety disorder.
    d. Autism.

22. Which disorder most clearly represents a failure to negotiate developmental issues faced by all children?
    a. Conduct disorder.
    b. Autism.
    c. Anxiety disorder.
    d. Attention deficit/hyperactivity disorder.

23. Given his developmental history, which psychological disorder would Malcolm have been most likely to experience?
    a. Anorexia.
    b. AD/HD
    c. Anxiety disorder.
    d. Depression.

24. Given her developmental history, which psychological disorder would Meryl have been most likely to experience?
    a. Anorexia.
    b. Hyperactivity.
    c. Anxiety disorder.
    d. Depression.

25. Given her developmental history, which psychological disorder would Maggie
    have been most likely to experience?
    a.   Anorexia.
    b.   Hyperactivity.
    c.   Anxiety disorder.
    d.   Conduct disorder.

MATCHING QUESTIONS:

Match the following key terms with their definitions:

1.   ___ Risk factor

2.   ___ Generalized anxiety disorder

3.   ___ Model

4.   ___ Attention deficit/hyperactivity
        disorder (AD/HD)

5.   ___ Anorexia nervosa

6.   ___ Protective factor

7.   ___ Conduct disorder

8.   ___ Separation anxiety disorder

9.   ___ Bulimia

10. ___ Autism

A.   A persistent pattern of repeatedly
     violating either age-appropriate
     social norms or the basic rights of
     others.

B.   Eating binges followed by self-
     induced vomiting to avoid weight
     gain.

C.   Excessive anxiety precipitated by
     separation from someone to whom
     the child is emotionally attached.

D.   Any factor that increases the
     likelihood of a negative
     developmental outcome.

E.   A disorder characterized by very
     general and pervasive worries and
     fears.

F.   A framework for explaining why
     things happen, a set of ideas and
     assumptions about causes and
     effects.

G.   A behavior pattern exhibited by
     children of normal intelligence that
     is characterized by extremely high
     activity levels coupled with
     attention-related difficulties.

H.   A rare, severe developmental
     disorder, featuring a powerful
     insistence on sameness, extreme
     social isolation, and severe
     language deficits.

I.   Any factor that promotes or maintains healthy development.

J.   A serious eating disorder characterized by extreme reduction in food intake and loss of at least 25 percent of normal body weight.

SHORT-ANSWER QUESTIONS:

1.   List three ways taking a developmental approach has enriched our understanding of emotional and behavioral disorders.

  (a)

  (b)

  (c)

2.   List four major **risk factors** for childhood psychiatric disorders.

  (a)

  (b)

  (c)

  (d)

3.   Explain how **protective factors** influence the development of psychological problems.

4.   The model of psychopathology that holds that psychological disorders should be considered mental illnesses is the _____ model.

5.   List four models of psychopathology that emphasize environmental factors.

  (a)

  (b)

  (c)

  (d)

6.   What aspects of the environment do behavioral models focus on?

7.   **Autism** affects about _____ children in 10,000; **autistic spectrum disorders** affect about _____ children in 1,000.

8.   Explain the difference between **life-course-persistent conduct disorders** and **adolescent-limited conduct disorders**.

9.   List the major characteristics of children with **attention deficit/hyperactivity disorder**.

10. _____ refers to situations in which a person's pattern of symptoms fits more than one disorder.

11. The disappearance of a disorder without professional treatment is called _____ _____ _____ _____.

12. What is the long-term outlook for children with anxiety disorders?

13. Explain why depression is often difficult to diagnose in children.

14. List three factors that contribute to the development of anorexia nervosa.
     (a)

     (b)

     (c)

15. Give two possible reasons for the widespread **comorbidity** in children's psychological disorders.
     (a)

     (b)

ESSAY QUESTIONS:

1. Discuss how **risk factors** and **protective factors** interact in determining the outcomes of children's development.

2. Explain the purpose of a psychopathology model. Identify and compare the major models that have been used.

3. Describe four ways mental health professionals distinguish among different types of **conduct disorders**.

4. Discuss the interaction of biological and environmental factors in the development of **AD/HD**.

5. Discuss the ways that the study of developmental psychopathology can further understanding of normal development.

6. Suggest some guidelines for parents and teachers who want to know how to judge whether a child has a psychological disorder that warrants treatment. In particular, what problems should they be particularly concerned about at each stage of development (infancy, toddlerhood, etc.)?

7. Discuss the protective factors that may have prevented Malcolm, Meryl, Maggie, and Mike from developing any serious childhood psychological disorders.

ANSWER KEY

MULTIPLE-CHOICE QUESTIONS:

1. d   Answers *a-c* all lie within the realm of developmental psychopathology.

2. c   Risk factors are not necessarily *causes* of psychological problems. The presence of risk factors does not guarantee that problems will develop, nor does their absence guarantee that there will be no problems.

3. a   For many negative developmental outcomes, the sheer number of risk factors seems to be more important than the specific risk factors that are present.

4. d   Most disorders share risk factors with other disorders.

5. c   Peer problems in elementary school represent a failure to negotiate a basic developmental task and are therefore more likely to have long-term repercussions.

6. b   Children seen at the clinic did have an above average rate of serious psychological disorders in adulthood. Childhood conduct disorders predicted several adult problems, including depression and schizophrenia, but shyness and anxiety did not predict adult problems. Virtually all of the adults diagnosed as sociopathic had shown sociopathic behavior as children.

7. b   Modern neurological and physiological models focus on chemical imbalances rather than structural brain damage. They tend to assume a genetic basis for imbalances that lead to psychological problems, but they do not focus on recessive single-gene traits.

8. a   Psychodynamic models assume that thoughts and feelings produced by life experiences are the underlying causes of psychological problems; therefore, they also assume that psychotherapy is the most appropriate form of treatment.

9. d   Answers *a-c* are all included in the developmental perspective.

10. b   Autistic children typically insist on *sameness* in the environment, and aggression is not a core feature of the disorder.

11. c   There is research evidence linking genetic factors, neurological abnormalities, and prenatal complications to autistic spectrum disorders, but studies have found no evidence of a causal link between immunizations and autism.

12. a   Conduct disorders are among the most common and persistent psychological problems of childhood.

13. b   Successful intervention programs for conduct disorders typically last at least two years and do involve the child's family. Chemical imbalances have not been found to be a major factor in conduct disorders.

14. b   Children with AD/HD often have symptoms of other psychological disorders.

15. b   Stimulants are effective for children with AD/HD because they enhance their ability to concentrate. They do not reduce children's overall level of activity; they *increase* activity levels in unconstrained settings, as well as heart rates and blood pressure. They do not remain effective indefinitely, but provide a window of opportunity for children to learn more effective ways of managing their behavior and dealing with their environment.

16. a   Anxiety disorders typically do not lead to serious problems in adulthood. Children with these disorders are less likely to be seen in clinics, probably because they are less likely to cause trouble for other people. However, anxiety disorders are actually more readily treatable than many other childhood psychological problems.

17. d   A number of family factors have been identified that seem to contribute to anxiety disorders in children, including cold, distant fathers, anxiously overinvolved mothers, high levels of family stress, and a history of anxious/resistant attachment.

18. a   Neither genetic nor biochemical markers have been found for childhood depression. Although antidepressants are increasingly being used to treat children with depression, it is not clear whether they are the most effective or appropriate treatment; attention to contextual factors that may have contributed to the depression is probably even more important in treating depressed children than in treating depressed adults.

19. c   There is much more evidence for family and cultural factors than for physiological ones.

20. b   Behavioral therapy is effective in the short term, but family therapy seems to have more long-term effectiveness, especially for younger patients with less chronic conditions.

21. d   The social and linguistic abnormalities associated with autism are more severe and pervasive than the abnormalities associated with the other disorders listed.

22. c   Anxiety disorders seem to be related to difficulties with the developmental issues of trust and autonomy.

23. a Without loving guidance and clear limit setting from his family, Malcolm's high energy level and tendency toward impulsiveness might have predisposed him to AD/HD.

24. c Meryl's early irritability and history of anxious-resistant attachment were both risk factors for anxiety disorders, but positive changes in her relationship with her mother and the added stability provided by Joe helped her avoid this outcome.

25. a As a bright, high-achieving girl, Maggie is in the group most at risk for eating disorders. In addition, her tendency to internalize problems in her family and her high standards for herself, combined with her doubts about her own attractiveness to men, could have contributed to the development of anorexia nervosa.

MATCHING QUESTIONS:
1. D   4. G   7. A   10. H
2. E   5. J   8. C
3. F   6. I   9. B

SHORT-ANSWER QUESTIONS:
1. (a) It has encouraged exploration of both the origins of abnormal behavior and the ways abnormal behavior changes over time; (b) it has focused attention on resiliency; (c) it has encouraged exploration of the ways disorders have their roots in major developmental issues.

2. There are many possible correct answers. Major categories of risk factors, listed in Table 15.1, include health history, demographic factors, adverse conditions, and stressful life events; more specific factors from within any of these categories could also be given. Other factors mentioned in the textbook include low IQ, parental criminal activity, aggressiveness, genetic factors, anxious attachment, and peer rejection.

3. Protective factors counteract the effects of risk factors or prevent a disorder from arising.

4. medical

5. Sociological, behavioral, psychodynamic, and family models.

6. Behavioral models focus on specific rewards, punishments, and modeled behaviors in a child's environment.

7. 4; 6.

8. Life-course persistent conduct disorders typically show up as aggression and antisocial behavior early in life, persist throughout childhood, and predict problems in adulthood. Adolescent-limited conduct disorders do not appear until adolescence and typically do not predict problems in adulthood.

9. Children with attention deficit/hyperactivity disorder are a heterogeneous group and do not all share the same characteristics. Some are impulsive, but not all. Some are more easily distracted and have a harder time concentrating than others, but all have some sort of attentional problems. They generally have particular trouble paying attention to routine tasks and often seem careless and hurried, with work that is sloppy, incomplete, or superficial. Many of them are restless and fidgety, which often prompts them to do things that get them in trouble. They are sociable, but often have trouble with peers.

10. comorbidity

11. spontaneous remission

12. The long-term outlook is very positive for children with anxiety disorders. These disorders are more likely to go away without treatment than other childhood problems, they are highly treatable, and they do not predict adult psychological problems.

13. Depression is difficult to diagnose in children because they typically have different symptoms than adults do; they are more likely to show somatic complaints, irritable mood, and social withdrawal and less likely to show motor slowing and despondency. In addition, childhood depression often occurs along with other disorders, such as AD/HD or anxiety disorders.

14. Factors that contribute to anorexia nervosa include a history of sexual abuse; overinvolved families; parents who expect perfection or discourage questioning or expression of anger; a tendency toward perfectionism; and a cultural emphasis on extreme thinness as beauty.

15. One possibility is that children have limited ways to manifest psychological problems, resulting in overlapping symptoms for different disorders. Another is that childhood problems may not fit into broad classes of problems rather than distinct syndromes.

ESSAY QUESTIONS:

1. Risk factors are any factors that increase the chances of a negative developmental outcome, whereas protective factors are any factors that promote or maintain healthy development. Together, risk and protective factors influence children's developmental outcomes. All five levels in Bronfenbrenner's model must be considered in examining risk factors and protective factors; in other words, risk and protective factors can be genetic, familial, socioeconomic, cultural, or developmental. The presence of risk factors does not guarantee that a child will develop problems, nor does the presence of protective factors offer absolute protection against negative developmental outcomes; risk factors simply raise the likelihood of problems while protective factors lower it. Individual risk and protective factors do not predict children's outcomes very well, but in combination their predictive power increases. The presence of multiple risk factors greatly increases the likelihood of developmental problems; several researchers have discovered that about 75 percent of children who have three or more common risk factors go on to develop problems of various sorts. However, protective factors can greatly lower this risk; in one study, the presence of a loving, dependable parent reduced the likelihood of problem behaviors for children with three or more risk factors to only 25 percent. Protective factors operate either by counteracting the effects of risk factors or by overriding them, preventing the development of problems.

2. A psychopathology model provides assumptions and explanations for the cause of psychological disorders, along with implications for possible treatments. The major models that have been used are the traditional medical model, modern neurological and physiological models, genetic models, sociological models, behavioral models, psychodynamic models, and family models. The first three models rely on biological factors to explain disorders; the others rely on environmental factors. Among the biological models, the medical model is the most vague about the nature of the biological cause. Neurological and physiological models specify imbalances in brain chemistry as the likely cause, and genetic models attribute disorders to groups of genes. The environmental models attribute disorders to varying aspects of the environment. Sociological models emphasize the broad social context, while family models narrow the focus to the family system. Behavioral models focus on specific features of the environment that provide reinforcement, whether they involve family or non-family members. Finally, psychodynamic models emphasize internal reactions to external events that may have happened in the distant past and often involve family members.

3. The first way mental health professionals distinguish among conduct disorders is in terms of degree of severity (from mild to severe), depending on the extent to which the child's actions harm others. Second, they distinguish between conduct disorders that involve aggressive behavior and those that do not. Third, they distinguish

between conduct disorders in which the child is able to form normal bonds of friendship and affection (socialized) and one in which the child seems to have no feelings for others (undersocialized). Finally, they distinguish between life-course-persistent conduct disorders, which begin early in life, remain stable across childhood, and predict problems in adulthood, and adolescent-limited conduct disorders, which do not appear until adolescence and do not predict problems in adulthood.

4. There is no specific biological marker for AD/HD, but it is widely assumed to have an organic cause. Different biological and environmental factors may be more prominent in different children. There is some evidence for genetic factors, including one particular gene that may interfere with the neurotransmitter dopamine and lead to difficulty inhibiting behavior. Some children may have a biological predisposition toward hyperactivity or attentional problems. If children with these predispositions receive responsive care from parents who help them develop self-regulation, they may not develop AD/HD. On the other hand, if they receive intrusive and overstimulating care, they may later be unable to regulate their own arousal and may be prone to attentional problems and hyperactivity.

5. The study of developmental psychopathology increases our understanding of normal development in many ways. Following are several ideas from the chapter; you may be able to think of others. Studying specific developmental problems can enhance understanding of normal abilities and highlight their significance. For example, the problems faced by children with autism highlight the importance of social interaction and verbal and emotional communication in children's development. The course of various problems sheds light on the role of continuity and change in children's development; the differences between life-course-persistent and adolescent-limited conduct disorders, for example, help to clarify factors involved in both continuity and change. Studying developmental problems can enhance understanding of the significance of major developmental issues; for example, anxiety disorders and anorexia both demonstrate problems that arise when issues of trust and autonomy are not resolved successfully in early childhood. The study of psychopathology provides particularly good opportunities to examine interactions between genetic and environmental factors and between risk and protective factors in development.

6. Parents and teachers often have difficulty deciding whether a child has a problem that warrants treatment. Four possible guidelines follow; you may be able to think of others:
    (a) Consider the developmental appropriateness of the child's behavior; for example, it is common for 3-year-olds to wet or soil their pants because they have not yet completely mastered bowel and bladder control, but this behavior could be a sign of trouble in an older child.

(b) Consider how common or uncommon the child's behavior is. For example, the majority of parents of preschool boys believe their sons are more active than average and may wonder if they are hyperactive. However, a high activity level by itself is quite common and does not indicate a problem.

(c) Consider whether the child seems to be having trouble dealing with a basic developmental issue. For example, difficulty separating from parents in early childhood may give rise to an anxiety disorder, and difficulty establishing relationships with peers in middle childhood is a strong predictor of later psychological problems.

(d) Consider whether the child's daily functioning and well-being are being negatively affected. Some behaviors that parents worry about, such as daydreaming, an active fantasy life, or typical childhood fears, do not interfere with normal interaction with others or with a child's overall sense of well-being. If these behaviors begin to disrupt other aspects of the child's life, treatment may be warranted, but under most circumstances it is not necessary.

7. Malcolm's neighborhood increased his risk for conduct disorders, but the clear standards, strong sense of family unity, and warm support provided by his family made this outcome unlikely. Although his energy level and tendency toward impulsiveness might have predisposed him to hyperactivity or attentional problems, the structure provided by his family helped him to control and direct his energy and attention. Meryl's developmental history placed her at risk for an anxiety disorder, but when her mother became involved with Joe, he provided warmth and consistent discipline for her and social support for her mother. These factors, along with her friendship with Amy and her responsibilities as a big sister, increased her self-esteem and willingness to tackle unfamiliar situations. Maggie was at risk for eating disorders or depression because of her strong achievement orientation, her distant relationship with her father, and her inability to control events in her family as her parents' relationship deteriorated and finally ended in divorce. Her solid attachment history, easy-going nature, and healthy development through middle childhood gave her a solid base for dealing with the stress that her parents' problems brought into her life. Her relationships with her mother, her grandmother, and her friends all helped her to deal with the changes brought by her parents' divorce and her mother's remarriage, and her improving relationship with her father offered additional support for dealing with the stresses of adolescence. Mike was at risk for depression because of his feelings of helplessness at not being able to prevent his parents' divorce and because of his loss of his father to the divorce and a new family. Initially, his relationship with his mother served as a protective factor. Later, his high school biology teacher and his stepfather served the same function after his relationship with his mother became more distant.